DERBY COUNTY
a season review

DERBY COUNTY
a season review

Edited by Gareth Davis

breedon **books**
PUBLISHING

First published in Great Britain in 2007 by
The Breedon Books Publishing Company Limited
Breedon House, 3 The Parker Centre,
Derby, DE21 4SZ.

Pictures courtesy of

and

ISBN 978-1-85983-602-6

Printed and bound by Scotprint, Haddington, Scotland.

Contents

Introduction

When you sit down and reflect on 2006–07, you find yourself looking at a season of twists and turns, of ups and downs, and ultimately of great memories.

Even right back on the opening day the dramatic 2–2 draw at home to Southampton set the tone for what was to follow.

It was a season that everyone involved with Derby County Football Club can be very proud of.

There were a number of hoodoos that needed breaking, from the poor away record to no victories at Leeds United since the 1970s, among numerous other fine achievements by the players.

Reaching the fifth round of the FA Cup for the first time since 1999 was something we were rightly proud of.

As the season went on it was clear that something special was happening.

Coming so close to automatic promotion and pushing Sunderland and Birmingham all the way, and putting Derby County back up at the right end of the table after years of relegation battles, gave us the chance to push on for Wembley.

The drama of those two legs against Southampton, the wonderful feeling after the penalty shoot-out victory, they are emotions that will stay with everyone present.

As for Wembley, what else can be said – it was a great team performance, backed by the usual wonderful support, and we did it.

We are Premier League!

Billy Davies

June

Billy Davies has been appointed as the new manager of Derby County. The Scotsman arrived at Moor Farm by helicopter – courtesy of club director Jill Marples – before being introduced to the media. And he cited the 'passion, enthusiasm and ambition' of the club as major factors in his switch from Preston North End.

He said 'I'm proud to be the new manager of Derby County, it's a tremendous club. We're starting with a blank sheet of paper in that there's lots of changes to make, but there'll need to be a bit more patience because we need time to make sure we bring in the right people and do the right things. But I'll be doing all I can to bring success to Derby.

'Every club is a big challenge. Staying at Preston would have been a big challenge and coming to Derby is of course a very big challenge, but there's a real passion and enthusiasm right through this club now, and I'm delighted to be part of that and very much now looking forward and eventually getting this club to where it belongs – in the Premier League.'

In the interview, and before that in his first press conference as Derby manager, Davies was keen to stress that patience still needs to be very much a key word as the club strives to move forward.

'There's real optimism throughout Derby County and that was important to me, but what I do want to say to the fans is that none of us has a magic wand and that getting the right personnel and setting the right things in place will take time.

'The process must be done slowly to get it right. We know where we want to get to, but the ambition is clear for everyone to see and this club is geared up for success with the facilities, supporters and staff it has in place.

'Now we have to look forward, not behind us. What lies ahead is the key now, and I look forward to the changes that have to be made – it took me time to get things right at Preston and the same will be the case here at Derby, but the most important thing is moving this club forward.

'We will now sit down and look at the pre-season plan in terms of games and everything else. I'm looking forward to meeting the staff and the players and working with everyone here to try and bring success to this great football club.

'There's great competition in the Championship and many great clubs in there who want to be in the Premier League, not least ourselves.'

Davies arrives at Pride Park having been in charge at Preston North End since September 2004.

In his two seasons with the Lilywhites he guided them to successive Play-off campaigns, first losing in the 2005 Final to West Ham then going down in the semi-final to Leeds a year later.

The appointment of a new manager was one of the first items on the agenda for the new consortium that took over the club in April 2006.

Managing director Mike Horton said it had been a thorough process and feels that the right man is now on board.

'The appointment of a manager is the biggest decision a club has to make, and in the past month we've been working flat out to make the right appointment,' said Horton.

'A manager is as good as two players on the pitch so, while we were conscious of the need to act as swiftly as possible, we were determined to be thorough.

'Billy is a great fit for this club. He is still young, but he has experience. Although he has tasted a bit of success by steering Preston to the Play-offs during the past two seasons, we were not interested in someone who didn't have anything to prove.

'The appointment is not a quick fix, it's for the long haul, and we believe we can provide Billy with the platform to take the club to the next level.

'We're unwilling to set timescales or promise any quick fixes. When the board took over the club it was on the back of a difficult season and there were a lot of problems.

'But we'll give Billy all the support we can. We'll be sitting down over the coming days to discuss his backroom staff and players to ensure he has the best possible start.'

Fixture release day has pitted the Rams against one of their former bosses to open up the 2006–07 campaign.

George Burley, who was in charge of Derby from 2003 to 2005, will bring his Southampton side up to Pride Park on 5 August.

He'll be pitting his wits against new Rams gaffer Billy Davies once more – the pair met in the 2005 Play-off semi-final when Burley's Derby lost to Davies's Preston.

It's a typical footballing twist but one that Davies is playing down and instead prefers to concentrate on the wider picture.

He said 'It's a great challenge and there's some exciting looking matches ahead, that's why it's imperative that we concentrate on fully preparing ourselves and making sure we are ready when the first whistle blows.'

The Rams' full pre-season friendly campaign has been confirmed – and it includes a trip to Austria.

It will all get under way on Wednesday 12 July with a game against FC Gratkorn from the Red Zac Erste Liga, Austria's equivalent of League One.

The game against Gratkorn is part of a four-day overseas visit that will include training and team bonding.

Three days later Derby take on their first domestic game under new boss Billy Davies when they travel to the National Hockey Stadium for a game against League Two side Milton Keynes Dons.

Away trips on the 19th and 22nd follow, to Mansfield Town and Burton Albion, then it all comes to a close on Saturday 29 July with the visit of Premiership side Bolton Wanderers.

July

Kevin Thelwell has been appointed as the Rams' new Academy manager. The 32-year-old joins from Preston North End, where he was previously director of youth and a colleague of Derby boss Billy Davies.

He's a former Shrewsbury Town player and is looking forward to working with Davies again after their time together at Deepdale.

'To team up with Billy at a fantastic club with a huge tradition and reputation for bringing through exciting young players was not a difficult decision,' Thelwell said.

'The manager believes in a club culture that sees every aspect of the playing side of the club coming together as one entity, and I'll be working with him to ensure the youth development side forges closer links with the senior set-up.'

Davies is convinced he has the right man for the job.

'Kevin is a first-class organiser, who is very good at his job,' said Davies.

'His reputation goes before him. He is a very well liked lad throughout the game. Also he is a very good disciplinarian, which is always important.'

The changes at Moor Farm are continuing with the departures of coach Steve Taylor, physiotherapist Dave Galley, sports therapist Faz Page and sports scientist Wayne Campbell.

Another new addition to the coaching staff is Pete Williams.

Williams arrives as goalkeeping coach from Preston North End and is another to be reunited with his former gaffer.

He arrived in time to join the squad for their trip to Austria, and Davies is pleased to have another old Deepdale colleague on board.

'I'm delighted to be teaming up with Pete again,' said Davies.

As the pre-season matches got under way the Rams recorded a victory in their first game under the new boss.

Tommy Smith opened the scoring nine minutes in to the friendly against FC Gratkorn and the lead was doubled nine minutes after the interval through teenager James Meredith.

Meredith is a graduate of the Rams Academy and signed a two-year professional deal over the summer after progressing through the ranks.

Gratkorn pulled one back late in the game when Daniel Braumeis converted from the spot after Meredith was penalised for a foul, but it was the Rams who ended the game in command.

Davies, in his first friendly, used 20 of the 21 players he took to Austria, with Meredith and Lewin Nyatanga playing the full 90 minutes, while only goalkeeper Steven Cann missed out altogether.

Paul Boertien got 45 minutes under his belt at left-back, while there were also starts for Nathan Doyle and Ainsworth, who partnered Smith in attack.

Adam Bolder took the captain's armband in the first 45 minutes with Marc Edworthy leading the side after the break.

The Rams came through unscathed injury-wise, but there were bookings in the second half for Michael Johnson and Inigo Idiakez.

RAMS: Camp (Grant HT), Jackson (Edworthy HT), Moore (M. Johnson HT), Nyatanga, Boertien (Holmes HT), Doyle (Bisgaard HT), Bolder (Barnes HT), Thirlwell (S. Johnson HT), Meredith, Smith (Peschisolido HT), Ainsworth (Idiakez HT).

'It was a good exercise, a good finish to a hard-working few days and a good step towards our preparations for the new season,' Davies said of the game.

'Fielding two different teams went as well as planned as everyone got some match practice.

'It was a very good few days for the boys to get their relationships going too.

'Fitness-wise everyone is fine, and we will have a tough training session on Friday morning before we go into the Milton Keynes game.'

Four of Derby County's Academy players sign new contracts with the club, pictured, L-R, front: Mike Horton, James Meredith. Back: Tom Cumberworth, Stephen Cann, Theo Streete.

MK DONS: Bankole (Baker 62), Jamie Smith, Lewington (Hastings 62), Mitchell (Lewis 62), Morgan (Murphy 76), Diallo (Page 62), McGovern, Gary Smith, Platt (Wilbraham 62), McLeod (C) (Taylor 62), Rizzo (Tillen 48).

DERBY: Camp, Edworthy (Jackson HT), Boertien (Doyle 80), Bisgaard (Meredith 70), Nyatanga, M. Johnson (C), Idiakez (Bolder HT), Barnes, Peschisolido (Ainsworth 66), Smith (S. Johnson HT), Holmes (Thirlwell HT).
UNUSED SUB: Grant.

ATTENDANCE: 3,014.

Giles Barnes in a pre-season friendly.

REPORT – 15 JULY 2006
MK DONS 1
DERBY COUNTY 2
PRE-SEASON FRIENDLY

The visitors had the game's first chance when good work down the left between Tommy Smith and Lee Holmes created a chance for the latter, but the winger dragged his shot well wide.

They almost forced an own-goal just six minutes in when Paul Peschisolido crossed low from the right, but Jamie Smith scrambled the ball out for a corner after originally slicing it towards the net.

From the flag-kick, Inigo Idiakez's swinging delivery struck the crossbar and bounced to safety.

And 15 minutes in the Rams were ahead. Smith found space down the left and fed Peschisolido, who laid the ball off for Morten Bisgaard to curl home beautifully from the edge of the box.

The lead was almost doubled nine minutes before the interval as Idiakez stepped up in a central position, 20 yards out, to curl a free-kick just past Ademola Bankole's left-hand post.

Derby should have made it two three minutes into the second period. Adam Bolder released Peschisolido, who waited before pulling the ball back for Seth Johnson, but the midfielder placed his shot wide of the upright. Bolder was again instrumental in Derby's second goal on 57 minutes.

It was his well-placed low cross that gave the home defence no chance of cutting out, and Seth Johnson rushed in at the far post to drive in from five yards.

Camp's hands were warmed by Scott Taylor with 25 minutes left.

MK Dons should have pulled one back with 17 minutes remaining, but Taylor, in plenty of space, could only head over a perfect cross from Joe Tillen.

Derby broke immediately and Meredith, scorer of the winner in Gratkorn, saw his low shot well saved by substitute 'keeper Matt Baker.

The Rams hit the woodwork for the second time in the game when Meredith broke down the left and his cross dropped on to the bar, but Ainsworth couldn't force the loose ball home.

Ainsworth was denied by Baker before Camp was stretched by Jamie Smith's effort as both sides came close to adding to the score sheet in the final stages.

Gary Smith's 30-yarder forced Camp into a flying save, and after Derby failed to clear their lines Smith drove the ball back in towards the far post where Wilbraham dived to head home from close range.

Seth Johnson came close to sealing the game as stoppage time began, but once again Baker pulled out a good block after the midfielder's clever run.

REACTION
Rams boss Billy Davies says his side still have a lot of hard work ahead of them in preparation for the 2006–07 season – but is delighted with the way they have come through so far.

Derby made it two wins out of two pre-season games by beating Milton Keynes Dons 2–1 on a sweltering hot Saturday afternoon at the National Hockey Stadium.

Once more, Davies gave all of his outfield players a game – as he did at FC Gratkorn on Wednesday night.

Davies said 'It was another good test for us. Their manager and staff like to put a lot into any game, they are very committed, and they made it hard for us. We are delighted to have come through it.

'The boys have worked ever so hard since day one, though we are still a little bit away so we've got to continue the hard work. But the response has been excellent from them so far, and we will continue to work towards that first League game.'

Paul Boertien is hoping the 2006–07 season will be a fresh start for him as he bids to get his Derby County career back on track.

The defender has not played a competitive game for the Rams since the FA Cup fourth-round replay defeat at Fulham in February 2005 – and that was only his second outing since April 2004.

But with a new manager in Billy Davies in charge, a new board of directors at the top and a new season about to get under way, the 27-year-old is hopeful about his prospects for the immediate future.

'Yes, it's a fresh start for me,' he said, after an 80-minute outing in Saturday's 2–1 friendly win over MK Dons.

'Things weren't the best last season – they were very up and down, and I was injured all the time. But now we have got a new manager, a new chairman, it's a new start. I'm fit now so hopefully I'll get a chance.'

REPORT – 19 JULY 2006
MANSFIELD TOWN 1
DERBY COUNTY 1

PRE-SEASON FRIENDLY

John Mullins was clear in the box with only Lee Grant to beat on two minutes – the Rams stopper spread himself and saved well from point-blank range.

Mullins threatened again three minutes later with a power drive from outside the box on the right, which Grant gathered well once more.

The home side were proving lively and netted in the 12th minute, although Dawson was judged offside as skipper Barker headed home from a Hamshaw free-kick.

Birchall's low drive flew past Grant's right-hand post on 21 minutes and seconds later Brown beat the offside trap on the right, but his cross into the box was squandered by Barker whose header from close range flew over the crossbar.

The Rams, while playing decent possession football, were struggling to fashion decent chances – unlike the home side, who won a corner after Grant was forced to tip over the bar from Brown's strong shot from the edge of the box.

Paul Peschisolido fired wide across the face of the area from a Morten Bisgaard right-hand corner on 40 minutes – a move that summed up Derby's first 45 minutes.

Seth Johnson's low shot trickled inches past 'keeper Muggleton's post on 50 minutes, and Tommy Smith ended a super solo run a minute later by shooting high and wide.

Giles Barnes's shot on 54 minutes took a deflection and was gathered well by Muggleton at his near post after the Rams had started the second half brighter.

Idiakez's 30-yard screamer opened the scoring on the hour mark.

PRE SEASON FRIENDLY

MANSFIELD TOWN
V
DERBY COUNTY

19TH JULY 2006
KO 7.45 PM

MANSFIELD TOWN	DERBY COUNTY
19. CARL MUGGLETON	1 LEE GRANT
2 JOHN MULLINS	2 MARK EDWORTHY
3 GARETH JELLEYMAN	3 LEWIN NYATANGA
4 JONATHAN D'LARYEA	4 ADAM BOLDER
5 JON HJELDE	5 DARREN MOORE
6 ALEX JOHN-BAPTISTE	6 MICHAEL JOHNSON
7 MATTHEW HAMSHAW	7 TOMMY SMITH
8 STEPHEN DAWSON	8 MORTEN BISGAARD
9 RICHARD BARKER	9 PAUL PESCHISOLIDO
10 SIMON BROWN	10 GILES BARNES
26 ADAM BIRCHALL	11 JAMES MEREDITH
	12 INIGO IDIAKEZ

SUBSTITUTES	SUBSTITUTES
15 GILES COKE	13 LEE CAMP
14 CHRIS BEARDSLEY	14 RICHARD JACKSON
22 CALLUM LLOYD	15 PAUL THIRLWELL
25 AUSTIN McINTOSH	16 LEE HOLMES
23 DANNY SLEATH	17 PAUL BOERTIEN
16 NATHAN ARNOLD	18 SETH JOHNSON
31 DANNY REET	
MICHAEL BOULDING	
RORY BOULDING	
PAUL COLLINS	

REFEREE: MR R BOOTH
YELLOW FLAG: MR S COOKE
RED/YELLOW FLAG: MR D COOTE
4TH OFFICIAL: MR M CHESTER

MANSFIELD: Muggleton, Mullins, Jelleyman, D'Laryea, Hjelde, John-Baptiste, Hamshaw, Dawson, Barker, Brown, Birchall.
SUBS (ALL USED): Coke, Beardsley, Lloyd, McIntosh, Sleath, Arnold, Reet, Boulding, Collins.

DERBY: Grant, Edworthy, Nyatanga, Bolder, Moore, M. Johnson, Smith, Bisgaard, Peschisolido, Barnes, Meredith, Idiakez.
SUBS (ALL USED): Camp, Jackson, Thirlwell, Holmes, Boertien, S. Johnson.

ATTENDANCE: 2,971 (1,032 Rams fans).

Inigo Idiakez celebrates after scoring his goal in the second half of the game.

Boertien's cross into the box from the left was headed down and cleared to the feet of the Spaniard, who fired the ball into the bottom right-hand corner of Muggleton's net.

Smith was down in the Mansfield box on 65 after clashing with Hjelde – the referee waved away penalty calls, but the Derby front-man was clutching his ankle and required physio attention.

Beardsley's shot from range flew through four players and forced a good save from Grant, who dived to his right to palm away on 80 minutes.

At the other end, Barnes's speculative volley from the right hit the side-netting a minute later.

Smith headed into Muggleton's arms from a Johnson corner on 84 minutes before Boulding levelled the scores two minutes from time with a low shot from inside the box.

Derby County are back in the transfer market with a bang after landing Luton Town striker Steve Howard in a million-pound deal.

The 30-year-old front-man has scored more than 100 goals in five years with the Hatters and becomes Billy Davies's first signing since taking over as Rams boss in June.

He is the most expensive incoming transfer since Francois Grenet in November 2001 and has been given the number-nine shirt immediately.

'This is the peak of my career so far, without a shadow of a doubt,' Howard said. 'Right now I am just itching to get going. I can't wait for the season to start and hopefully I can beef up the strike-force at Derby County.

'It's about me getting my head down and doing my best for Derby County.'

Davies was understandably delighted at his first bit of business.

'Steve is a top signing for us,' said the boss. 'He is the right age, has great experience and is a player who will help take this club forward in the next few years.

'To say we are happy to have him on board is an understatement because there was a lot of competition for his signature.

'Players of Steve's quality are difficult to find, and it helps too for team spirit that he's also a fantastic guy.'

Derby County's first summer signing, striker Steve Howard, with manager Billy Davies.

REPORT – 22 JULY 2006
BURTON ALBION 1
DERBY COUNTY 3

PRE-SEASON FRIENDLY

Only three minutes were on the clock when home goalkeeper Stuart Tomlinson was picking the ball out of the net.

Adam Bolder played a tidy ball in to Barnes inside the area. Out came Tomlinson to challenge, but the ball bobbled into the path of Barnes, who was left with a simple tap-in.

On five minutes the visitors were almost further ahead when Bolder rose well to head Marc Edworthy's cross down and to the bottom corner, only to see Tomlinson dive and save superbly.

The game then became a much more even affair as bolts of lightning lit up the Pirelli.

On 32 minutes Idiakez cut open the Burton defence with a lovely low

BURTON: Tomlinson, Rowett, Webster (Brayford), Tinson, Austin, Fowler (Corbett), Clare (Stride), Ducros, Gilroy (Holmes), Hall, Scoffham (Harrad).
UNUSED SUBS: Taylor, Brayford, Clough.

DERBY: Camp (Grant 46), Edworthy (Jackson 46), Boertien (Meredith 65), S. Johnson, Moore, M. Johnson (Nyatanga 77), Smith, Bisgaard (Holmes 46), Barnes, Idiakez (Thirlwell 46), Bolder (Peschisolido 46).

ATTENDANCE: 2,711 (1,475 Rams fans).

ball through the centre that released Barnes, and he was left one-on-one with Tomlinson, but his low shot was saved by the 'keeper's feet.

As the rain continued to pour, the players of both teams continued to try and get the ball down and play on an increasingly slippery surface.

Six minutes before the break Andy Ducros worried the Rams with a low effort that fizzed along the wet pitch and just wide.

Within seconds of the restart, Barnes latched on to a bad Aaron Webster pass and hit a splendid swirling 25-yarder that Tomlinson did superbly well to tip over.

On 51 Barnes opened up the opposition defence with a flicked ball into the path of sub Holmes, who was left with a race through on goal. He took it in his stride well but hit his shot straight at the 'keeper before Barnes did exactly the same with the rebound.

Eight minutes later the Rams were two up, once again thanks to Barnes – and this time it was a lovely goal. The teenager skipped past a sliding tackle on the right side of the area with ease and angled a low, unstoppable drive past Tomlinson.

Within 60 seconds a jubilant Barnes had completed his hat-trick. Fellow striker Tommy Smith took a pot-shot from range that looked to have beaten Tomlinson.

He got a hand to it but could only look on in disbelief as Barnes tapped in the rebound with his left foot.

At the other end Brewers' centre-half Darren Tinson charged forward from the back and let fly with a cracker from 30 yards that seemed to be heading goalwards until Grant flung himself to his left and plucked the ball out of the air.

Grant was forced into another excellent fingertip save from a Darren Stride diving header and was then in action again, palming behind a Corbett header as Burton piled on the pressure.

Ex-Derby man Gary Rowett grabbed a late consolation, but it was simply that as Billy's boys picked up another pre-season win.

REACTION

Rams boss Billy Davies insists his side are showing the right signs of being able to play the game the way he wants it to be played.

Davies saw Derby record a 3–1 win at Burton Albion on Saturday after a 90-minute performance that included plenty of flowing football.

It was a vast improvement on the previous Wednesday's 1–1 draw at Mansfield Town and left the gaffer encouraged by the progress his side is making.

'That's the style of play we want and that is what we are all about,' he said. 'We will have to adapt from time to time, we will have to play a certain way at certain grounds, but in general we want to move it around in that fashion. We want to play the game the way we believe it should be played, which is the passing game.

'With the chances we created, the shots at goal and the crosses we put into the box, I'm sure the Derby fans will have gone away happy with what they saw.

'There was much more energy than at Mansfield, and we played more on the front foot, which we're all about. With the players we've got we have to be on the front foot and playing with that level of energy.'

The Rams attacking options look set to be further boosted soon with news that the club has agreed a fee with Premiership giants Arsenal for exciting young winger Ryan Smith.

Smith, 19, is a player Derby boss Billy Davies rates as having enormous potential, and he is trying to tie down a deal ahead of Saturday's pre-season friendly with Bolton Wanderers.

'We're down to the final details of negotiations with player and agent, and we are hoping that within the next two or three days that it can be concluded,' he revealed.

'We would like him in the squad for Saturday so fingers crossed.

'It is a great opportunity for him, he would be a great addition for us, and we are hoping we can get him on board.'

Smith, an England Youth international, is a left-sided winger who spent a spell on loan at Championship side Leicester City last season.

He has yet to make a League appearance for the Gunners but has made six Carling Cup outings, including a debut at the age of 16 in October 2003.

While with the Foxes, Smith made 19 appearances in all competitions with 17 in the Championship – including 10 starts – and scored one goal.

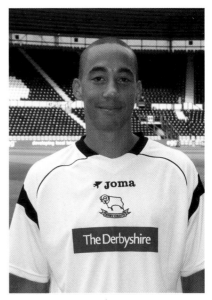
New signing Ryan Smith.

REPORT – 29 JULY 2006
DERBY COUNTY 2
BOLTON WANDERERS 0
PRE-SEASON FRIENDLY

The game opened slowly, and it wasn't until 15 minutes had passed when the first chance arrived, but Ricardo Vaz Te, with plenty of time just eight yards out, chose spectacular over making certain and managed to completely miss the ball with his scissor-kick.

Vaz Te came closer six minutes later after being picked out by Stelios's inch-perfect right-wing cross, but the Portuguese youngster headed just over the bar.

Howard had Rams' first opportunity with a 20-yard snap-shot that went just wide of the post, with Jussi Jaaskelainen completely beaten. And it was Derby who opened the scoring on the half-hour mark.

Barnes had been hacked down on one of his trademark powerful runs, some 30 yards from goal but right in the centre of the pitch. Inigo Idiakez lined it up and showed once again why he is the master in those situations – Jaaskelainen stood no chance with his perfectly-placed curling effort.

Howard came close to adding a second with a stooping header from Idiakez's right-wing free-kick.

Neither side made a half-time change, and once again it was the Rams on the attack as the second period got under way.

Smith robbed Tal Ben Haim and began a move that saw Barnes fire across goal for Jaaskelainen to palm the ball out to Howard. The striker had to hit his shot on the turn, however, and flashed his effort just wide of the far post.

Jaaskelainen denied Tommy Smith with a fine low save on 63 minutes as Derby pressed for a second goal.

The Rams then doubled their lead with five minutes remaining, with Barnes once again poaching from close range.

Paul Peschisolido had gone through against Al Habsi, but the 'keeper denied him with a fine low save, though the ball rolled loose for Barnes to tap home his fourth goal of pre-season.

DERBY: Camp, Edworthy (Meredith 81), Moore, Johnson (C) (Nyatanga 81), Boertien (Jackson 53), Idiakez (Thirlwell 74), Bolder, Bisgaard (Peschisolido 53), Barnes, Smith, Howard (Holmes 73).
UNUSED SUB: Grant.

BOLTON: Jaaskelainen (Al Habsi 74), Hunt (Perez 41), Fortune (Fojut 53), Nolan (C) (Charlesworth 72), Ben Haim (Sissons 67), Speed, Stelios (Wolfe 61), Campo, Vaz Te, Diouf (Blazey 78), Ellis.
UNUSED SUBS: Tal, Howarth.

ATTENDANCE: 9,135.

Giles Barnes celebrates after scoring Derby's second.

With Idiakez off the field, free-kick duties were left to Barnes, and he was just off target with a late 20-yard curler.

REACTION

Boss Billy Davies admits he shouted to Inigo Idiakez to pass the ball wide seconds before the Spaniard stepped up to hit a 25-yard free-kick special for the Rams' opener against Bolton on Saturday.

'Yes, I was screaming at him to pass to Mark Edworthy because I thought he was too far out to score,' Davies said.

'But I know better now! I'm glad Inigo proved me wrong, in fact I'm delighted. I will apologise to him later and take back the stick I was giving him.'

As for the 2–0 victory over Premiership opposition, Davies described the friendly as 'a nice workout against a very good team'.

'Every game we play without getting beaten breeds confidence,' the gaffer said. 'We have to get into the habit of becoming a winning team, but the most important thing in pre-season is to come through games injury free.

'I thought we moved the ball around pretty well at times today, but there's still a lot of rebuilding to do, and I hope the fans appreciate that.'

Marc Edworthy.

August

One of the most hotly-anticipated days in the footballing calendar is just around the corner, with the 2006–07 season about to get under way. It's the beginning in earnest of a new era for Derby County, under the guidance of Billy Davies after his summer appointment.

It's always important to start well, and the Rams have a tricky opening month, with former boss George Burley's Southampton standing in their way on the opening day.

Boss Billy Davies has released the 2006–07 Rams squad numbers.

There are first-team squad places for youngsters James Meredith, Tom Cumberworth, Theo Streete, Jeremy Bossekota and 'keeper Steven Cann.

Lee Camp will once again pull on the goalkeeper's number-one jersey – although Davies has yet to reveal his first-choice 'keeper.

He's also leaving fans guessing the identity of his skipper with Inigo Idiakez, Adam Bolder, Michael Johnson and Darren Moore all pulling on the captain's armband during the pre-season campaign.

'We have a number of players with the right kind of character to take on the captain's role,' said Davies.

'There's also the possibility of a player from outside the club taking it on.'

Lee Grant keeping warm during half time.

Nathan Doyle on the ball against Birmingham City in 2005 is off to Bradford City on loan until the new year.

THE RAMS 2006–07

1	Lee CAMP
2	Marc EDWORTHY
4	Adam BOLDER
6	Michael JOHNSON
7	Tommy SMITH
8	Morten BISGAARD
9	Steve HOWARD
11	Paul PESCHISOLIDO
12	Paul THIRLWELL
13	Lee GRANT
14	Richard JACKSON
17	Paul BOERTIEN
18	Seth JOHNSON
19	Nathan DOYLE
20	Lee HOLMES
23	Darren MOORE
27	Inigo IDIAKEZ
28	Giles BARNES
29	Lionel AINSWORTH
30	Lewin NYATANGA
31	James MEREDITH
32	Tom CUMBERWORTH
33	Theo STREETE
34	Jeremy BOSSEKOTA
35	Steven CANN

Winger Lee Holmes and midfielder Nathan Doyle, both 19, are joining Bradford City – managed by Derby legend Colin Todd – until the end of the year.

Holmes is Derby's youngest-ever player, having appeared for the first-team on Boxing Day 2002 at the age of 15 years and 267 days.

Giles Barnes is making the headlines once more after signing a new four-year contract with the club.

Barnes penned his first professional deal on his 17th birthday in August 2005 and made his senior breakthrough during the last three months of last season.

Derby have already rejected two offers from Premiership clubs for the midfielder and are understandably delighted that he has agreed a new deal.

Barnes had no hesitation about staying at Pride Park and wants to continue the progress he has made over the last 12 months.

'You can always develop, I'm always learning and always picking up things,' he said.

'It's the same for every single player – whether it's Darren Moore and his physique, or Steve Howard in attack holding the ball up.

'You're always learning from everyone in every year, and that is how I will continue.

'When I step on to the pitch I always want to give my best because that is how you improve.

'In training I've tried to do my best as well and you get the rewards at the end.'

And there will be two more additions to the squad list after the Rams completed a pair of signings – one expected, one out of the blue.

The expected deal is that to bring 19-year-old Arsenal winger Ryan Smith to Pride Park after he decided to make the switch from the Emirates Stadium.

But the unexpected capture sees experienced central-midfielder Matt Oakley arrive on a free transfer from Southampton.

The 28-year-old has put pen to paper on a three-year contract and will go straight into the squad for Sunday's season-opener against his former club.

'Matt Oakley is a tremendous signing for us who has vast experience from a long time at Southampton, where he was a former club captain, and played a huge amount of games in the Premiership,' the boss said.

'I have been chasing Ryan for a few days because of his great potential, his pace and wonderful left foot.

'We are delighted to have signed both players.'

Oakley insists it was the 'infectious enthusiasm' of Rams boss Billy Davies that persuaded him to leave Southampton after 14 years.

He claims Davies is in the same mould as former Saints boss Gordon Strachan and rejected other offers to team up with the Scot at Pride Park.

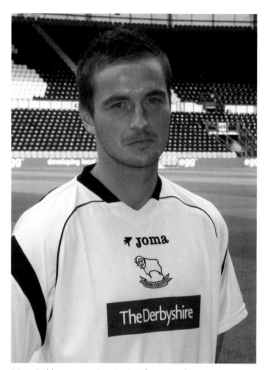

Matt Oakley: a surprise signing from Southampton.

'I've spent my whole career at Southampton and felt it was time for a fresh start and a new challenge,' said the 28-year-old midfielder.

'It's strange to think that I am almost 29 and this is the first medical I've had!

'I was impressed with what Billy had to say and that's why I'm here today.

'I had a number of options – including a new one-year deal with Southampton – but once I started talking football with Billy I knew this was the place I wanted to be.

'His knowledge, his infectious enthusiasm and, of course, his plans for the future were very persuasive.'

Smith, meanwhile, has vowed to do to other Championship clubs what he did TO the Rams last season.

The 19-year-old left-sided star, who has joined Derby on a three-year deal from Arsenal, came on twice as a sub in both games against the Rams last year when on loan at Leicester.

So the Pride Park faithful will have some idea what to expect from confident Smith – who has been handed squad number 15 – if he makes his debut against Southampton on Sunday.

Smith said 'I definitely promise that I'll do some damage to the opposition, that's my aim.

'I have pace and will be running at defenders all day long, hoping to create and score goals.

'I'm hungry to get started with my Derby career as soon as possible, hopefully by playing on Sunday.

'To be honest I can't wait, this is a challenge I'm really looking forward to.'

DERBY: Camp, Edworthy, Moore, M. Johnson (C), Jackson, T. Smith, Idiakez (Bolder 78), S. Johnson (Peschisolido 82), R. Smith (Bisgaard 62), Barnes, Howard.
UNUSED SUBS: Oakley, Nyatanga.

SOUTHAMPTON: Davis, Pele, Lundekvam (C) (Ostlund 3), Skacel, Rasiak, Wright, Fuller (Wright-Phillips 53), Belmadi, Baird, Bale, Viafara.
UNUSED SUBS: Poke, Dyer, Surman.

ATTENDANCE: 21,939.

Seth Johnson taps in Derby's first goal of the new campaign.

REPORT – 6 AUGUST 2006
DERBY COUNTY 2
SOUTHAMPTON 2

Understandably there was a cagey opening to proceedings with neither side willing to give anything away in the early stages of the new season.

Saints forced a couple of corners around the quarter-hour mark, and from the second of Skacel's deliveries Jhon Viafara rose to head wide at the far post.

Derby's first opportunity came 19 minutes in, although it was a difficult one for Darren Moore, and he was only able to head Inigo Idiakez's corner wide while under pressure.

Howard had the chance for a debut goal a couple of minutes later following great work by Giles Barnes down the right, but the million-pound man couldn't get his shot away.

He was closer seconds later with a header that arrowed just over from Richard Jackson's left-wing cross. And on 34 minutes Derby were in front from a goal that owed much to Howard's power in the air. Richard Jackson crossed for Howard to head down for Seth Johnson, and, although his first effort was superbly saved by Kelvin Davis, the ball rolled kindly out for Johnson to drive home.

Davis then saw his fingers stung by Idiakez's powerful 30-yard free-kick that looked destined for the top-corner three minutes before half-time.

Southampton came perilously close to an equaliser just two minutes into the second half as a cross was allowed to bounce all the way through to Ostlund, but the full-back's shot flew only into the side-netting.

And they were level on the hour. Ryan Smith hauled down Belmadi 20 yards out, in the inside-right channel, and Gareth Bale stepped up to beautifully curl home the free-kick.

Derby had a clear penalty claim rejected when Tommy Smith robbed Chris Baird and had his heels clipped by the full-back.

And by 68 minutes Southampton had turned things around.

Ex-Ram Grzegorz Rasiak held the ball up well and laid it off for Wright-Phillips to take a touch before firing emphatically past Camp from just inside the box.

Derby almost hit back immediately when Idiakez saw his shot saved by Davis, and Smith's effort from the rebound was deflected wide.

The Rams were an inch away from levelling on 82 minutes as Michael Johnson rose to meet Seth Johnson's free-kick, but his headed effort dropped just over.

Howard's headed effort stretched Davis as Derby looked to find a leveller, while Camp was busy at the other end when Rasiak cracked one goalwards from a narrow angle.

The goalkeeper's fingers prevented Skacel from extending the lead with three minutes to go as Southampton found themselves on top. But cometh the hour cometh the man, and that man was substitute Paul Peschisolido. Bisgaard's through ball was dummied by Barnes into the path of Peschisolido, who showed typical composure to find the bottom corner from 14 yards.

REACTION

Derby manager Billy Davies said he was disappointed with his side's performance in the final half-hour of Sunday's 2–2 home draw against the Saints.

'I thought for 60 minutes we did what we wanted to do, but after that too many players ran too deep and stopped pressing,' he said.

'For an away team we allowed them too much time on the ball. That said, Southampton have already been crowned champions of this League by some pundits.

'They have signed many new players and are two years into their development so we have to be pleased in one sense because we have a lot to do.

'For me, the last 30 minutes was a learning curve because I saw far too many of my players not competing. I am not fooled by the draw – we are not there yet.

'It was a reasonable performance and a decent point, but there's a lot to come from certain individuals.'

Paul Peschisolido admitted it was critical that the Rams didn't get their season off to a losing start – and was happy to be in the right place at the right time to ensure they took a point from the opening-day battle against Southampton.

It looked as though the visitors would take away all three points after Gareth Bale and Bradley Wright-Phillips had turned things around once Seth Johnson put Derby in front before half-time.

But as stoppage time approached the ball broke to Pesch just inside the box, and in that situation there was only one thing about to happen.

'Super-sub!' he said after the 2–2 draw.

'I loved it, that has happened on a few occasions over the years here and at other clubs.

'It was a shame we didn't win because we would have liked to have given the crowd something to cheer about from the first game, but there were plenty of positives.

'We will get stronger and stronger, and I guess a draw was a fair result.'

Peschisolido's goal celebration.

Howard's dominance in the air was evident from the opening match.

STOKE: Simonsen, Hoefkens, Higginbotham (Dickinson 68), Duberry (C), Hill, Chadwick (Paterson 64), Brammer, Russell, Sweeney, Sidibe, Pericard (Sigurdsson 84).
UNUSED SUBS: Pulis, Duggan.

DERBY: Grant, Edworthy, Moore, Nyatanga, M. Johnson, T. Smith, Oakley (C) (Idiakez 70), S. Johnson (Peschisolido 60), R. Smith (Bisgaard 60), Barnes, Howard.
UNUSED SUBS: Bolder, Jackson.

ATTENDANCE: 20,013.

Inigo Idiakez is shown a yellow card.

Rams boss Billy Davies has announced that new signing Matt Oakley will be Derby's team captain for the 2006–07 season.

The 28-year-old central-midfielder, who joined the Rams in a three-year deal on Friday and was an unused substitute in the 2–2 draw with his former club Southampton, has a wealth of experience having been a one-club man with the Saints for 14 years.

Veteran defender Michael Johnson, who wore the armband for the Pride Park clash on Sunday, has been named as club captain.

Davies said 'Matt is an experienced pro who is a good leader and very vocal out on the pitch, and Jonno knows the club and all the players inside out. That's why I felt they were both suitable for these roles.'

REPORT – 8 AUGUST 2006
STOKE CITY 2
DERBY COUNTY 0

Neither side threatened at all in the early stages, and it took until 16 minutes were on the clock for the game's first chance to come as Peter Sweeney crossed from the left for Mamady Sidibe, but the big front-man directed his diving header wide. But just a minute later the home side were in front.

Sidibe laid the ball off inside the box for Sweeney to cross low from the left, and Vincent Pericard stretched out a long leg to poke home from close range.

The Rams came close to a quick equaliser when Tommy Smith's cross was headed away from Steve Howard, and after Stoke failed to clear the corner Oakley's 20-yard drive was deflected and caused Steve Simonsen a few problems.

Teenage winger Ryan Smith forced Simonsen into his first real save of the night four minutes before the interval with a cracked 25-yard effort that the goalkeeper had to turn over the bar.

Derby faced some late Stoke pressure as half-time approached, though Grant was called into action to grab Luke Chadwick's 20-yard volley.

Stoke had the second half's first opportunity from a training ground free-kick, but Sweeney volleyed wide from a narrow angle.

Derby actually started the second half strongly, but it was Stoke who almost made it two 11 minutes in. The Rams were split open as Pericard went through one-on-one with Grant and cracked a powerful shot against the underside of the bar. The home faithful were appealing for a goal as the ball bounced down, but the well-placed assistant referee kept his flag down.

But just seconds later the lead was doubled. Pericard drove the ball low from 20 yards, and as the ball bounced up from Grant's save Russell was there first to head home from close range.

Brammer's 30-yard shot whistled just wide of the post as Stoke looked to be taking control with a passage of flowing football.

It was looking increasingly unlikely that the Rams would be taking anything home from the game, and Moore's tug on Sidibe took their yellow card total to four.

The Rams were even presented with four minutes of stoppage time to try and attempt a dramatic recovery, but they never looked like doing so.

There could be no argument that Stoke deserved the win.

REACTION

Rams boss Billy Davies had no complaints with the result as his side went down to a 2–0 defeat at Stoke City.

Goals in either half from Vincent Pericard and Darrel Russel condemned Derby to their first defeat of the new season at the Britannia Stadium. And Davies admitted that his side had 'failed the test' that the Potters put in front of them.

'No, no complaints when you analyse the game,' he said. 'In the end we were probably out-fought and out-run at times. It was a test we came here to take on, and it was a test we have failed in. We now know the situation, it has been staring us in the face for a long time and we are not surprised.

'We have got to work that little bit harder, be more determined, be more passionate, and we have got to come to places like Stoke City and battle more than we have done.'

New skipper Matt Oakley has revealed he rejected the chance of a Premiership return in favour of a move to Derby County. He left Southampton in the summer and had spent pre-season training at Charlton Athletic, who wanted him to sign on for a year.

But speaking after making his debut in the 2–0 defeat at Stoke City, Oakley revealed he is targeting a return to the top-flight with the Rams.

'I had offers on the table from other clubs and Charlton offered me a year,' he said.

'But I spoke to Billy [Davies], and he impressed me unbelievably, which is why I am here.

'I want to win things, I want to be back in the Premiership, and I think Billy is the manager to do it.'

Billy Davies has delivered on his promise to add further names to his Derby County squad with three captures in as many days.

Thursday's late-evening capture was defender Dean Leacock, a 22-year-old snapped up from Premiership side Fulham.

Experienced left-back Mo Camara was next through the door, on a free from Scottish giants Celtic.

And completing the trio is goalkeeper Stephen Bywater, who has signed on an emergency loan deal that allows him to play at Hull City this evening.

Of Leacock, Davies said 'Dean is a player with plenty of potential, and we're pleased to have him on board.

'There's room for improvement, he's not the finished article, but we'll be working hard to develop that potential.

'He's quick and good on the ball and will add to our defensive options.'

And the gaffer added of Camara, 'We are delighted Mo has decided to join us as part of our rebuilding process as we continue to develop the squad.

'He is a great player with a terrific engine and will be a very good asset for the club.'

Mo Camara.

Dean Leacock.

Stephen Bywater.

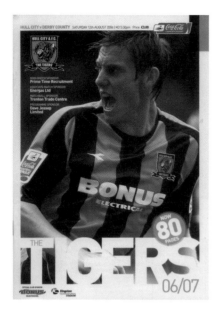

HULL: Myhill, Dawson, Turner, Parkin, Duffy (Barmby 34), Ricketts, Marney, Collins, Livermore (Andrews 80), Fagan, France (Elliott 79).
UNUSED SUBS: Duke, Thelwell.

DERBY: Bywater, M. Johnson, T. Smith, Howard, Jackson (Leacock 78), Boertien, S. Johnson (R. Smith 58), Oakley, Moore, Idiakez, Barnes (Bolder 85).
UNUSED SUBS: Bisgaard, Peschisolido.

ATTENDANCE: 15,261.

REPORT – 12 AUGUST 2006
HULL CITY 1
DERBY COUNTY 2

Derby found themselves in front with only seven minutes on the clock. Tommy Smith played the ball to skipper Matt Oakley 20 yards out and, despite protestations from the home crowd who thought he was offside, he clinically despatched the ball across 'keeper Bo Myhill and into the bottom corner.

The livewire Craig Fagan then curled an angled thunderbolt just past Bywater's right-hand post from the right and then, in what was becoming an end-to-end game, Idiakez looped a 30-yard free-kick just over the bar.

Myhill palmed out another Idiakez set-piece on 18 minutes, but the resulting corner was wasted by Seth Johnson, who sent his left-footed effort well over everyone.

Six minutes later the visitors produced a nice flowing move that ended in Seth Johnson heading narrowly over.

Derby continued to dominate, but they were hit by a sucker punch deep into injury time when Paul Boertien mistimed a sliding challenge on Fagan. The referee pointed to the spot and up stepped Jon Parkin to slot the ball low past Bywater.

With eight minutes of the second half played, a loose Idiakez back-pass to Bywater was under-hit and very nearly let in Barmby, but the 'keeper was off his line smartly to clear the danger.

With 20 minutes left, Howard nodded a ball down perfectly into the path of advancing Tommy Smith. He controlled well and created a clear opening, but his weak shot from 12 yards was straight at Myhill.

On 73 minutes the Rams were offered a lifeline when Andy Dawson handled a Barnes cross from the right inside the area.

Smith stepped up to take the penalty, and though his effort lacked power it had plenty of direction and nestled in the bottom corner.

Fagan curled a shot wide as Hull pushed on for an equaliser, and on 87 minutes Bywater did well to cling on to a Parkin shot on the turn from the edge of the box.

The Rams defended their lead well and saw the game out with Moore making an amazing last-gasp block late on to deny Parkin once again.

Matt Oakley about to score Derby's first goal.

Tommy Smith's penalty gives Derby the lead.

REACTION

Billy Davies knows that picking up points is the most important part of football so was happy that his side came away from the KC Stadium 2–1 winners.

But the manager wasn't overly pleased with aspects of his team's display – most notably a nervousness that seemed to surround the defending at times – and said that he hopes there's better to come.

Davies said 'I'm very pleased because we came here to win the game and we achieved our aim.

'I think that overall we deserved it.

'We need to take the positives from the performance, and there were plenty of them, but I wasn't happy with the nervousness we showed at times.

'There's still plenty of work to be done on that front.'

Three new arrivals in as many days last week have given the Rams plenty of competition for places as they prepare for Saturday's visit of Norwich City to Pride Park.

Rams boss Billy Davies wants to build on the win at Hull in front of Derby's own fans and is looking forward to working with his new signings once more.

'We need to build on the result at Hull but put in a better performance,' said Davies.

'Norwich have started the season well and have a good squad. In Darren Huckerby and Robert Earnshaw they have two lively forwards, and we'll need to match their energy.'

He's added some energy and experience to the Rams ranks over the past few days with three new signings – defender Dean Leacock and 'keeper Stephen Bywater featured at the KC Stadium last weekend, while Mo Camara prepares for a possible debut this Saturday.

'We're increasing the competition in different areas and a selection headache is a great problem to have. It keeps all the players on their toes.

'The new players are good personalities to have around the place and have settled in well.

The minutes count down to Derby's first win of the season.

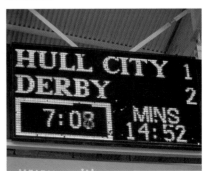

Arturo Lupoli joins the Rams on a season-long loan from Arsenal.

DERBY: Bywater, Edworthy, Moore (Nyatanga 33), M. Johnson (C), Camara, Bisgaard, Barnes, Idiakez (Bolder 75), T. Smith, Peschisolido (Lupoli 54), Howard.
UNUSED SUBS: R. Smith, S. Johnson.

NORWICH: Gallacher, Drury (C), Shackell, Huckerby, Croft (McVeigh 71), Earnshaw, Safri, Etuhu, Colin, Doherty, Robinson.
UNUSED SUBS: Fleming, Hughes, Jarvis, Lewis.

ATTENDANCE: 22,196.

'Leacock is a young player with lots of potential. He's composed on the ball, has great ability and has a bright future.

'At 31, Camara is more experienced but still very fit and athletic with real pace. He's bringing competition to the left-back position.

'Bywater is a good communicator on the pitch – he talks to his defenders and has great presence.'

And Davies has taken his signings total to seven with the loan capture of exciting Italian teenager Arturo Lupoli from Premiership side Arsenal. The 19-year-old has arrived from the Emirates Stadium until the end of the season and comes with a glowing reference. Gunners legend Thierry Henry likens the diminutive striker to Italian World Cup winner Paolo Rossi.

'I was very pleased with Thierry's comments,' smiled Lupoli. 'It's great to hear that sort of thing from him. I just hope to score as many goals as him because that would be an amazing career.'

REPORT – 19 AUGUST 2006
DERBY COUNTY 0
NORWICH CITY 0

Norwich had the ball in the back of the net with two minutes on the clock as Gary Doherty powered home a header from Darren Huckerby's corner, but it was ruled out for a push by the centre-half.

Steve Howard nodded down neatly for Bisgaard, who should have done better from inside the box, before the big number nine tested Paul Gallacher with a 25-yard drive.

Bisgaard then landed a shot on the roof of the net from fully 35 yards out that caught everyone inside the ground by surprise, including Norwich 'keeper Gallacher, who wouldn't have got near it.

Barnes tried to beat Gallacher from 10 yards closer in after good work by Howard and Peschisolido, but was also just off target. The 18-year-old was having plenty of joy down the right and went on one of his powerful runs before feeding Howard, who turned well on the edge of the box and forced Gallacher into a low 24th-minute save. Howard's luck was out again in the 26th minute as he couldn't have come any closer to his first Rams goal.

Idiakez swung over a free-kick from the left-hand touchline, and Howard rose highest to get a flick to the ball as Gallacher came out, but it hit the bar and bounced back into the hands of the grateful custodian.

Derby went to sleep five minutes before the break and nearly paid for it as Robert Earnshaw found space on the left to whip over a superb cross that Carl Robinson headed over from eight yards.

Bright sunshine had greeted the players at the start of the game, but they returned for the second half to be met by grey skies, rain and the floodlights on.

Derby were almost the architects of their own downfall nine minutes in as a poor Idiakez corner led to Norwich breaking at pace and Earnshaw shooting just over from 20 yards.

Norwich were offering more of a threat on the break with the pace of Huckerby, Earnshaw and Croft causing Derby a few headaches in the first quarter of an hour after the break, and it was only Earnshaw's misplaced header that stopped them opening the scoring.

On 69 minutes they broke with four on three as Huckerby ran at Michael Johnson, but the Rams skipper produced a perfectly-timed tackle to halt the winger in his tracks.

The game seemed to be opening up as time ticked on, but Derby were too often guilty of sloppy errors as they looked like breaking away.

Having played so well in the first half, Derby looked like they were in serious danger of blowing things with a performance that got sloppier and sloppier as the second period went on, and with two minutes left they had an escape as Earnshaw blazed over from the edge of the box.

REACTION

Billy Davies says every point his side pick up during their transitional phase is invaluable.

Speaking after Saturday's second home draw on the trot, Davies said 'Drawing against Norwich is a decent point for us right now. It was a game of two halves really.

'After a bright first 45 minutes we caused ourselves too many problems in the second half, but a point keeps us moving along. We have to become a side that's hard to beat.

'Until we reach the transfer window at the end of August, and we know what we are working with, we will just grind away and pick up something wherever we can.

'Ideally today we would have wanted three points, but we've been up against two teams at home in Southampton and Norwich who will be right up there at the end of the season, and every point is vital to us right now.

'We had a few chances, hit the bar and got at Norwich in the first half.

'Considering the changes we are making, I'm relatively satisfied, but it's important we keep our discipline.

'You could see in the second half it was important we matched them three for three in midfield and that's a battle we lost.

'We know the situation and we aren't fooled, but we have nudged forward and have become a tough team to crack.

Mo Camara receiving his first yellow card.

Lupoli came on for Peschisolido as a second-half substitute.

Stephen Bywater revealed that he chose squad number 43 in tribute to his former goalkeeping coach Les Sealey.

Sealey, the former Coventry City, Luton Town and Manchester United star, looked after the goalkeepers at West Ham United until his tragic death from a heart attack on 19 August 2001.

He was a great mentor for Bywater, who joined the Rams from West Ham, and was 43 years old at the time of his death – something the former England Under-21 international was keen to recognise.

'Last year I was number one at West Ham when Roy Carroll came in, and they asked me what number I wanted,' the 25-year-old said.

'I was thinking about it, and I wanted 43, but they couldn't give it to me.

'Les Sealey, who played at Manchester United and was my coach at West Ham, died at the age of 43 – which was no age to die.

'It was the fifth anniversary of his death on Saturday so I thought it would be fitting.

'I know he is watching over me, I know he wants me to do well, so that is for him. He was a nice bloke and looked after me like a father.'

'31 August is just around the corner and that's when the hard work starts, when we know what squad we are working with.'

Arturo Lupoli lapped up the Pride Park atmosphere during his Derby County debut – and said it reminded him of Highbury.

The 19-year-old striker moved to Derby on Friday for a season-long loan from Arsenal, where he had found opportunities hard to come by in the two years since joining from Parma.

But he has sampled the special atmosphere at Highbury and also played at Old Trafford and the City of Manchester Stadium – and reckons Pride Park can match the best of them.

'It was amazing to play in front of so many people,' he said after getting his Rams career under way with a 36-minute substitute appearance in the 0–0 draw with Norwich City.

'I only had a few chances in the first-team with Arsenal: in the Carling Cup, at Old Trafford, the City of Manchester Stadium and at Highbury. It has been great for me to play in front of so many people at Derby. The atmosphere here reminds of the one at Highbury so it is very special.'

Derby County are preparing to get their Carling Cup campaign under way with a first-round trip to Stockport County.

The Rams' recent history in the competition is littered with Cup upsets by lower-division teams, and the League Two Hatters will prove a tricky test at Edgeley Park.

Boss Billy Davies is determined to condemn Derby's dire record to the history books.

'We are taking this game as seriously as any other,' he insists. 'We've been preparing in the same manner as we do League games. We have had Stockport watched, we know what they're about, and we've been working hard to ensure our name is in the hat for the second round.'

The Rams were dumped out in the first round of the Carling Cup by Grimsby last season, Lincoln City during 2004–05 and Huddersfield Town a year earlier.

After a first-round win at Mansfield Town in 2002–03, Oldham were the victors in a Pride Park second-round tie.

The boss continued: 'Cup games are potential banana skins, as this club knows, so we have the right mental attitude – we must be professional and prepared to battle.

'We're taking the Carling Cup seriously, as a competition in which we want to progress and as a chance to foster a winning mentality. Whether it's a League, Cup, friendly or training ground match, it's all about winning.'

REPORT – 22 AUGUST 2006
STOCKPORT COUNTY 0
DERBY COUNTY 1
CARLING CUP FIRST ROUND

The game's first shot came almost quarter of an hour in, and it was only a yard or so away from opening the scoring as Morten Bisgaard curled a low 20-yarder that left James Spencer grasping at thin air.

Adam Bolder was on target with a dipping volley that Spencer grabbed at the second attempt.

But Derby had an escape on 22 minutes as Michael Rose broke free down the Stockport left and whipped across a lovely low ball that Adam Proudlock was an inch away from getting a vital touch on.

Ryan Smith linked well with Bisgaard for the Dane to fire in a 25-yarder that Spencer did well to turn over the bar as Derby looked to build a head of steam up just before the half-hour mark.

The lively Liam Dickinson had Stockport's first shot on target 10 minutes before the break after being fed by Tommy Smith's poor back-pass, but he failed to test Camp from the edge of the box.

Derby couldn't have been much closer to opening the scoring just two-and-a-half minutes before the interval, and this time it was Barnes with the dipping 20-yard effort that was turned out for a corner via the post by Spencer.

From the corner-kick Ryan Smith found space and drove goalwards, and although Spencer parried his shot Michael Johnson was on hand to poke in the rebound from six yards.

Stockport came out for the second half looking for a quick route back into the game, but the closest they came to an equaliser was when Raynes headed over from eight yards.

Briggs broke through midfield and shrugged off the challenge of Bolder, only to fire just wide of Camp's right-hand post having made good ground.

Arturo Lupoli had a good chance to open his account in the 70th minute after he had cleverly created space for himself from Howard's knock-down, but having done the hard work he fired over when well-placed.

A second goal would have settled any Derby nerves, but with 12 minutes remaining it still hadn't arrived, despite the best efforts of Lupoli, who stretched to toe-end Idiakez's cross just over the bar.

Briggs fired straight at Camp, but there were no real late scares for the Rams, who recorded their first League Cup win for four years and were good value for it, despite the apparent closeness of the score line.

REACTION

Billy Davies was delighted to end another hoodoo as Derby County recorded their first League Cup win in four years.

STOCKPORT: Spencer, Bowler, Rose, Williams, Owen, Allen (Briggs 6), Taylor, Dinning, Griffin, Proudlock (Raynes HT), Dickinson (Le Fondre HT).
UNUSED SUBS: Deasy, Robinson.

DERBY: Camp, Edworthy, Nyatanga, M. Johnson, Camara, Barnes, Bisgaard (Idiakez 62), Bolder, R. Smith (Peschisolido 84), T. Smith (Lupoli 62), Howard.
UNUSED SUBS: Grant, S. Johnson.

ATTENDANCE: 3,394.

Michael Johnson celebrates scoring the only goal of the game.

The Rams earned a place in the second round for the first time since the 2002–03 season thanks to a 1–0 win away at League Two side Stockport County.

Davies was pleased with the way his side stood firm to keep the home side at bay.

'Four years is a long time and to be asked who we fancy in the next round sounds nice,' he said. 'Again that is another hoodoo we have broken – after the away record – and we're delighted. It has been an awfully long time and psychologically that can be damaging.

'It is another good clean sheet with one defeat in five, and with the injuries we've got we are obviously delighted to avoid what was very much a potential banana skin.'

Tommy Smith takes on a Stockport defender.

The trip to Stockport also saw a new face on the Derby County bench for the first time. Andrew Balderston began matchday work as the club's new head physiotherapist following his arrival from Preston North End, and Davies is backing him to be a successful appointment.

'I am delighted to be welcoming Andrew to the football club,' Davies said. 'He is a young man who already has plenty of experience and the qualifications. I genuinely believe that he can go right the way to the top.'

Balderston's move to Pride Park sees him re-united with Julian Darby, Pete Williams, Kevin Thelwell and Glyn Salmon, who were all together under Davies at Deepdale.

Having recorded success at Stockport, the Rams now travel to Colchester United on Saturday for their first-ever League game at Layer Road.

Derby have only ever faced the Essex side – promoted to the Championship for the first time in their history this season – in FA Cup games. The most recent came in January this year when the Us, then in League One, triumphed 3–1 in a fourth-round encounter.

Since their elevation to the Championship they have lost all five of their games, but boss Billy Davies is warning his players to be on their guard.

'If we remain disciplined and focused we have a side good enough to win the match,' he said. 'But this will be another tough game and many of our players already know what it is like to lose at Colchester.'

REPORT – 26 AUGUST 2006
COLCHESTER UNITED 4
DERBY COUNTY 3

COLCHESTER: Davison, Halford, Brown, Watson, Duguid, Cureton (White 83), Izzet, Iwelumo (Guy 79), Baldwin, Garcia, Barker.
UNUSED SUBS: Gerken, Richards, King.

DERBY: Camp, Leacock, Nyatanga, M. Johnson, Camara, Barnes, Idiakez (T. Smith 46), Bisgaard (S. Johnson 59), R. Smith (Peschisolido 81), Lupoli, Howard.
UNUSED SUBS: Grant, Edworthy.

ATTENDANCE: 4,574.

Derby launched the first attack of the game immediately from the kick-off, but the move resulted in an over-hit cross by Giles Barnes that sailed over the bar.

The hosts responded and following a corner from the left an unmarked Jamie Cureton volleyed just wide of Lee Camp's right-hand post when he should have hit the target.

On six minutes Cureton got in behind the Derby defence and had another gilt-edged chance, but instead of squaring the ball to a teammate he drove his effort over.

On 14 minutes Cureton came spectacularly close with a six-yard overhead kick that thumped off the bar following a Colchester corner, before Camara headed behind for another set-piece.

And with 28 minutes on the clock Colchester went ahead courtesy of the livewire Cureton. He pounced 10 yards out to latch on to Chris Iwelumo's flick-on and half-volley the ball home.

Exactly on the half-hour mark things got even worse for the visitors when Cureton scored his, and his side's, second goal of the game.

His far-post stooping header was clinical following Kevin Watson's crossed free-kick.

On 38 minutes Cureton very nearly completed his hat-trick when he picked up a pass from captain Karl Duguid. He nipped in behind the defence and only a good Camp save prevented his low shot from going in.

With three minutes left until the break, Derby were handed a lifeline courtesy of Lupoli. The front-man scored his first goal for the Rams with a low curler into the bottom corner from the edge of the area.

Deep in first-half injury time Camp produced an excellent fingertip save to prevent Iwelumo's header.

Two minutes into the second half Richard Garcia had a fantastic opportunity to further the home side's lead, but got under the ball and sent it over from six yards.

Then, just a minute later, Garcia was released early down the right by a quick-thinking Davison who threw it to the winger who charged down the right, all the way to the other end of the field. As he belted the ball into the box he was upended by an over zealous Lewin Nyatanga, and the referee pointed straight to the spot. Up stepped Iwelumo, and he made no mistake with a low finish past Camp.

Colchester had the ball in the back of the net again on 64 minutes when Camp went over the line while in possession, but he was clearly barged by Iwelumo and a free-kick was awarded to Derby.

Three minutes later Cureton completed his hat-trick with a goal that had pure class written all over it.

Once again he found himself in behind the Derby defence, and he showed great composure in lifting the ball over Camp into the top corner with an exquisite lob from an angled position 10 yards out.

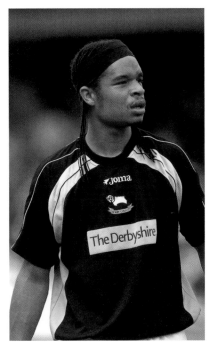

Dean Leacock during the warm-up before making his first start.

Lupoli tries to curl a free-kick around the Colchester wall.

Steve Howard tries to find a way through the Colchester defence.

With 10 minutes to go Lupoli bagged a second goal with a sweet finish past Davison from 16 yards – another curler into the bottom corner, after a neat Ryan Smith through-ball.

On 89 minutes super sub Paul Peschisolido gave Derby even more hope when he flicked home an in-swinging Seth Johnson corner at the near post.

In injury time it almost got better when Howard rose highest to meet a Seth Johnson cross, but his header looped narrowly over the bar.

REACTION

Rams manager Billy Davies has his work cut out this week as he bids to strengthen his squad ahead of Thursday's transfer window deadline.

Talking following his side's 4–3 defeat at Colchester, Davies revealed he has his sights set on bringing more new faces into the club.

He said 'We know what we need to do and we'll be working extremely hard to make as many improvements as we can. We've known for a while what we need to do, the situation has not changed just because we've lost at Colchester.

'There's always a lot up in the air as a transfer deadline approaches, and things can happen right up to the deadline. Taking this club forward, as I've said many times, is the aim.'

Having scored his first Derby County goals at Colchester on Saturday, Italian striker Arturo Lupoli vowed to hit the net even more frequently – if he gets the service. And the 19-year-old hit man, who bagged a clinical brace in the 4–3 defeat at Layer Road, says the international break next weekend should be used wisely.

Tommy Smith, off to join Watford in the Premiership.

Lupoli said 'I was happy with my goals, they were good finishes, especially the second, as me and Steve [Howard] linked up well.

'But I'm disappointed by the performance and the result as we are a better team than that. I feel there is no time to rest while we have the international break. I need to train more with the team as I have only trained a few times with them.

'We are not fully understanding one another as there were times in the game when I had made runs that would have put me in front of goal, and I wasn't found.

'If we can train hard together I will score more goals.'

Transfer deadline week looks like being a busy time at Pride Park with potential movement in and out of the club.

But the Rams have been dealt an early blow in their attempts to further bolster Billy Davies's playing squad.

USA striker Josh Wolff has been a target for a number of weeks but won't be joining after his appeal for a work permit was turned down as he has not played the required amount of games for his national side.

Club officials put forward their case to the Home Office in a bid to land the 29-year-old Kansas City Wizards striker.

Managing director Mike Horton said 'We are especially disappointed as it was Billy's belief he would have formed the perfect partner for Steve Howard.'

And the first departure from Pride Park has been confirmed with forward Tommy Smith returning to his former club Watford.

The 26-year-old, Derby's current player of the year, has spent just over two seasons with the Rams, but he is heading back to Vicarage Road, where he started his professional career.

The undisclosed fee for the striker, who signed on for the Rams on a free transfer from Sunderland after one season on Wearside, is thought to rise from around half-a-million pounds to a higher figure dependant on appearances and Watford retaining their new Premiership status.

Inigo Idiakez has also followed Smith out of the exit door. The 32-year-old Spanish midfielder has joined Southampton, where he is re-united with George Burley – the man who initially signed him for Derby in 2004.

Idiakez, player of the year in 2004–05, had two seasons left on his contract but opted to make the move to St Mary's after 95 games and 22 goals in a Derby shirt.

But the deadline has passed with no further movement in or out at Pride Park – despite the club's best efforts to bring in new faces. A number of targets – including Josh Wolff, Freddy Eastwood and Celtic midfielder Stephen Pearson – were earmarked, but for a variety of reasons deals could not be reached. And managing director Mike Horton said 'panic-buying' was off the agenda.

'Yes we were disappointed to miss out on some of our targets ahead of the deadline, but by Thursday we knew there was no incoming business to be done. We certainly didn't want to panic buy,' he said.

'So while two players have gone in the last couple of days, that only happened after we had brought in seven.

'The ones who left – Tommy Smith and Inigo Idiakez – were players Billy Davies had made clear did not fit in with his plans.

'On that basis my job was to get the best possible deal for Derby County. I believe I did that.'

Idiakez leaves to join former Rams manager George Burley down at Southampton.

TABLE

	P	W	D	L	F	A	Pts
Cardiff	5	4	1	0	7	2	13
Norwich	5	3	1	1	10	4	`0
C Palace	5	3	1	1	9	6	10
Birmingham	5	3	1	1	5	4	10
Wolves	5	3	1	1	5	4	10
Burnley	5	2	2	1	6	4	8
Plymouth	5	2	2	1	7	6	8
West Brom	5	2	2	1	5	4	8
Southampton	5	1	4	0	7	5	7
Luton	5	2	1	2	7	6	7
Leeds	5	2	1	2	4	4	7
Leicester	5	2	1	2	4	4	7
Coventry	5	2	1	2	3	4	7
Barnsley	5	2	1	2	9	12	7
Stoke	5	1	3	1	5	4	6
Preston	5	1	3	1	5	5	6
Southend	5	2	0	3	5	7	6
Sheffield W	5	1	2	2	3	4	5
Derby	**5**	**1**	**2**	**2**	**7**	**9**	**5**
QPR	5	1	2	2	6	8	5
Ipswich	5	1	1	3	5	7	4
Colchester	5	1	0	4	7	10	3
Sunderland	5	1	0	4	6	9	3
Hull	5	0	1	4	3	8	1

September

September sees Billy Davies come up against his former colleagues at Preston North End for the first time since leaving in June to take over at Pride Park.

Before that the Rams will have time to reflect on that defeat at Colchester thanks to an early-season international break. Then it all gets going again with the visit of Sunderland – a side struggling to come to terms with the Championship following their relegation from the Premiership last season.

Derby County chairman Peter Gadsby has paid tribute to former Rams owner Lionel Pickering, who died on Saturday morning, aged 74.

'This comes as very sad news for Derby County Football Club and its supporters, and our first thoughts are with Lionel's family and close friends,' said Peter, who served as a vice-chairman during Lionel's time with the club.

'One of the first things this board did on taking over the club last spring was approach Lionel with a view to creating some permanent recognition of his very considerable commitment to the club, most especially the move to Pride Park under his leadership.

'This is something the club's directors will be discussing in the immediate future in consultation with his family.

'Like many fans Lionel felt a powerful emotional commitment to the Baseball Ground and was initially reluctant to leave, but he was far-sighted enough to understand the need to move to Pride Park and provide some of the best facilities in the English game.

'It is a move which has been an enormous success and Lionel's personal reward came when the stadium was officially opened by the Queen. He told me at the time that it was the finest and proudest day of both his and his wife Marcia's life.

'Lionel was a maverick who put his money where his heart was, and the fact that his chairmanship ended unhappily should not disguise the fact that he had overseen a period of huge achievement both on and off the field.

'He could be a tough man to deal with and a tenacious opponent in business, but he was above all a fan who loved this club and had an especially close affinity with its former players.

'Most people who knew Lionel could tell you of having at least one pretty fierce argument with him – but they would also tell you of a great number of terrific nights in his company, many of them after matches at Pride Park.

'Lionel played a major part in an important stage of the club's history and we will hold a minute's silence in his memory before the next home game against Sunderland.'

Former Rangers man Bob Malcolm has completed his move to Derby County and signed a two-year deal.

Ex-Rangers man Bob Malcolm joins the squad on a two-year deal.

The 25-year-old was out of contract having negotiated his release from his Ibrox contract ahead of last week's transfer deadline, which allows him to make a permanent move to Pride Park.

Malcolm, a Rangers youth product, can operate comfortably in defence or midfield.

Rams boss Billy Davies said 'I'm delighted to have Bob here. He's a player that will bring a bit of quality to our squad, and he has vast experience of playing at a great club like Rangers. I'm looking forward to seeing Bob getting involved in the Championship.'

Malcolm made his Rangers debut in April 2000 and added a total of 89 starts with 26 substitute appearances, along with three goals.

Football League clubs are also allowed to sign players on loan outside of the transfer window – and that has seen two players heading out for temporary switches.

Derby-born goalkeeper Lee Camp has joined Coca-Cola Championship rivals Norwich City on a three-month loan.

The 22-year-old will give the Canaries cover after they were left with one senior goalkeeper due to injuries.

Camp started the opening game of the season but was replaced by Lee Grant for the second, and then Stephen Bywater's arrival further increased the competition.

And midfielder Paul Thirlwell has moved to League One side Carlisle United, also for three months.

The 27-year-old, signed on a free transfer from Sheffield United at the start of 2005–06, has yet to feature for the Rams under new boss Billy Davies.

The international break means it seems like a while since Derby were last in action – but they have a big match to look forward to.

Sunderland have a new man in charge in the shape of legendary player Roy Keane – taking his first managerial role after a glittering playing career with Nottingham Forest, Manchester United and Celtic.

Derby go into the game with injury concerns over four players – Stephen Bywater, Darren Moore, Richard Jackson and Matt Oakley.

Midfielder Oakley and Richard Jackson have been out since before the game against Norwich City on 19 August with groin and calf problems respectively.

Centre-half Moore and goalkeeper Bywater joined them on the sidelines after that game with hamstring and groin injuries.

All four are now back in training, and Davies will assess them on Friday ahead of the Saturday clash with Roy Keane's Black Cats.

'The four players who have been out are now back in training, which is good,' Davies said.

'I'm hoping we will get the majority back into the squad for Saturday.

'We will have to look at training on Friday to make the decision as there are still one or two who need that little bit extra. But it is nice to see them running, joining in, and being part of the squad.'

New signing Bob Malcolm, meanwhile, hopes he is arriving in a 'winning environment' at Derby County.

The 25-year-old put pen to paper on a two-year deal after his release by Scottish giants Rangers before the transfer deadline.

And he had no doubts about making the move to Pride Park after speaking to Davies.

'This is a massive club,' he said. 'The chance to sign here came up, and I spoke to the gaffer; he sold the club to me straight away.

'I came down earlier in the week and was shown around the stadium and the training ground. The facilities are unbelievable and that was a major part of my decision.

'Hopefully I am coming here to a winning environment, but we have a hard game on Saturday so we will have to see what happens and take it from there.'

Derby's young 'keeper Lee Camp joins Norwich for a three-month loan.

REPORT – 9 SEPTEMBER 2006
DERBY COUNTY 1
SUNDERLAND 2

The match was preceded by an emotional minute's applause in memory of former club chairman Lionel Pickering, who passed away seven days ago.

In the game, the visitors enjoyed much of the early possession, backed by a sold-out away end, but had very little by way of a serious threat in the first 15 minutes.

Steve Howard had Derby's first effort on target, a 23rd-minute header from Ryan Smith's right-wing cross, but it was no trouble for Ben Alnwick.

Howard came closer to breaking his goal duck with a thunderous shot from just outside the box that smacked against the crossbar and bounced out as far as Barnes, who could only head a difficult effort over the target.

The big number nine was enjoying an effective first 40 minutes against a physical Sunderland defence, and he again came close with a header that Alnwick grabbed. Derby were beginning to get a grip on the game, and Alnwick had to be sharp to dive down low to his left and keep out Smith's 25-yard drive.

And having stepped their game up, the Rams deservedly found the back of the net in first-half stoppage time. Mo Camara hoisted a cross over from the left which was met at the far post by Howard, who headed down intelligently for Oakley to drive home from 10 yards out.

Miller worked well to feed Connolly inside the box as Sunderland looked for a leveller after the break, but the former Wigan man completely missed his kick with only Bywater to beat.

Sunderland were getting up a head of steam, and after Derby failed to get close enough to Kavanagh the equaliser came on 61 minutes. The Irishman fed Miller, picked up the return pass and crossed low for Chris Brown to force the ball home at the near post. The visitors struck again just two minutes later. Derby failed to deal with a long ball that found its way to Ross Wallace inside the penalty area, and the former Celtic man cracked a firm left-footed drive beyond the dive of Bywater.

Sunderland were controlling proceedings with time ticking by, and they looked well set for the win having defended solidly and given Derby nothing by way of a sniff.

Kavanagh was cautioned for a stoppage time foul on Smith out on the Derby left, but once again the home side failed to make the most of a set-piece situation.

As in their first home game of the season, Derby had led at half-time, only to see things turned around thanks to two quick goals midway through the second period.

This time, however, there was to be no late drama.

REACTION

Billy Davies says his young players need to grow up quickly if the Rams are to make an impact on the Championship this season.

Speaking after Saturday's 2–1 home defeat against Roy Keane's Sunderland, the Derby boss said 'This is the starting point. We have an opportunity to build on what we have got, but the youngsters need to learn that when you have teams down on the ground you have to bury them.

DERBY: Bywater, Edworthy (Bolder 88), Camara, Leacock, M. Johnson, Howard, Peschisolido (S. Johnson 56), Smith, Lupoli, Oakley (C), Barnes.
UNUSED SUBS: Grant, Malcolm, Nyatanga.

SUNDERLAND: Alnwick, Delap, Cunningham, Whitehead (C), Brown, R. Elliott, Varga, Kavanagh, Connolly (S. Elliott 82), Wallace, Miller.
UNUSED SUBS: Ward, Hysen, Leadbitter, Collins.

ATTENDANCE: 26,502.

Derby celebrate the opening goal.

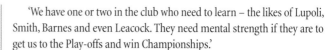

'We have one or two in the club who need to learn – the likes of Lupoli, Smith, Barnes and even Leacock. They need mental strength if they are to get us to the Play-offs and win Championships.'

The good side of a busy Coca-Cola Championship fixture list means that the opportunity to put right a defeat is rarely too far away. And that's exactly the case as the Rams prepare for a trip to Wolverhampton Wanderers on Tuesday evening.

It's the perfect chance to try and get three more points on the board after the disappointment of Saturday's defeat at home to Sunderland.

Wolves were live on Sky Sports on Sunday lunchtime – giving Derby boss Billy Davies time to sit and assess his side's next opponents.

'I watched the game and was not surprised with what I saw,' he said of the Molineux club's late 1–0 win at Leeds United.

'Every game in this League is tough and this will be no different for us. We have got to go down there and do what we did in the first 60 minutes at home on Saturday. We have got to try and finish the team off if we get the opportunity, but it certainly will be another tough match.'

Goalkeeper Stephen Bywater is another who can't wait for the Wolves game to come around after Derby suffered defeat at the weekend. The 25-year-old admits that the disappointment of losing drives his hunger for victory in his next outing.

'It's about winning games – you can't have a sloppy five minutes every game because it costs you,' he said. 'It hurts, and I don't want that feeling again.

'At the weekend I want to be able to go out and relax, and have a good meal with my family and friends. It ruins your weekend, but that makes you even hungrier to win the next game.

'The games are coming thick and fast now so for us it's a matter of not getting down, we have got to move on and concentrate on the next game.

'I only saw the last minute of their game on Sunday, but they won it with a good strike.

'Getting the wins is what this division is about – it doesn't matter how you do it, in the first minute or the last minute, it doesn't matter how they come.'

WOLVES: Murray, Olofinjana, Breen, Craddock (C), Henry (Clarke 77), Bothroyd (Cort 57), Edwards, Johnson, Potter, Jones (Ricketts 57), Little.
UNUSED SUBS: Ikeme, Cort, Mulgrew.

DERBY: Bywater, Edworthy, Camara, Bolder (Nyatanga 90), Leacock, M. Johnson, Bisgaard (Barnes 68), Howard, Lupoli (Smith 77), Oakley, Malcolm.
UNUSED SUBS: Peschisolido, S. Johnson.

ATTENDANCE: 21,546.

Ex-Manchester United star Roy Keane's first job in management is at struggling Sunderland.

REPORT – 12 SEPTEMBER 2006
WOLVERHAMPTON WANDERERS 0 DERBY COUNTY 1

Craddock's mistake in defence gifted the ball to Howard on four minutes, but his tame shot was saved by Murray low to his left.

A Potter ball in from the right on 16 found Bothroyd in the centre of the Rams penalty area with his back to goal. Turning under pressure from Leacock, his hooked shot flew over the bar from seven yards.

Bisgaard's power drive from the left-hand edge of the area forced a diving save from Murray on 20 minutes, and seconds later Howard's flick-on from Edworthy's angled long ball found Lupoli in space – he sliced his shot narrowly over the bar from 10 yards.

Michael Johnson was adjudged to have been holding Olofinjana as a

Jones corner kick flew in on 22 minutes. Bywater dived low to his left to smother Bothroyd's spot-kick.

Howard's first Derby goal came on 34 minutes. A clever flick out by Oakley released Bolder who had acres of space to run into.

He found Lupoli to his left, who drove down the flank and, after turning Edwards and Craddock inside out, his chipped cross to the near post was met by Howard in the six-yard box – he headed past the stranded Murray.

Bothroyd beat off the challenge of Lupoli to unleash a rocket-shot from 22 yards that landed in the arms of the unflinching Bywater.

On 53 minutes it appeared Lupoli only had to walk the ball into the back of the net after a great passing move from Oakley and Howard.

After rounding the 'keeper, he dwelled on the ball, got it caught under his feet and was muscled out of a certain goal by the Wolves defence.

Jemal Johnson's ball into the box from the left on 65 minutes saw Bywater stretch to gather it, and seconds later Edwards couldn't find a clean contact on a ball in the area under pressure from Michael Johnson – it looped into the arms of Bywater.

Olofinjana left a foot in on Smith as the wide man went at Wolves' last man, Craddock – conceding a free-kick 25 yards out on 81 minutes. Camara's free-kick was a curling left-foot strike that was tipped over by Murray.

Three minutes from the end Ricketts rattled Bywater's left-hand post with a low shot.

The Rams were rattled, too, as Wolves looked to provide a grandstand finish – laying siege to Bywater's goal in the dying minutes.

Clarke's header flew over from close range on 89 minutes, and the Rams 'keeper was booked for time-wasting as he prepared for the resulting goal-kick, but Derby saw it through for an important victory.

REACTION

More of the same please – that's the message from Billy Davies to his players after the Rams produced their best performance of the season in winning 1–0 at Wolves on Tuesday.

Derby defended stoutly when required to, took their big chance of the night for Steve Howard's goal, and could have added others to increase the victory margin. And Davies says the Molineux performance is the kind of display he wants to see on a regular basis.

'I've said before that it will take time, that things are not going to happen overnight,' he said. 'To the fans I would say again that they have got to be patient, that they have got to let us develop this team, work with individuals and continue to build over the next transfer window and beyond.

'We have always said that it is a long-term plan as there is not a short-term fix.

'But against Wolves we looked like an organised unit, we looked like a team that knows what it is all about. Hopefully that message is beginning to drop.'

Steve Howard celebrates scoring his first goal for Derby.

Bisgaard has a shot at the Wolves goal in the first half of the match.

Striker Steve Howard claimed to be the happiest man in the Midlands after scoring his first goal for the Rams.

The summer signing stooped to nod home Arturo Lupoli's 34th-minute cross and seal a hard-fought win for Derby against Wolves.

He declared 'I'm the happiest man in the Molineux tonight! It's a massive relief to score my first goal and claim three valuable points.

'It's been a long time coming, and I'm just glad to get off the mark.'

And on the back of winning at Wolves, Derby are now preparing for the visit of Preston North End to Pride Park on Saturday.

Recent history has seen the Lilywhites see off the Rams in the Play-offs two years ago, while there are many more current connections between the two sides.

Preston boss Paul Simpson is a Derby hero who was part of the 1996 promotion side. While in the home camp are Billy Davies, Julian Darby, Kevin Thelwell, Pete Williams, Glyn Salmon and Andy Balderston – all having left Deepdale in the summer to join Derby.

But Davies is playing down the significance of Saturday's opponents as he bids to build on Tuesday night's win at Wolverhampton Wanderers.

He is aware of the connections in both camps but sees the game as the next step in Derby's progression.

'One or two people will try to make something of it,' he said. 'But I would prefer to be talking like that in April if both of us are going for promotion, then it would be different.

'In September I can't really get too excited about anything else except that it is the chance for another three points and another game in Derby County's season.'

Simpson, meanwhile, has his sights firmly set on extending his Preston side's five-match unbeaten Championship run when they visit Pride Park on Saturday. He took the Deepdale job in the summer when previous incumbent Billy Davies left to join Derby.

A lot has been said about Saturday's game but both managers are only looking at the task in hand, and for the fourth-placed Lilywhites that means building on two impressive home victories this week.

'We want to stay unbeaten, that's the first thing we need to do, and if we can go and get another three points then even better,' Simpson said.

'It's early on in the season, but I'd rather be sat fourth top of the table than fourth bottom. If we want to stay in at least fourth position then we need to go and get a positive result at Pride Park, and that is what we will be getting the players focused to do.'

REPORT – 16 SEPTEMBER 2006
DERBY COUNTY 1
PRESTON NORTH END 1

Preston started the game brightly and forced a few set-pieces on the right that gave Danny Pugh the chance to put his left foot to good use, though the Rams held out without any real scares.

And at the other end they nearly took a 12th-minute lead as Steve Howard – fresh from his first goal for the club in midweek – rose to meet Matt Oakley's right-wing free-kick, and only the sprawling save of Carlo Nash prevented him making it two in two.

Howard, with his confidence clearly up, controlled a long ball well and turned to let rip with a dipping 20-yard volley that Nash appeared to touch over the bar, though a goal-kick was given.

The visitors' first effort on target came 21 minutes in as Patrick Agyemang turned and shot from close range, though his effort was no trouble for Stephen Bywater.

The Rams had a spell of giving the ball away cheaply, and it almost cost them as Whaley curled an effort wide.

On 41 minutes they won a penalty, and it was all down to the individual brilliance of Lupoli. The Italian intercepted a cross-field pass near the halfway line and made ground into the box only to be felled by Sean St Ledger.

There was a penalty-taking vacancy to be filled after the departures of Inigo Idiakez and Tommy Smith, but one man was first to the ball – Howard, who stroked confidently home and sent Nash the wrong way to open the scoring. But within three minutes the visitors were level.

Derby failed to clear a Chris Sedgwick cross then sat off Pugh and allowed him the time and space to pick his spot in the bottom corner from 20 yards.

Bisgaard forced Nash to dive and grab his 25-yard free-kick in the 49th minute as the Rams came out looking to re-assert themselves after that late blow before the break.

A wonderful move almost restored Derby's lead in the 55th minute as Bob Malcolm strode forward to feed Howard, who in turn cleverly flicked the ball into the path of Lupoli, only for Nash to deny him with a fine save.

The Rams kept up the pressure as Bisgaard played in Oakley, who found the hands of Nash after turning his shot goalwards.

A mix-up between Bywater and Edworthy let Nugent in on a long ball, but the striker's touch took him to the by-line, and by the time he curled the ball towards goal Bywater was back in position to claim.

Howard was an inch away from making it 2–1 as he rose to head Oakley's corner powerfully towards goal, only to see his effort hit the crossbar once more – it was in front of the South Stand, and pretty much the same spot of the bar he had already hit twice this season.

Nash grabbed Malcolm's curling 25-yard free-kick with ease, but the whistle blew to leave the Rams still waiting to taste victory in front of their own fans this season.

DERBY: Bywater, Edworthy (Barnes 62), Leacock, M. Johnson, Camara, Bisgaard (Peschisolido 81), Oakley (C), Malcolm, Bolder, Lupoli, Howard.
UNUSED SUBS: S. Johnson, Moore, Nyatanga.

PRESTON: Nash, Alexander (C), Pugh, Sedgwick, Agyemang, Dichio (Nugent 45), St Ledger, Chilvers, Whaley (Anyinsah 81), McKenna, Hill.
UNUSED SUBS: Lonergan, Jarrett, Wilson.

ATTENDANCE: 22,260.

Steve Howard makes it two in two games with a penalty against Preston.

A Preston player receives a yellow card following a challenge which left Arturo Lupoli needing treatment.

The Rams players celebrate Steve Howard's penalty in front of the home fans.

REACTION

Manager Billy Davies says he's gutted for his centre-forward Steve Howard, who once again hit the woodwork at Pride Park with a crashing header that could have given the Rams all three points against Preston.

'We deserved to win that game because we kept them down to minimal shooting opportunities,' Davies said after Saturday's 1–1 draw.

'On the amount of chances we created we deserved three points and for Steve to go and hit the bar at that stage in the game shows our luck is slightly down at the moment.'

Howard – a scorer at Wolves on Tuesday night – had tucked away a penalty to give Derby the lead just before half-time, only for Davies's former club to equalise through Danny Pugh two minutes later.

'That was a disappointing goal to concede,' said the boss. 'It was a lack of concentration and a poor time to lose it because I thought there was only one team trying to pass the ball.

'We looked comfortable but when we needed that bit of luck we couldn't get it.'

Dean Leacock feels familiarity is the key as the Rams look to progress this season.

Manager Billy Davies was able to field an unchanged line up for the first time this season as Derby faced Preston on the back of a midweek win at Wolves.

Across the park the Rams performed exceptionally well at Molineux and there were signs of bonds forming in all areas during the 1–1 draw with the Lilywhites.

'The back four played against Wolves and did really well so I think the gaffer had an easy choice to make about playing the same team,' defender Leacock said.

'I thought in the first half today we did well but died a bit in the second, though we will take the point and move on to the next game.

'We are doing well now, the team is getting together and there is a good bond here now. Training is good, everything at the moment is gelling really well and hopefully the form on the pitch can continue.'

Adam Bolder insists the Rams are well prepared for the Carling Cup challenge of Doncaster Rovers.

Boss Billy Davies has been putting his troops through their paces this week in a bid to ready them for the Earth Stadium encounter. And Bolder reckons this week's efforts at the training ground will stand Derby in good stead.

'They are a good team, but we have done our homework on them,' the midfielder said. 'We have watched videos, seen their strengths and weaknesses and looked at how we are going to go about the game.

'They have got some quick players up front and plenty of options, and a couple of decent players in midfield who like to pass the ball. We know we have got to be on our guard and pick things up nice and early.'

REPORT – 20 SEPTEMBER 2006
DONCASTER 3
DERBY COUNTY 3 aet
CARLING CUP SECOND ROUND
Doncaster won 8–7 on penalties

Barnes shot into the arms of Budtz from a tight angle on the left after Howard had won a flick-on from Roberts on five minutes. Within seconds the home side were ahead. O'Connor's driven through-ball caught Nyatanga napping, allowing Guy to pull the ball back to Forte, whose drilled effort beat Grant in the centre of his net.

The Rams almost hit back from the restart as Jackson's angled cross was headed two yards over Budtz's right-hand upright by Howard.

On 26 minutes Malcolm was dispossessed by Heffernan, who drove at the Rams defence. His pass to Forte was cut out by Nyatanga, and Grant gathered the loose ball – the move was unfairly judged by the referee as a back-pass, leaving a free-kick from 12 yards out.

A cleverly worked indirect set-piece saw Stock calmly side-foot low through the goalline wall at the near post to double the lead.

A break from a Rovers corner saw Barnes run the length of the left flank before finding Howard, whose neat chest control allowed him space to volley at goal, but his effort was cleared by Lockwood.

O'Connor unlocked the Rams defence on 55 minutes when his through-ball found Forte as the Derby back line attempted to play the offside trap. His initial shot was saved well by Grant, who could only watch as it looped over his head and dropped over the line to put Doncaster three-up.

Bolder set the recovery ball rolling when he made it to the by-line and cut a ball back for Howard, whose turn and shot was heading into Budtz's right-hand corner when Rovers skipper Lockwood slid in to make certain.

After more pressure, the Rams clawed it back to 3–2 with Bolder again the provider with a right-wing cross which caused uncertainty in the Rovers box, and Moore was quickest to react with an eight-yard header.

Rovers introduced Jason Price and his first involvement was to fire a 22-yard shot that was spectacularly tipped over by Grant. This only spurred on the Rams, as within two minutes Lupoli was driving at a back-tracking Rovers back line.

As the Italian bore down on Budtz, his initial shot was parried, but the striker was quickest to react, and he steered home from four yards to level on 88 minutes.

With extra-time under way, Griffith's driving running shot from the right was halted by the referee, who brandished a second yellow card for Lupoli, who was adjudged to have hauled back the Rovers defender.

Grant was at full stretch for McDaid's near-post header from a Griffith cross from the right 10 minutes into the first period.

The Rams were under pressure when Stock found himself free 25 yards out and

DONCASTER: Budtz, O'Connor, G. Roberts, S. Roberts (Griffith 90), Guy, Lockwood (C), Heffernan (Thornton 105), Forte (Price 85), McDaid, Stock, Green.
UNUSED SUBS: Horlock, Smith.

DERBY: Grant, Jackson, Moore, Nyatanga, Camara, Bolder, Oakley (C), Malcolm (S. Johnson 45), Barnes (Smith 80), Peschisolido (Lupoli 45), Howard.
UNUSED SUBS: Leacock, Boertien.

ATTENDANCE: 5,598.

PENALTIES
S. Johnson scored 1–0
Green scored 1–1
Howard scored 2–1
Thornton scored 2–2
Oakley scored 3–2
Price scored 3–3
Bolder scored 4–3
McDaid scored 4–4
Smith scored 5–4
Stock scored 5–5

Sudden-death
Moore scored 6–5
Roberts scored 6–6
Camara scored 7–6
Lockwood scored 7–7
Nyatanga wide 7–7
O'Connor scored 7–8

Darren Moore celebrates his goal, Derby's second, making the score 3–2.

his low drive was gathered at the second attempt by Grant seconds before the whistle blew.

The home side were struggling to make the extra man count as the second period wore on, but, with four minutes to go before penalties, Guy's run up the right caused jitters in the Rams defence as his shot was deflected wide.

As the final whistle brought a dramatic and absorbing two hours of football to a close, the lottery of penalties lay between the Rams and the third round.

REACTION

Darren Moore had plenty of words of encouragement for fellow centre-half Lewin Nyatanga after the Rams' Carling Cup defeat at Doncaster Rovers.

The epic encounter saw Derby trail 3–0 with just over quarter-of-an-hour remaining, then mount a dramatic comeback to take the game to extra-time, only to get reduced to 10 men and ultimately go out 8–7 on penalties.

Unfortunately someone has to miss in a shoot-out, and it was Nyatanga's off-target effort that gave Doncaster the chance to go through and cause another Cup upset after their exploits last year.

Experienced stopper Moore feels that Nyatanga, at only 18 and the opposite stage of his career, will learn from the occasion and says Derby lost as a team.

'Unfortunately it's a cruel way to go out, but Lewin will learn from it, and I'm sure in the future he will take a penalty in a Cup game,' Moore said. 'It is all about learning. He is a young man, a very good player, and he will be a great player for Derby County, but unfortunately here he missed a penalty.

'But we don't hold that against him as it is a team game, and when you lose you lose as a team – not as an individual.'

Billy Davies wants his Derby County side to carry on with the progression of their last two League games when they travel to Sheffield Wednesday on Saturday.

The Rams were the better side in the 1–1 draw at home to Preston North End last week, a result that came on the back of an impressive 1–0 win at Wolverhampton Wanderers. And Davies says that the forthcoming clash at Hillsborough will give them another chance to keep building on recent positives.

'As well as those games, I thought in the second half and extra-time at Doncaster we also performed reasonably well,' he said.

'We gave ourselves a mountain to climb because of a terrible start but there were a lot of positives in there. We have just got to carry on with the League form of Preston and Wolves because there were a lot of good signs.

'The building continues.'

Goalkeeper Stephen Bywater is the Rams' biggest doubt ahead of the trip to Hillsborough. The 25-year-old sat out the midweek Carling Cup exit to Doncaster Rovers after picking up a tweak to the inside of his thigh – and Rams boss Billy Davies says he will be given a late fitness test ahead of the Hillsborough encounter.

'Stephen picked up a slight knock in training this week, though it was more a precaution to keep him out,' Davies said. 'He is back in

Arturo Lupoli celebrates his goal with Ryan Smith, making the game level with only two minutes to go.

Giles Barnes runs with the ball.

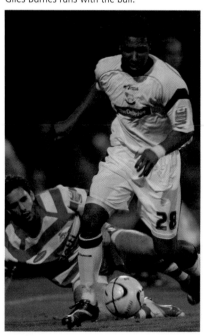

training so we will have a look tomorrow and hopefully have him back for the game on Saturday.'

Academy product Theo Streete has joined Doncaster Rovers on a month's loan. The young defender teams up with Sean O'Driscoll's Rovers two days after the League One side dumped the Rams out of the Carling Cup.

Streete was handed a short-term deal at the end of 2005–06. He began that season playing football for Solihull College and didn't even receive any professional coaching of note until he was picked up by the Rams. He was a regular in the table-topping Under-18 side during 2005–06 and was given his chance to impress with more senior players in the regular behind-closed-doors games at Moor Farm.

REPORT – 23 SEPTEMBER 2006
SHEFFIELD WEDNESDAY 1
DERBY COUNTY 2

The game took a while to get going, but on 13 minutes the Rams won a free-kick in the inside-right channel that caused panic in the Wednesday area.

Matt Oakley's delivery was scrambled out to Seth Johnson, who drove goalwards from the edge of the box, and the home side escaped after scrambling the ball away when Chris Adamson fumbled the shot.

Wednesday came close when Frank Simek created space for himself after Chris Brunt's excellent pass but fired over Grant's goal from just inside the box.

The dangerous Brunt, a left-footer playing on the right of the attack, flashed an effort inches wide with the home side enjoying a spell of pressure.

Derby had a golden opportunity on 36 minutes, and it came from the industry of Smith, who had moved over to the right and escaped the challenge of Tommy Spurr.

Smith got to the by-line and pulled the ball back for Oakley, who only succeeded in blazing wildly over the bar from 10 yards. Smith then cut in from the right and cracked a low 25-yarder with his left foot that fizzed just wide of Adamson's post, with the 'keeper beaten.

Grant made the game's first real save an hour in after the Owls broke quickly again through Majid Bougherra and then Tudgay, who crossed for Burton – left in acres of space at the far post – to crack in an effort that Derby's number 13 did well to turn around the post.

The Wednesday fans had plenty to cheer shortly afterwards when they opened the scoring.

Derby failed to deal with a long throw into the box, as they had done all afternoon, and Bougherra's flick-on found Brunt close in on goal for the simple task of firing home.

Derby's afternoon got doubly difficult on 73 minutes as they found themselves reduced to 10 men for the second time in two games.

This time it was Barnes – who had only been on for 19 minutes – who saw a straight red for a late challenge on home skipper Coughlan.

The teenager had gone on a mazy run but lost the ball and in an over-

WEDNESDAY: Adamson, Lunt (Talbot 81), Coughlan (C), Whelan, Tudgay (Corr 83), O'Brien, Burton (MacLean 61), Brunt, Simek, Bougherra, Spurr.
UNUSED SUBS: Bullen, McAllister.

DERBY: Grant, Edworthy, Leacock, M. Johnson, Camara, Bisgaard, Bolder (Malcolm 21), S. Johnson (Peschisolido 74), Oakley (C), Smith (Barnes 54), Howard.
UNUSED SUBS: Cann, Moore.

ATTENDANCE: 23,659.

Barnes saw a straight red for a late challenge on Wednesday skipper Coughlan.

Howard, Bisgaard, Leecock and Oakley all confront the referee after Barnes is sent off.

Paul Peschisolido scoring and celebrating after netting Derby's equaliser late in the second half.

zealous attempt to win it back he caught the centre-half, and referee Wright pulled out the red card with little hesitation.

Billy Davies changed things around again with 14 minutes left as he introduced Paul Peschisolido for Seth Johnson – to almost immediate effect.

The Rams won a corner, and, after Leacock's effort was cleared off the line, Wednesday failed to get it away and Peschisolido did what he does best – putting the ball in the back of the net.

The game looked to be heading for a hard-fought draw with four minutes of stoppage time signalled, but that was still enough to allow for some late drama.

Howard picked up a long ball on the edge of the Wednesday box and, with no other Derby player near him, the sensible option might have been to head for the corner.

However, the number nine – chasing his fourth goal in as many games – had other ideas and shook off the challenge of his marker before finishing expertly past Adamson to seal all three points.

REACTION

Rams boss Billy Davies told supporters to 'enjoy the win' after seeing his side sensationally fight back from one down to take all three points at Hillsborough.

As with the fightback at Doncaster in midweek, there were bucket loads of character on show as 10-man Derby – sub Giles Barnes was sent off in the 74th minute – came back from the brink.

Sub Paul Peschisolido tapped in from close range seconds after coming on, and in-form striker Steve Howard put the icing on the cake with a superb finish in the 94th minute.

With the club having had so much upheaval on and off the pitch in recent years, Davies said that it was the fans – who were in great voice again on their travels to South Yorkshire – who deserved the victory most of all.

The manager said 'The fans should enjoy this victory, once again they were in great voice, and they should celebrate this one when they get home tonight because it's the least they deserve.

'This club has been through a lot in recent times so everyone – from the players through to all the staff at the club and the supporters – should make sure they enjoy it.

'As with the game at Doncaster, we showed lots of character and determination and that's extremely pleasing.

'Even when we were down to 10 men we never gave up the fight and in the end got what we deserved.'

Striker Steve Howard was beaming from cheek to cheek after his fourth goal in as many games gave the Rams the most dramatic of wins at Sheffield Wednesday.

Howard celebrates at the end of the game.

The big man manufactured space on the edge of the box in the 94th minute and unleashed an unstoppable shot that flashed past Chris Adamson in the home goal.

Howard left it late, but the successful strike meant he became the first player in five years – Fabrizio Ravanelli in 2001 the last – to score goals in four consecutive games.

After the match the former Luton man said 'I'm over the moon, not just for me but for the whole team. We worked so hard, never let our heads go down and thoroughly deserved the win in the end.

'Once again we had to do it in adversity after Giles [Barnes] was sent off, but Pesch did brilliantly to score straight after coming off the bench, and I'm pleased to have got my opportunity.

'When the ball came to me I managed to create a bit of space to my right, and it opened up for me. I kept it hard and low and thankfully it went in.

'It's nice to have scored four in four, but I won't be looking too much into that, I'll just keep working hard and we'll see what happens. But my goalscoring record has always been good so let's hope that continues.'

Paul Peschisolido celebrating in front of the Rams fans.

Giles Barnes misses the next three games for the Rams.

Midfielder Giles Barnes will sit out a three-match suspension after the Rams failed in their attempts to have his red card at Sheffield Wednesday overturned.

Barnes, 18, was dismissed 19 minutes after coming on as a substitute in Saturday's 2–1 win at Hillsborough for a challenge on home skipper Graham Coughlan.

Derby submitted an appeal to the Football Association at the start of the week, but this was rejected, meaning Barnes will miss this Saturday's visit of Southend United to Pride Park, as well as the trips to Plymouth Argyle and Queen's Park Rangers.

'That is a blow and a disappointment having seen the tape and what I felt was a blatant handball just before,' boss Billy Davies said. 'But life moves on and we have to accept the decision now.'

Arturo Lupoli returns to the Derby County squad for Saturday's Coca-Cola Championship game at home to Southend United.

The Italian front-man sat out last week's 2–1 win at Sheffield Wednesday through suspension after being dismissed in the Carling Cup exit at Doncaster Rovers.

But Lupoli, on a season-long loan from Premiership side Arsenal, has looked sharp in training this week and is figuring strongly in the thoughts of manager Billy Davies.

'He has looked very bright in training, a handful as he always is,' Davies said. 'Arturo is a great young player to have in the squad. He is a tremendous goal threat and it is good to have him back for this weekend.'

Davies confirmed that his major injury headache, goalkeeper Stephen Bywater, 'looks as if he might be struggling' to make the game against the Shrimpers.

Bywater missed the game at Doncaster with a thigh injury that also kept him out of the Hillsborough clash and it is still giving him problems.

Davies admits it would be nice to go into the October international break having secured a first home win of the season.

No team has won more away games in the Coca-Cola Championship this season than Davies's Derby, though the side are yet to taste success in front of their own supporters.

Three of the four Pride Park games have been drawn this season, but with a little more luck the Rams could have had at least two more wins on the board.

'We know the importance of trying to pick up three points and our first home win, which we have been very unlucky not to have collected so far,' Davies said. 'The away form has been first-class, but at home we have been a little unfortunate so this weekend would be a nice time to end that.

'We have taken seven points from our last nine in the League, and it should have been nine, as we should have beaten Preston, but that was not to be.

'The confidence is there, the team spirit is there, and you can certainly see that the belief is there to win matches. It would be nice to get the three points going into the break, and that is the most important thing.'

REPORT – 30 SEPTEMBER 2006
DERBY COUNTY 3
SOUTHEND UNITED 0

A clever free-kick in the third minute saw Derby go close thanks to Morten Bisgaard's curling effort that dipped just wide from 25 yards.

Southend were playing some nice one-touch football and almost opened the scoring with a move on the break after 20 minutes.

Eastwood held the ball up well down the left and crossed for skipper Kevin Maher at the far post to crack in a low volley that Lee Grant did superbly well to push away for a corner.

The best chance of the game so far came just before the half-hour mark as Derby broke quickly down the left through Arturo Lupoli, whose low cross found the foot of Steve Howard six yards out. But the striker, looking to score in his fifth consecutive match, could only steer the ball over the Southend bar.

Lupoli was having a bright few minutes and followed that up with a low shot from the right that curled narrowly past Darryl Flahavan's post.

Derby were having their best spell of the match, and a nice move gave Camara space down the left to curl over a cross that Lupoli headed up rather than down.

But they kept going and almost got their reward on 36 minutes as, from Lupoli's missed kick, Bolder found himself in the six-yard box with the time and space to compose himself before smashing in a shot that Flahavan did well to block.

And on 39 they took a deserved lead. Matt Oakley's fine through-ball sent Lupoli scampering clear, but he was forced wide in the penalty area by the out-rushing Flahavan. However, the little Italian wasn't flustered. He took his time, got the ball under control, and from a narrow angle fired into the far corner of the net with defenders rushing back to try and block on the line.

Just two minutes into the second half the lead was doubled. Oakley curled over a fine free-kick from the inside-right channel and Michael Johnson peeled away from his marker at the far post to plant a header past Flahavan and back across goal.

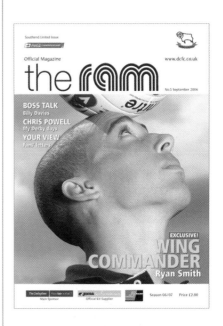

DERBY: Grant, Edworthy, Moore, M. Johnson, Camara, Malcolm, Bisgaard (Smith 74), Oakley (C) (S. Johnson 80) Bolder, Lupoli, Howard.
UNUSED SUBS: Boertien, Jackson, Nyatanga.

SOUTHEND: Flahavan, Francis (Campbell-Ryce 80), Hunt, Barrett, Gower, Maher (C), Eastwood, Guttridge, Clarke, Hammell, Hooper (Ricketts 67).
UNUSED SUBS: Collis, Sodje, Paynter.

ATTENDANCE: 22,395.

Lupoli returns with a brace of goals against Southend.

Mo Camara heads clear.

Bolder saw a header from Bisgaard's cross cleared off the line as the Rams looked to put the game completely to bed.

But they were given a wake-up call as Simon Francis whipped over a cross from the right that found Eastwood on the far post, though the prolific front-man could only steer his shot into the side-netting.

Derby were still having by far the best of things and could have added further to the lead through Bisgaard, who saw his shot well saved by Flahavan after Oakley's good build-up work.

And it was three on 63 minutes. Bisgaard cleverly fed the ball through to Lupoli just inside the box, and once more the on-loan youngster finished superbly.

Bolder did well to rob Francis and feed Howard, who saw his low 20-yard effort comfortably saved by Flahavan, as the white tide flowing forward continued.

Howard had a chance to make it five in five but could only curl his shot wide from inside the penalty box.

The big number nine kept at it though and his header from Seth Johnson's left-wing corner dipped just over the bar with just three minutes left.

Howard chanced his arm after Seth Johnson drove forward, but this time Flahavan was equal to his effort.

Seconds of the 90 minutes remained when Southend had their best chance of the game as Mark Gower's cross was met by the head of Rickets just six yards out, but Grant – who had otherwise been untroubled all afternoon – pulled a flying save right out of the top drawer.

REACTION

Billy Davies didn't want to talk about summer target Freddy Eastwood as his side comfortably recorded their first home win of the season over the striker's club Southend United.

'Our focus is on the players we have got, not Freddy Eastwood,' the Derby boss said.

'Yes we will have targets going into the next transfer window, and in the meantime we are looking to bring in a couple of loan signings, but today my side put in some excellent performances from back to front.

'We started nervously and perhaps let the home record get to us early on. But sometimes we need to forget the crowd and the beautiful playing surface and just concentrate on our strengths.

'That's what we did – we started to move the ball around like we are capable of doing. I have been saying for weeks there is a real spring in our step, and that showed today.'

A training ground move couldn't have worked out better as Michael Johnson scored his second goal of the season.

Jonno was on target two minutes into the second half as the Rams recorded their first home win of the campaign with a resounding 3–0 success against Southend United.

Matt Oakley's right-wing delivery was perfectly placed and was a deserved reward for working hard on the training ground.

'It's always delightful when you score like that,' he said. 'That was something we have worked long and hard at on the training ground. I managed to escape my marker and the ball in from Matt was inch-perfect. It was like Christmas Day when I came out of the pack and nobody was around me so it was just a matter of guiding it towards the goal.'

TABLE

	P	W	D	L	F	A	Pts
Cardiff	10	7	2	1	22	8	23
Birmingham	10	5	3	2	14	11	18
Preston	10	4	5	1	11	8	17
C Palace	10	5	2	3	13	11	17
Southampton	10	4	4	2	15	11	16
West Brom	10	4	4	2	14	10	16
Plymouth	10	4	4	2	15	12	16
Wolves	10	5	1	4	8	10	16
Derby	**10**	**4**	**3**	**3**	**15**	**13**	**15**
Luton	10	4	3	3	15	13	15
Burnley	9	4	2	3	14	11	14
Ipswich	10	4	2	4	14	13	14
Colchester	10	4	2	4	13	13	14
Sunderland	10	4	1	5	14	14	13
Coventry	10	4	1	5	8	8	13
QPR	10	3	3	4	12	14	12
Norwich	9	3	2	4	14	14	11
Barnsley	10	3	2	5	15	21	11
Leicester	10	2	4	4	6	9	10
Leeds	10	3	1	6	9	15	10
Stoke	10	1	6	3	9	11	10
Southend	10	2	3	5	9	17	9
Hull	10	2	2	6	8	14	8
Sheffield W	10	1	4	5	6	10	7

The Derby players celebrate one of Lupoli's two goals.

October

Once again the Rams have got to wait to get their month's fixtures under way due to another international break.

It's frustrating for Derby, who ended September with two successive victories and will want to build on that momentum.

They're only at home once during October, to much-fancied Birmingham City, with long and difficult away trips to Plymouth Argyle, Queen's Park Rangers and Cardiff City on the agenda.

Billy Davies has confirmed that striker Paul Peschisolido is facing a spell of six weeks on the sidelines after picking up a thigh injury during the warm-up for Saturday's game against Southend.

The Canadian was due to be among the substitutes against the Shrimpers but injured himself while taking a shot at goal.

Pesch's injury leaves Derby with two fit front-men in Steve Howard and Arturo Lupoli, and with Giles Barnes also suspended Davies is considering re-inforcements.

'It's something we've got to think about as we're left short, especially with Giles Barnes suspended,' he said. 'Pesch has got a nasty thigh strain that he picked up making a side-footed finish before the game, and is looking at six weeks out.'

Davies does, however, remain hopeful that injured goalkeeper Stephen Bywater and defender Dean Leacock will be available for the Plymouth Argyle trip on Sunday 15 October.

Sunderland striker Jon Stead has joined the Rams on loan until the New Year. The 23-year-old will take squad number 10 and is expected to be drafted straight into the squad to face Plymouth at Home Park on Sunday. He will remain with the Rams until 2 January, making him available for the trip to Preston North End on New Year's Day.

Boss Billy Davies was delighted to land his man after having his eyes on Jon Stead for a number of years.

Davies first admired the former England Under-21 international when he first broke on to the senior scene with a flurry of goals, while he was at Huddersfield Town and Davies was with Preston North End.

'I liked the lad then as he showed a lot of good things when he played,' Davies said.

'I liked the attitude he displayed and that is why he experienced the Premiership and a move to a big club like Sunderland.

'He is now ready for that next challenge in his career, and I feel that is at Derby County.

'Hopefully we can get him scoring goals, get a smile on his face, and hopefully he will like what he sees here and his move will become long term.

'I think he has got lots to do in his career, there is a lot more ahead for him.'

Stead is 100 percent certain he has made the right move in joining Derby.

'I am delighted. There were decisions to make, but I'm here and 100 percent confident that it is the right move.

'I spoke with the manager and was very impressed with what he had to say. I was also very impressed with the set-up of the club at the moment as it is really going places. That is important as a club that is moving forward is a nice place to be. I feel that it is a place where I can get games, and with the squad we have got here we can really do things this season.

'For the next three months, and if it is going to be longer than that, I want to be a part of it.'

England Under-21 international striker Stead made his name as a youngster at Huddersfield Town when he broke through to score 24 goals in 76 League and Cup games.

That form earned him a £1.25m move to the Premiership with Blackburn Rovers in February 2004, and he was an immediate top-flight hit with six goals in his first 13 games, including a winner against Manchester United.

However, the following season was less successful for the Huddersfield-born front-man, who took until March 2005 to get off the mark and added only one more goal before the end of the campaign.

Newly-promoted Sunderland splashed out £1.8m to take Stead from Ewood Park during the summer of 2005.

Stead has started just once for Sunderland this season, scoring in a 3–1 defeat at Southend United in August, and hasn't featured for the Black Cats since Roy Keane took over as manager.

New loan signing Jon Stead.

PLYMOUTH: McCormick, Nalis, Norris, Buzsaky (Samba 77), Ebanks-Blake (Aljofree 50; Summerfield 73), Hayles, Kouo-Doumbe, Capaldi, Wotton, Seip, Connolly.
UNUSED SUBS: Larrieu, Djordjic.

DERBY: Grant, Edworthy, Camara, Bolder, M. Johnson, Bisgaard (Smith 68), Howard, Stead, Lupoli, Oakley (S. Johnson 77), Moore (Leacock 56).
UNUSED SUBS: Jackson, Bywater.

ATTENDANCE: 13,622.

Stead steps straight into the starting line up against Plymouth.

REPORT – 15 OCTOBER 2006
PLYMOUTH ARGYLE 3
DERBY COUNTY 1

Paul Connolly's long throw from the right into the box was headed safely into the arms of Lee Grant by Matt Oakley within the first minute.

Oakley found Jon Stead storming into the box on the right, he pulled the ball back from the by-line and his cross found Adam Bolder, whose header from close range landed in the arms of Luke McCormick on three minutes.

Stead, looking lively early on, met Grant's long ball in the box with his back to goal on six minutes. Under pressure, he turned and fired over, with the ball taking a deflection. From the corner, Howard's header flew over the crossbar from six yards.

Lupoli's header from an Oakley free-kick from the right landed in McCormick's arms on 12 minutes.

Nalis fired a foot over Grant's crossbar from 35 yards after a good ball from the left from Hayles on 22 minutes.

Bisgaard's left-foot shot flew just wide of McCormick's right-hand post on 24 minutes after good build-up play from Oakley and Bolder. Then Bisgaard's pin-point cross from the right found Lupoli arriving in the box on the left on 26 minutes – his dangerous header was palmed away by McCormick for a corner.

The defender was booked for the challenge, with Hayles landing in the ref's book for his elbow-raising reprisal. Capaldi's resulting free-kick flew low into Grant's arms.

Camara's rash challenge on Ebanks-Blake on 43 minutes, after the Plymouth man had beaten the offside trap, saw skipper Wotton step up to fire home from the penalty spot.

Two minutes into injury time, and seconds before the break, Lupoli levelled the score after latching on to Johnson's speculative, long-range shot that looked to be flying wide and steering it into the back of McCormick's net.

Grant's double save on 50 minutes kept the Rams in the game as he parried away Norris's power drive and Buzsaky's close-range follow-up.

Within seconds Kouo-Doumbe was given his marching orders for a second bookable offence after going in on Bisgaard with his studs up.

Johnson's alleged tug on Hayles, who had his back to goal in the box on the hour mark, saw Wotton step up to net his second penalty of the afternoon to restore the home side's lead. An angry Johnson was booked for what appeared to be a legitimate challenge.

Seip's far post header from a corner looked to have wrapped up the points on 77 minutes. Capaldi's set-piece from the right was headed on by Hayles at the front post to be met by Seip for Argyle's third goal.

Lupoli lost his footing and the ball with just the 'keeper to beat as the four minutes of extra time kicked in, and it was Plymouth who took their place in the Play-off spots.

REACTION

Billy Davies was left to rue the performance of referee Paul Taylor after his side's first League defeat in five games.

Taylor's harsh decision to award a second-half penalty against defender Michael Johnson changed the face of the Home Park clash, claimed Davies – and he revealed that the official had apologised to the Derby defender after the game, which ended 3–1.

'I thought we played some good stuff in the first half, we were the brighter side and deserved to equalise after their first penalty,' he said. 'I can't argue with that penalty, although the ref should have blown up for Jon Stead being impeded seconds earlier.

'He did apologise to Jonno for the second penalty but by that time it was too late. We'd played some good stuff, they were down to 10 men and we were well in the game – but that decision was a turning point.

'We should have kept our heads, though, and when their third goal went in we became a little erratic.'

Celebrations as Derby equalise.

Defender Darren Moore will sit out the Coca-Cola Championship game at Cardiff City after picking up his fifth booking of the season. Moore, 32, was cautioned during Sunday's 3–1 defeat at Plymouth Argyle – taking him over the threshold for a one-match ban.

FA regulations state that the punishment kicks in seven days after the fifth card was accrued, with the player then being suspended for the next first-team match, which sees Moore ruled out of the 28 October encounter at Ninian Park.

Moore will be available for Tuesday night's trip to Queen's Park Rangers, a game Billy Davies is targeting three points from after seeing his side beaten at Plymouth Argyle two days ago.

The 3–1 Home Park reverse was Derby's first in normal time in six games – Doncaster Rovers put them out of the Carling Cup on penalties – but they have been presented with a quick chance to put things right at Loftus Road.

Davies admits he isn't keen on a second run of two games in 48 hours this season but says the players now have to put the Plymouth result out of their minds.

'We have got to put that behind us as the most important thing to remember is that we have lost just one in six,' he said.

'If we could have got a point at Plymouth and a point at QPR we would have been delighted.

'So the target now must be three at QPR to put us a stage further forward in our development.

'It's another tough away game, we know that, and every game in this Division is tough, but it is one we're looking forward to.

'The team spirit is very much where I want it to be, and we have got to take the good from the bad.

'There certainly were some good signs of progress on Sunday, and plenty of good play, but again that inconsistency in the second half has to be addressed.'

Meanwhile, team skipper Matt Oakley says the Rams remain confident on the road – and are given a lift by the tremendous travelling support.

Derby have already won three League games away from home this season and go looking for a fourth at Queen's Park Rangers.

They will once again be backed by some vocal support from the away end at Loftus Road, a factor Oakley credits in helping to turn things around after the Rams won only twice last season.

'They are really helping us,' Oakley said. 'I think that is why we are playing so well away from home – we've got the fans there to see what we're doing on the pitch, rather than them sitting at home listening to it on the radio.

Adam Bolder fights off a Plymouth attacker.

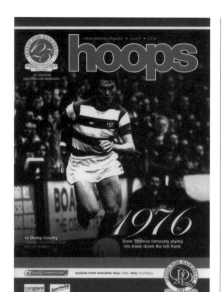

QPR: P. Jones, Bignot, Rehman, Bircham (C), Rowlands, Lomas (Donnelly 82), Cook, Stewart, R. Jones (Gallen 73), Blackstock, Smith.
SUBS: Royce, Ward, Mancienne.

DERBY: Grant, Edworthy, Leacock (Boertien 90), M. Johnson, Camara, Bisgaard (Moore 84), Oakley (C), S. Johnson, Bolder, Lupoli (Stead 61), Howard.
UNUSED SUBS: Bywater, Smith.

ATTENDANCE: 10,822.

'It's nice for them to travel away and think "we are going to get something here," and that is the way we are feeling.

'There is something happening in the dressing room, our mentality is changing and we feel we are going to win games now.

'If we can match our home record with our away record we will be up there or thereabouts at the end of the season.'

REPORT – 17 OCTOBER 2006
QUEEN'S PARK RANGERS 1
DERBY COUNTY 2

Only five minutes were on the clock and the Rams were in front thanks to Bisgaard's first goal of the season. Rangers failed to deal with a long ball and it fell to the Dane 20 yards out, who curled his shot beautifully past Paul Jones and into the bottom-left corner.

The home side had a great chance to equalise immediately as Dexter Blackstock met Lee Cook's left-wing cross with a firm header, but Lee Grant was equal to it with a fine save.

But equalise they did just two minutes later with a thunderous volley from the edge of the box.

Derby failed to clear their lines and the ball dropped to Jimmy Smith, who cracked home his shot and left Grant with no chance.

The goal gave Rangers an immediate lift and they peppered the Derby box with crosses to their two tall strikers, but each time they met with a confident fist from Grant.

Derby should have been back in front on 18 but were denied by a wonder-save from Jones.

Bisgaard found himself in space on the right and his cross was inch-perfect for the head of Lupoli, but Jones's reactions were equal to the close-range effort. Jones then showed agility beyond his 39 years to tip over a powerful Seth Johnson 25-yarder that looked destined for the top-left corner.

Derby were back in front 12 minutes before half-time after breaking quickly down the left through Bolder and Mo Camara.

Camara's cross was blocked out to Lupoli, whose 14-yard shot was well saved by Jones, but Howard was on hand to ram home the rebound from close range.

Bisgaard scores his first of the season.

Derby opened up the second half on the attack and came close to extending their lead in freak circumstances as Bolder got in the way of Rehman's clearance only for the ball to bounce just over Jones's bar.

Martin Rowlands saw his 16-yard drive flash just over as the second half promised to continue in the same vein as the first.

From a free-kick Jones made another fine save – this time following Bisgaard's low effort.

Derby had a great chance to make it three when Rehman failed to deal with a long ball and let Howard through, but the big number nine never quite got the ball out from under his feet and Jones saved well.

Stead then struck a post from 20 yards with a shot that came completely out of nowhere, and as Rangers failed to clear their lines Howard headed Camara's cross against the bar.

The understanding between Howard and Stead produced another golden chance for Derby and this time Bolder was the guilty party as all he had to do was make contact with Stead's low cross five yards out, but somehow the midfielder missed his kick.

Grant produced a fine diving save to push away Bircham's 25-yard pile-driver and Blackstock headed over from close range with three minutes left as the Rams lived a little dangerously from Cook's in-swinging free-kick.

Stead did well to hold up Camara's ball and turn cleverly past Damion Stewart on the edge of the box, but once again Jones pulled out a fine save from the striker's low shot.

Gallen missed a stoppage time sitter for the home side, but Derby held out for their fourth win on the road this season.

REACTION

Billy Davies felt only a wonderful performance from QPR goalkeeper Paul Jones prevented the Rams from winning at Loftus Road by more than the one goal.

Morten Bisgaard and Steve Howard struck in the first half to give Derby all three points from a 2–1 success, but a string of fine saves from Jones kept them to two and left the game always on a knife-edge.

Jimmy Smith had equalised for the Hoops, but Jones was by far the busier 'keeper on the night and showed his best form on numerous occasions.

'I thought their goalkeeper was magnificent, and I don't know how many saves he made, but he kept them in the game,' Davies said. 'We created a lot of chances and played very well. We had to battle as it was a scrappy game at times, and a difficult match for the referee, but it was a fantastic three points for us.

'I said previously that the two games in three days was a big test for us, with QPR having that extra day's recovery, but I felt we looked far fitter this time around than the first time it happened this season.'

Defender Dean Leacock will see a doctor on Thursday afternoon to assess whether or not he's able to play in the Championship clash with Birmingham City at Pride Park Stadium on Saturday.

The centre-half suffered minor concussion in a clash of heads in the last couple of minutes of the 2–1 win at Queen's Park Rangers on Tuesday night, and a decision will only be taken on whether or not he can feature against the Blues once the medical advice has been received.

The Rams boss said 'Dean was not fully unconscious but had not fully come round after physio treatment so he was taken to hospital.

'He was released from hospital the same night, came back to Derby and will see a doctor tomorrow afternoon to assess his condition and give us a view on his availability for Saturday.'

Leacock battles in the air to stop another Rangers attack.

Two of the Rams' 18-year-olds have headed out on loan. Centre-half Lewin Nyatanga has joined Coca-Cola Championship side Sunderland until 2 January after only starting four times for Derby this season, and Academy product James Meredith will spend a month on loan with Nationwide Conference side Cambridge United. The 18-year-old Australian is making the switch to the Abbey Stadium and is eligible for their encounter with table-topping Oxford United on Friday night.

On-loan Italian Arturo Lupoli insists the Rams have nothing to fear from Saturday's visit of Birmingham City.

Derby have crept above the Blues in the Coca-Cola Championship table on the back of four wins and a draw from their last six games. Birmingham, on the other hand, have not won in five and have taken only two points in that time.

'We do not need to be afraid,' the teen ace – Derby's leading scorer this season with six goals – said. 'They have lost their last two games so they will want to put it right, and we have to take our opportunities if we are to get the three points.

'If we are able to do it we will be in a very good position at the end of the weekend.

'Birmingham have some very good and experienced players so we need to be focused on getting another win at home.'

Nyatanga goes out on loan to Sunderland until the start of the new year.

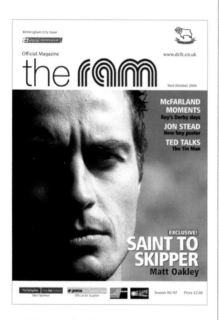

DERBY: Grant, Edworthy, Moore, M. Johnson (C), Camara, Bisgaard, Bolder, S. Johnson, Lupoli, Howard, Stead.
UNUSED SUBS: Bywater, Jackson, Smith, Boertien, Barnes.

BIRMINGHAM: Maik Taylor, Kelly, Jaidi, Martin Taylor, Sadler, D. Johnson (C), Clemence, Nafti (Larsson 81), McSheffrey (Danns 87), Bendtner, Dunn (Jerome 23).
UNUSED SUBS: Doyle, Campbell.

ATTENDANCE: 25,673.

REPORT – 21 OCTOBER 2006
DERBY COUNTY 0
BIRMINGHAM CITY 1

The Rams started well as Jon Stead shot over from the corner of the box on eight minutes, after being well fed by Steve Howard. They broke from the edge of their box through Arturo Lupoli, who started the move after picking up the ball from Marc Edworthy's tackle and almost finished it from just outside the Birmingham area after Stead's initial shot had been blocked, but the Italian saw Maik Taylor comfortably save his low shot.

Derby had an escape with 11 minutes on the clock when Lee Grant dropped Gary McSheffrey's cross, with David Dunn ready to pounce. The ball was scrambled away and Dunn went down appealing for a penalty, but referee Uriah Rennie was un-moved.

Nicklas Bendtner broke away after a long ball and eased off the challenge of Michael Johnson but could not force his shot past Grant, who produced a fine save and then a confident punch from the resulting corner.

The game began to open up around the half-hour mark and another inch on Steve Howard's stretch would surely have seen him poke home Morten Bisgaard's excellent cross from the right.

Cameron Jerome, still looking for his first Blues goal after a big-money summer move from Cardiff City, couldn't have asked for a better opportunity after being found in plenty of space by Bendtner's intelligent back-heel.

However, with time to pick his spot, the England Under-21 international rolled the ball tamely into the hands of Grant – who had dived early but was left to wait for the ball to come to him, such was the lack of power on Jerome's shot.

Bendtner turned McSheffrey's 35th-minute corner goalwards, but it stayed out thanks to a combination of Grant, the post and a Derby body on the line.

Howard had the second half's first real opportunity three minutes in, but his shot from just inside the box was deflected over by Jaidi for a corner.

Bisgaard broke down the right and struck the outside of a post with his low cross-shot on 56 minutes.

Jerome picked up on Stead's loose pass and advanced to the edge of the Derby box, but this time he could only fire straight at Grant.

There were 20 minutes on the clock when Maik Taylor was given his first serious test, but he passed it well as Bisgaard advanced down the right before cracking in a shot from the edge of the box that the Northern Ireland international turned around the post.

Birmingham broke with seven minutes left on the clock and peppered the Derby box with crosses, until the Rams' resistance finally cracked. Derby failed to clear their lines and Clemence drove in a 20-yard shot that took a wicked deflection and spun away from Grant's dive before finding the net via a post.

Stead saw his shot sail wide of the target as the Rams looked for a late recovery. Bolder then saw an effort wide for a corner as the end of stoppage time approached, but after a mad scramble the ball ended up safely on the roof of the net.

REACTION

It was a game of two halves for manager Billy Davies, who continues to be frustrated with his side's performances at Pride Park Stadium.

'The first half was disappointing – we didn't pass and again we didn't play in our home environment,' Davies said after the 1–0 defeat. 'We have to handle that better.

'We improved in the second half, but they got a deflected goal and there was nothing we could do about that. Sometimes sides need a bit of luck like that.

'To be honest I was expecting we would be leggy after our travels. Birmingham were able to make around six changes today – you need that depth of squad and the ability to bring in quality. We played with great energy after the break, but it wasn't enough.'

Seth Johnson felt the Rams were caught by a 'freak' Birmingham City goal as they fell to their second home defeat of the season.

Eighth hosted ninth in the Coca-Cola Championship, and it looked like a point each after a tight encounter at Pride Park. But with Derby on the attack Birmingham broke quickly and stole all three thanks to Stephen Clemence's wickedly-deflected 83rd-minute effort.

'That was the only way they were going to get a goal, they caught us on the counter-attack and got a freak deflection,' Johnson said. 'We didn't seem to get the rub of the green today as their goal came from a deflection and it went in, while our deflections were going wide.

'I thought we were well on top in the second half and the longer the game went on the more we had them camped inside their own half.

'It has been a tough week for us and we are disappointed not to have got more points.'

Defender Theo Streete will spend a second month on loan at League One side Doncaster Rovers.

The 18-year-old signed a short-term professional deal with Derby over the summer and joined Rovers for an initial month during September.

Streete, an Academy product, has made one start and two substitute appearances and has shown plenty of good signs to new Doncaster boss Sean O'Driscoll.

Billy Davies has admitted that losing midfielder Bob Malcolm for as

Howard wins the header.

Seth Johnson looks high for the ball.

long as three months comes as a big blow ahead of Saturday's trip to Championship table-toppers Cardiff City.

The Scotsman has undergone surgery this week to remove a piece of floating bone from his right ankle and is now expected to be sidelined until January next year.

It is a blow for Malcolm, who was building up his match-fitness after his arrival on a free transfer in September, while it leaves Davies's options limited ahead of the trip to Ninian Park.

'It is a blow for the player, for the club, as Bob is a key member of the squad, but that is part of football,' the gaffer said. 'We have got to get on with it and work with the squad we have, within the financial constraints we have, and do the best we can, and that is what we are doing.

'There is a great spirit in the squad, the players are working very hard to try and do what we can and that will continue into this Saturday's game.'

Malcolm first picked up the problem in the game against Preston North End on 16 September but battled on before aggravating it in training ahead of the Plymouth Argyle match a month later.

He underwent keyhole surgery to repair the damage after it failed to respond to treatment.

The trip to Cardiff is one that all of the players are looking forward to, according to on-loan striker Jon Stead.

Cardiff have enjoyed an excellent start to the campaign under Dave Jones and sit three points clear at the head of the pack.

But Stead is pleased with how Derby have performed in the three games he has played since joining on loan from Sunderland and believes the Ninian Park encounter holds no fears.

'It will be a tough game as they are doing well,' the 23-year-old said. 'They lost at the weekend but they are a good side. We know what they're about and it is a tough trip, but it is one that I can say everyone is looking forward to.'

Leacock jumps with Cardiff's Steven Thompson.

REPORT – 28 OCTOBER 2006
CARDIFF CITY 2
DERBY COUNTY 2

A wet afternoon in the Welsh capital was taking a while to ignite, and almost 15 minutes had passed before the game's first shot, but it never threatened a goal as the home side's Stephen McPhail fired safely over from 20 yards.

Joe Ledley then escaped down the left and put over a fine cross that was only half-cleared out to Kevin McNaughton, who drove his effort wide from the penalty spot.

Paul Parry should have done better 21 minutes in after the ball fell to him following Michael Johnson's strong challenge on Michael Chopra, but with space inside the box the winger blazed his effort well over the bar.

The Rams were forced into a defensive change as a result of the incident as Johnson was unable to continue, hobbling off to be replaced by Richard Jackson.

Jackson slotted in at right-back, his natural position, while Marc Edworthy moved across one place to partner Leacock in the centre of defence.

With the Rams still re-shuffling, Cardiff carved them open and should really have taken the lead when Chopra went through one-on-one with Bywater, but the striker inexplicably shot wide with the goal at his mercy.

Derby's first shot on target came on 26 minutes as Stead, with no other real option, cut in from the right to force Neil Alexander into a smart low save.

Stead thought he had broken his duck with 12 minutes to go before half-time after turning smartly on the edge of the box and smashing in a left-footer that Alexander could only drop badly over his line.

However, the goalkeeper was reprieved when Stead was penalised for tugging on the shirt of Darren Purse as he controlled the ball.

Chopra again should have opened the scoring five minutes before the interval after getting clear of the Derby defence, but again he shot wide with only Bywater to beat.

Bywater was back in action five minutes later with a smart sprawling save low to his left from Riccy Scimeca's effort, which the 'keeper couldn't have seen until late. And on 52 minutes the home side took the lead, as they had threatened to do since the second half kicked-off.

Parry's corner from the right swung in and was met firmly by the head of Glenn Loovens, who powered the ball down and past Bywater.

Derby had a loud shout for a penalty just before the hour when Stead was bundled over by home skipper Darren Purse, but referee Andre Marriner dismissed the appeals – much to the dismay of the visiting contingent.

But 67 minutes later the Rams were level.

Oakley and Bisgaard combined well down the right to free Jackson, whose fine cross was met powerfully by the head of Howard for an emphatic close-range leveller.

Cardiff looked to strike straight back and were inches away when Parry's cracking shot from the right flashed just past Bywater's right-hand post.

The home side restored their lead on 75 with a goal worthy of a team top of the table. Scimeca cleverly fed Chambers's pass into the path of Chopra, who from inside the box succeeded where he had twice failed and smashed the ball past Bywater.

Stead thought he had scored his first goal for Derby, only to have it disallowed for an earlier foul.

CARDIFF: Alexander, McNaughton, Purse (C), Loovens (R. Johnson 62), Chopra, Thompson, McPhail, Parry, Ledley, Scimeca, Chambers.
UNUSED SUBS: Howard, Flood, Campbell, Kamara.

DERBY: Bywater, Edworthy, Leacock, M. Johnson (Jackson 21), Camara, Bisgaard (Barnes 73), S. Johnson, Oakley (C), Lupoli, Howard, Stead.
UNUSED SUBS: Grant, Bolder, Smith.

ATTENDANCE: 17,371.

Lupoli weaves his way through a couple of Cardiff players.

Seth Johnson wins the ball in midfield.

Derby found themselves with plenty of possession midway through four minutes of stoppage time, and they levelled matters in dramatic style.

Jackson's cross from the right was deflected up in the air and it fell to Barnes, who crashed home a spectacular volley that wouldn't have looked out of place in a World Cup Final.

REACTION

First-team coach Julian Darby felt the Rams fully deserved their 2–2 draw at League leaders Cardiff City – and was full of praise for Giles Barnes's dramatic late equaliser.

Eighteen-year-old Barnes struck in the second minute of stoppage time with only his second senior goal to earn Derby a point at Ninian Park with a volley that would have graced any game.

Richard Jackson's cross looped up in the air and Barnes showed the technique of a world superstar to smash it past Neil Alexander and into the roof of the net.

'It was an absolutely fantastic strike, I can't say any more about it than that,' Darby said. 'In the second minute of injury time, with the ball up in the air for what felt like forever, and the lad has took his time – with 17,000 fans baying for his blood too. It's dropped and he's steamed it right past the 'keeper. He does it all the time in training. His technique is fantastic.'

Giles Barnes said modestly of his point-saving wonder-goal: 'I just thought why not?'

Barnes, 18, netted only his second senior strike with a thunderous volley two minutes into stoppage time at Ninian Park to rescue a point from table-topping Cardiff City.

He showed technique well beyond his years to finish superbly and send the Derby fans home happy but was more keen on recognising the importance of the draw when he spoke after the game.

'It was a decent finish to the game, but the important thing was we got a point out of it,' he said.

'I just saw it coming down after Jacko's cross had been deflected so I thought why not have a strike. I hit it cleanly enough and just got lucky really.'

TABLE

	P	W	D	L	F	A	Pts
Cardiff	15	10	3	2	29	13	33
Preston	15	8	5	2	26	16	29
Burnley	15	8	4	3	25	14	28
Birmingham	15	8	3	4	20	15	27
West Brom	15	7	5	3	27	16	26
Plymouth	15	6	7	2	22	16	25
Wolves	14	7	2	5	12	15	23
Coventry	15	7	1	7	14	13	22
Luton	15	6	4	5	23	25	22
Colchester	15	6	3	6	21	17	21
Ipswich	15	6	3	6	26	23	21
Leicester	15	5	6	4	15	15	21
Southampton	14	5	4	5	18	17	19
Derby	**14**	**5**	**4**	**5**	**20**	**20**	**19**
Sunderland	15	6	1	8	20	22	19
Norwich	15	5	4	6	21	27	19
Stoke	15	4	6	5	21	15	18
C Palace	15	5	3	7	17	20	18
Sheffield W	15	4	5	6	16	21	17
QPR	15	3	6	6	22	26	15
Leeds	15	4	1	10	14	30	13
Hull	15	3	3	9	12	21	12
Barnsley	14	3	3	8	18	28	12
Southend	15	2	4	9	14	28	10

November

Can that stoppage time equaliser at Cardiff prove a springboard for the Rams to push their season on? There's no better way to spark your campaign into life than a late goal to take a deserved point away from the League leaders.

And with six games to come in November – starting with two successive outings at Pride Park – Derby will fancy their chances of making further progress.

Defender Michael Johnson has been ruled out of action for up to four weeks with the hamstring injury he picked up in Saturday's 2–2 draw at Cardiff City.

The 33-year-old limped off 21 minutes into the Ninian Park clash after picking up the problem.

At first it was thought to be nothing more than a tweak, but further assessment over the last couple of days has found that the injury will keep Jonno on the sidelines for longer.

The Rams have Darren Moore back from suspension for Wednesday's game against Barnsley, while Marc Edworthy filled in admirably at centre-half on Saturday once Jonno went off.

However, Billy Davies is delighted at the perfect timing of Darren Moore's return to the squad. Moore missed out on Saturday's 2–2 draw away at Cardiff City through a one-match suspension, leaving Michael Johnson and Dean Leacock as the only recognised senior centre-backs at the club.

And with Johnson this week being ruled out for up to a month with the hamstring injury, Moore's availability is a great tonic ahead of the visit of Barnsley.

'Jonno's injury is not as bad as first thought as it's not a tear or a pull,' the boss said. 'It is just tightness which will probably keep him out for three to four weeks.

'We're welcoming Mooro back into the squad, which is a good thing, and Marc Edworthy's performance against a top side was first-class, he showed us that he can handle the centre-half position very well.'

As well as Johnson, Derby go into the game also missing striker Paul Peschisolido (thigh) and midfielder Bob Malcolm (ankle).

'The other 16 are fine, all ready and looking forward to the game,' Davies added.

Michael Johnson and Darren Moore.

REPORT – 1 NOVEMBER 2006
DERBY COUNTY 2
BARNSLEY 1

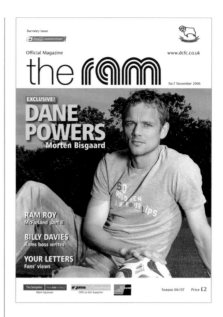

Barnsley had much of the early possession and were looking to ex-Ram Michael McIndoe to provide their creative force, but Derby were dealing well with his crosses from the left.

At the other end a skied clearance dropped in front of Barnes – 'shoot', cried the crowd – but the teenager couldn't repeat his spectacular effort from Ninian Park. But the visitors opened the scoring on 12 minutes with what could only be described as a sloppy goal given away.

McIndoe floated a corner over from the left, Stephen Bywater came out but got nowhere near it, and right-back Bobby Hassell rammed home the ball at the far post.

Seconds later Marc Richards broke through clear of the defence, and although Bywater came out to block the ball rolled dangerously towards goal before Darren Moore intervened.

Derby should have found themselves two behind on 18 minutes when Dean Leacock was caught in possession and Tommy Wright went through, but the Barnsley man forced his shot wide with just Bywater to beat.

Another McIndoe corner almost created another Hassell goal on 27 minutes, but this time the defender's shot was blocked in front of goal.

The Rams' first shot on target came 31 minutes in via Steve Howard's 20-yarder that was straight at Nick Colgan, although the Barnsley 'keeper could only grasp it at the second attempt with Jon Stead closing in.

Arturo Lupoli jinked and twisted on the left before firing in a low left-footer towards the near post that Colgan again failed to hold first time, but no Derby player could get to the loose ball.

Barnes had the ball in the back of the net shortly before half-time, though the whistle had already gone to pull him back for offside.

Barnsley had the first opportunity of the second half, though Wright couldn't make the most of a free header eight yards out and could only find the hands of Bywater.

Richards should have doubled the lead on 52 minutes as Derby once again gave away possession in midfield. This time Martin Devaney broke down the right and his excellent low cross found the front-man with the goal at his mercy, but somehow he stabbed his shot wide.

Seth Johnson warmed the hands of Colgan with a powerful 20-yarder – again, the 'keeper failed to hold it but again he grabbed it at the second attempt.

On 66 minutes the Rams were an inch away from levelling when the two old Arsenal teammates combined.

Ryan Smith found space on the left and pulled the ball back for Lupoli, whose shot from the penalty spot was deflected on to the post with Colgan totally beaten. Bywater let Sam Togwell's low drive squirm away from his grasp but then did well to recover as the Barnsley midfielder closed in.

But with 18 on the clock Derby were level as from a free-kick the visitors could only half-clear and the ball dropped to Barnes, who crashed another spectacular shot into the back of the net from the edge of the box.

The goal clearly lifted Derby and within three minutes they were in front – and once again, Barnes was the scorer.

DERBY: Bywater, Edworthy (Jackson 90), Moore (C), Leacock, Camara, Barnes, S. Johnson, Bolder (Bisgaard 59), Lupoli, Stead (Smith HT), Howard.
UNUSED SUBS: Grant, Boertien.

BARNSLEY: Colgan, Hassell (Austin HT), Heckingbottom, Reid (C), Togwell, McIndoe, Howard, Kay, Richards (Nardiello 83), Wright (Hayes 78).
UNUSED SUBS: Healy, Williams.

ATTENDANCE: 21,295.

Barnes scores from the edge of the box after a free-kick is only half cleared.

Stephen Bywater was the busier of the two 'keepers.

Giles Barnes celebrates his goal.

Barnsley failed to clear their lines from a corner and the ball rolled out as far as the 18-year-old on the edge of the box, and he found the top corner with a thunderous right-footer.

Nardiello thought he had equalised on 86 minutes when he tapped in after Bywater dropped McIndoe's edge-of-the-box shot at the striker's feet, but as with Barnes in the first half he was denied by a linesman's flag for offside.

There were some late nerves, but the whistle blew to much jubilation among the Pride Park faithful.

REACTION

Billy Davies declared, after his side's second home win of the campaign, 'We owe our fans an apology for that first-half performance.'

The Rams boss was furious with Derby County's sloppy approach in the first 45 minutes that saw struggling Barnsley go in at the interval with a 1–0 lead.

Davies responded by replacing Jon Stead with Ryan Smith at the break and later introducing Morten Bisgaard for Adam Bolder.

'The substitutions brought us more quality in the second half,' he said.

'We had been talking in the past few days about taking the right approach and bringing the right energy to this game, but one or two of my players simply turned up tonight and didn't listen to those words, so we got what we deserved in the first 45. It was unacceptable.'

Even after Giles Barnes won the game for the Rams with two stunning strikes, Davies stressed lessons had to be learned before the visit of West Brom this Saturday.

'We have to play with a lot more composure at Pride Park,' he said.

'Barnsley were a potential banana skin, so it's an important three points for us, but you can make life difficult for yourself against the bottom teams, and we certainly did that in the first 45.'

Giles Barnes spoke after coming to the fore again with two more spectacular strikes – and was as modest as ever about the impact he had on the 2–1 win over Barnsley.

Barnes had struck in the second minute of stoppage time to rescue a point in Saturday's 2–2 draw at Cardiff City. And he was the Rams' saviour once more on Wednesday night as Barnsley led for over an hour until the 18-year-old netted twice in three minutes with more explosive finishing.

'I don't know about being the Derby County hero!' he replied when asked how it felt to have been the hero of the last two games. 'I have just scored a few goals, as has Steve Howard, and Arturo Lupoli too. I wouldn't have got the chances if it wasn't for the other lads in the team so I can only thank them for that.

'A goal is a goal – the most important thing is the result, not how good the strike was or when it was.'

Darren Moore admits it will be a strange feeling to step out against West Bromwich Albion for the first time since leaving them in January – but says all that matters is three points for Derby County.

Defender Moore joined the Rams at the start of this year after a tremendously successful spell with the Baggies, during which time they won promotion twice and enjoyed Premiership football.

But come 3pm on Saturday, all memories of his time at the Hawthorns will be put to one side as Derby look to build on that midweek victory against Barnsley.

'It will feel strange to start with, but I'm professional enough to – if selected to play – put that to one side and concentrate on the game,' the big centre-half said.

'I had a great time at West Brom, everyone knows about my association with the football club, but now I'm committed to Derby and my aim is to be fully committed to the cause on Saturday.

'West Brom have a good team, and as players we will have to raise our game and push ourselves to get a result.'

REPORT – 4 NOVEMBER 2006
DERBY COUNTY 2
WEST BROMWICH ALBION 1

A Derby attack down the left six minutes in almost produced the game's first goal – though the Rams would have found themselves behind rather than in front.

Richard Chaplow broke up play and the ball was eventually fed to Diomansy Kamara, whose shot from the edge of the box was deflected over with Stephen Bywater beaten.

Bywater was called into serious action on 12 minutes, and he delivered when required with a fine sprawling save to push out Nathan Ellington's far-post header.

The 'keeper, who received criticism from some quarters for his performance against Barnsley in midweek, then produced another fine save to turn away Kamara's powerful drive after the striker had been fed clear inside the box.

But on 21 minutes he dropped Steve Watson's right-wing free-kick and was lucky to escape as Curtis Davies's effort struck the crossbar and bounced away. And the Baggies were in front four minutes later with another goal that Derby could have prevented.

Seth Johnson's misplaced pass in midfield was picked up by Ellington, and, although his pass had a bit of luck to find its way through to Richard Chaplow

DERBY: Bywater, Edworthy, Leacock, M. Johnson, Camara, Barnes, Oakley (C), S. Johnson (Smith HT), Bisgaard (Moore 90), Howard, Lupoli (Stead 58).
UNUSED SUBS: Bolder, Grant.

WBA: Hoult, Watson, Perry, Davies (C), Greening, Ellington (Phillips 58), Gera (Hartson 87), Chaplow, Albrechtsen, Kamara, Koumas.
UNUSED SUBS: Steele, McShane, Wallwork.

ATTENDANCE: 25,342.

Matt Oakley scores Derby's first goal in the second half of the game.

Morten Bisgaard, whose near-post cross was converted by Barnes for Derby's winner.

inside the Derby box, the midfielder did well to force his shot past Bywater then add the finishing touch from half a yard.

Too many passes were going astray, and while there was the usual work-rate from the Derby players, the quality was lacking.

In fact, the biggest cheer of the half from the home fans came when Bywater managed to put a clearance over the East Stand roof and out of the stadium – a rare feat indeed in the nine years since the Rams moved to Pride Park.

No sooner had the game restarted than West Brom should have made it two. Kamara did well to get in a shot from a narrow angle that Bywater blocked out, and the ball rebounded to Ellington at the far post, who had the simple task of tapping it into an empty net.

Somehow, the former Wigan man managed to shoot wide of the target from inside the six-yard box.

Kamara was proving a danger every time he got the ball, particularly when he pulled out to the left before cutting back in, and with his next effort he rattled the ball into Bywater's side-netting from just inside the box.

The Baggies were in again on 57 minutes when Ellington pounced on Ryan Smith's sliced clearance to feed Jason Koumas, but the Welsh midfielder showed a distinct lack of composure and shot wildly over from the penalty spot.

Just after the hour the Rams came as close as they had done all afternoon, and once again Howard was denied by the woodwork.

Good work by Bisgaard down the right allowed Oakley to cross from the by-line, but the ball was slightly behind Howard, who did well to head it back where Hoult had came from but rather than the back of the net he found the outside of the post.

Bywater produced a good low block to deny Koumas, who had ran clear from his own half after Derby wasted a free-kick at the other end. And out of nowhere, with the game getting stretched, Derby levelled on 68 minutes – in spectacular fashion again.

Oakley picked up the ball in the centre-circle and strode forward towards the Baggies box, and with space in front of him he paused some 25 yards out before unleashing an unstoppable drive into the top corner that Hoult stood no chance with.

And as they had done in midweek, the Rams turned things around with a second goal in the space of four minutes. Bisgaard found space down the right and whipped in a fine ball to the near post, where Barnes met it with a powerful downward header into the back of the net for his fourth goal in three games.

Bywater produced another fine save from Jonathan Greening's low edge-of-the-box drive after some intense pressure from the men in green and yellow.

Bisgaard was an inch away from making it three with another cracker from outside the box, but as the clock ticked over to 85 minutes nerves started to spread around Pride Park.

Howard could have wrapped it up in stoppage time but his close-range effort was deflected over.

REACTION

'It's a shame some of our games don't start at half-time, because if they did we would be top of the League!'

Billy Davies's tongue-in-cheek comment after his side again came from behind to record a second home win in three days struck a chord after another lacklustre first-half performance was followed by a display of real

passion in the second 45 minutes against a classy West Bromwich Albion outfit.

'They have got real quality in their side and throwing on Kevin Phillips and John Hartson shows what depth they have in their squad,' said Davies.

'In the first half we were again sloppy, but in the second we showed character, commitment and fitness. When players are giving their best you are always in with a chance, but I have said before we need to add quality. What we do have is a lot of bottle, and sometimes that's what counts.'

Matt Oakley went into the game against West Bromwich Albion dosed up on painkillers after suffering from a bout of sciatica – and came out of it feeling on top of the world.

Team skipper Oakley wasn't expected to face the Baggies due to the problem, but he was passed fit after making a quick recovery.

He responded with a superb 68th-minute strike that levelled matters after Derby had gone behind to Richard Chaplow's first-half goal – and then Giles Barnes won it for the Rams.

'That certainly released it,' Oakley said. 'I was very pleased with that one, it changed the game for us after we had been struggling up to that point.

'Everyone was shouting at me to pass it, but I thought I'd have a shot. The crowd were great after that, they really did lift us today, and then Giles popped up with another goal.'

Derby County manager Billy Davies feels the time is right for new faces to strengthen the Rams squad.

Having seen his side move up to eighth in the Championship, the gaffer believes that it is now the perfect period to add extra bodies to what is a fairly lean squad.

However, until the January transfer window opens Billy knows he has to be reliant on emergency loans – and he's certainly not prepared to compromise on quality.

He said 'Yes, I do feel that now is the right time to bring some new players in, if the opportunity presents itself.

'We've done very well in recent weeks and new faces would help build on that by adding even more competition for places.

Giles Barnes scores the winner, his fourth goal in three games.

Derby celebrate Barnes's goal.

'We know our options are slightly limited, but I have been making phone calls and hopefully things can happen in the coming weeks.

'But, as I've said all along, we'll only bring players in if they're good enough and if they have the right attitude and desire to play for Derby County. Supporters can rest assured about that.'

However, the gaffer could soon have two familiar faces available to him. Popular front-man Paul Peschisolido is nearing a return to action and could be back playing in around seven days.

Davies says the Canadian striker is making great progress after tearing a thigh muscle, and he could be in contention for the game at Luton a week on Saturday.

There's also good news regarding midfielder Bob Malcolm, who recently underwent surgery to remove floating bone in his ankle. He's off crutches and the injury is progressing well, although he's still likely to face another couple of months on the sidelines.

Davies said 'Both Pesch and Bob are making progress, in fact in Pesch's case he could well be back playing again in about seven days time. Bob's surgery went well, and I'm pleased to say he's now off his crutches and back walking on both feet, but he now enters a period of intensive rehabilitation twinned with rest and will not be available for selection for a couple of months.'

Derby travel to Coventry City on Saturday and defender Marc Edworthy claims the Rams can wipe the slate clean this weekend and put recent catastrophes there behind them.

Billy Davies's side have conceded six goals on each of their last two trips to Coventry – a 6–1 beating at the Ricoh Arena in January 2006, after a 6–2 reverse in the final game at Highfield Road in April 2005.

But former Sky Blues player Edworthy, who spent four seasons at Highfield Road, believes Derby can take heart from recent results as they prepare for the Ricoh Arena clash.

'We've had a good week with a draw against the League leaders and two home wins,' said Edworthy.

'We've managed to see off our home curse and now is the chance to put another to bed against Coventry.

'Last season was certainly a disaster, but we have a new squad, a new manager and the right mentality and, although we're not getting carried away, our away form has been good.

'We're ticking along and sneaking up the table and this weekend we have another chance to secure our place among the front-runners. But Micky Adams will have his side fired up and they're a tough, physical team with a great defensive record.'

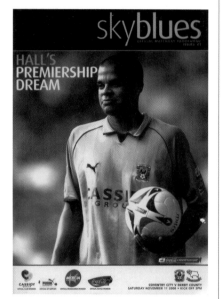

COVENTRY: Marshall, Hall, Page (C), Ward, Doyle, John, McKenzie, Tabb (Adebola 86), Hutchison (Cameron 87), Duffy, Clarke.
UNUSED SUBS: Gonzalez, Andrews, Birchall.

DERBY: Bywater, Edworthy, Leacock, M. Johnson (Moore 56), Bisgaard (Smith 59), Howard, Stead (Lupoli 72), Boertien, S. Johnson, Oakley (C), Barnes.
UNUSED SUBS: Grant, Bolder.

ATTENDANCE: 19,701.

REPORT – 11 NOVEMBER 2006
COVENTRY CITY 1
DERBY COUNTY 2

A long ball through the middle found Leon McKenzie, whose gentle touch to the right for Stern John saw the ex-Derby loanee fire over the crossbar from a decent position on eight minutes.

Jon Stead's first Derby goal in a Rams shirt came on 11 minutes.

A Steve Howard headed flick-on from a long Edworthy pass from the back found Stead with his back to goal – he turned on the edge of the box to fire past Marshall.

John responded to the constant taunts of the Rams fans by levelling on 21 minutes. The Rams failed to clear from a long throw-in near the left-hand corner flag with John popping up to fire past Bywater at the second attempt from close range.

Oakley fired over Marshall's goal within 30 seconds, and a minute later Doyle's power drive from outside the area was parried down by the diving Bywater.

Good work by Barnes down the left on the half-hour mark saw him skin Duffy and pull the ball back for Stead in front of goal – his low left footer hit Page and spun to safety.

The first bit of action of note after the break was a real dampener – literally – and it was when a pitch sprinkler accidentally came on as the match was being played, giving Bisgaard an early shower!

The Rams were forced into some desperate defending when McKenzie burst into the box and caused all sorts of problems, but the back line was resilient and Boertien got in a vital clearance.

On 54 minutes McKenzie was involved again as he twisted in behind the Rams back four and laid the ball back to John, who drove in a low shot that arced just wide.

Stead was close soon afterwards with a whipped low effort from 20 yards that Marshall was forced to dive to his right to save.

Coventry survived a penalty claim when Howard looked as though he may have been held in the area, and Derby were starting to rally, looking for the winner.

And the goal the noisy visiting fans sitting behind Marshall's net were looking for came on 76 minutes – another expertly taken header by Howard.

Smith floated over a lovely corner from the left, and the Rams striker floated an expert effort into the top corner of the net.

Rams fans had their hearts in their mouths on 84 minutes when Page

Rams players observe a minute's silence at the beginning of the game.

Rams players celebrate Jon Stead's opening goal.

Stephen Bywater saves from a Coventry attack.

David Jones joins Derby on loan until the New Year.

strode forward and unleashed a fierce drive that flew behind the outstretched palm of Bywater, but thankfully wide.

At the other end the visitors then had a chance to wrap the game up, but Lupoli's angled left-footer drifted just wide.

REACTION

Billy Davies praised the performance of players and fans as the Rams picked up their third consecutive 2–1 win – but he's refusing to get carried away by his side's top-five position.

Goals from Jon Stead and Steve Howard shot the Rams into the Play-off places, and they are 10 points better off than they were at the same stage last season.

But Davies will still not sneak a glance at the League table.

'Nothing is won or lost in November,' he insists. 'We need to be in this position in May. I am sure the fans are delighted with our position, and I am pleased that those who were at the Ricoh Arena today can travel home with smiles on their faces for a change.

'It was important to come here and pick up the points to keep our run going, keep us in with a shout and, of course, to reverse the hoodoo that has left us without a win in Coventry since 1997.

'The fans were fantastic again today – their vocal support from first to last played a part – and I would encourage our supporters to give us more of the same next weekend and, crucially, at home.'

'Really happy to have got off the mark, especially as we went on to pick up the win,' was the verdict of striker Jon Stead after he set the Rams on their way to a 2–1 victory at Coventry City.

Stead wasn't part of the Derby team that was crushed 6–2 and then 6–1 in successive seasons in Coventry, but he knew all about those humbling results and was pleased to have played his part in the visitors turning the tables.

After the match Stead revealed 'I'm really happy to have scored my first goal for the club. When the chance came about I only had one thing on my mind and am buzzing that it flew into the net.

'I've been working hard to improve my finishing and thankfully it paid off today. But the most important thing was that we came here and got a result, so to come away with all three points was tremendous.

'Coventry always make it tough for you, so it's a great result.

'I've heard all about the last two performances at Coventry – which I just want to point out I wasn't part of – and it's great for the lads, and the travelling fans who were once again in great voice today, that we won the game.

'The key to that was that we were a fair bit better in the first half than we have been in recent matches, and that gave us the platform to go on and get the victory.'

Central-defender Michael Johnson's fifth booking of the season in Saturday's 2–1 win at Coventry City rules him out of this week's visit to Luton Town. Jonno picked up the caution in the 25th minute of the Ricoh Arena success for a foul on the home side's Leon McKenzie.

The Rams will have one new face in their ranks when they visit Kenilworth Road on Saturday. Manchester United midfielder David Jones has joined Derby on loan until the New Year.

Manager Billy Davies is delighted to be bringing the 22-year-old to Pride Park.

'David has great ability, a super left foot and boasts a range of passing,' said Davies. 'I see him as a good old-fashioned midfielder. He's a creator and scorer of goals and can only get better. In fact, I believe he has the skill to shine on the international stage and will eventually turn out for his country.'

It's a ringing endorsement from the manager, who knows Jones well from his loan spell at Preston last season.

'He had a successful few months with me at Deepdale and put in some wonderful displays before his loan move to Holland,' the boss added. 'He became a firm fans' favourite, and I'm sure that will prove to be the case again during his time with Derby County.'

The trip to Luton gives Derby the chance to further cement their record as one of the Coca-Cola Championship's best away sides.

The Rams' away record is matched only by table-toppers Cardiff and third-placed Birmingham – all three sides have won five, drawn one and lost three on their travels – with Davies and his men hoping to make it six of the best at Kenilworth Road.

'We've almost sold out of our allocation of tickets so we'll have a large travelling support who I am sure will once again prove first class as they have been all season – vocally supporting us from the first whistle to the last,' he said. 'With the right approach and professionalism, we hope to once again send them home happy.'

It's been a turbulent week for Luton after boss Mike Newell's outburst at female match official Amy Rayner and club chairman Bill Tomlins.

Newell publicly apologised for his comments about Rayner and accepted that his remarks about the chairman were inappropriate, and he has been 'severely reprimanded' by the club. That all came on the back of five straight defeats in all competitions and injuries to a number of key players.

For Derby, one man well blessed with inside knowledge of the Hatters is striker Steve Howard, who spent five years at Kenilworth Road before joining the Rams in the summer.

'They had a cracking start, but now they are in a dip and off the pitch it isn't going too well,' Howard said. 'It may be the right time to play them. I think there is a lack of confidence in their squad so hopefully we can exploit that and really go to town on them.

'We will have to battle as it is a tight pitch with the crowd on top of you so it is not going to be easy. But if we stick together, I think we will have more than enough.

'The trouble off the field will filter through to the players, but that's the way it is.

'Obviously we have got to turn that to our advantage and go down there and produce a performance like we have been doing lately.'

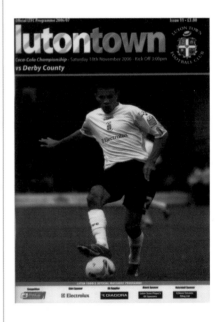

REPORT – 18 NOVEMBER 2006
LUTON TOWN 0
DERBY COUNTY 2

Rowan Vine had the game's first effort though his shot flew across goal, while at the other end Jon Stead flashed wide of the near post following Steve Howard's knock-down inside the box.

The ball was spending too much time in the air for both teams' liking,

LUTON: Beresford, Foley, Perrett, Edwards, Robinson (Bell 85), Vine (Morgan 71), Emanuel, Brkovic (Feeney 71), Boyd, Barnett, Heikkenen.
UNUSED SUBS: Holmes, Brill.

DERBY: Bywater, Edworthy, Leacock, Bisgaard (Smith 86), Howard, Stead, Boertien, S. Johnson (Jones 79), Oakley, Moore, Barnes.
UNUSED SUBS: Camara, Jackson, Lupoli.

ATTENDANCE: 9,708.

Steve Howard celebrates with Dean Leacock after scoring Derby's second goal.

The Rams celebrate Steve Howard's goal.

but on 16 minutes Derby came as close as anyone through Stead once more, as his 20-yard drive arrowed just over the bar.

Derby began to play some nice stuff, and on 25 minutes only a fine reaction save from Marlon Beresford stopped them going in front.

A good move involving Marc Edworthy and Morten Bisgaard led to Matt Oakley driving a low ball across that Perrett almost turned past his own goalkeeper.

Bisgaard then missed an absolute sitter on 31 minutes. Johnson released Oakley down the right and the skipper pulled the ball back to Bisgaard, who – on the edge of the six yard box – blazed wildly over.

Bywater produced an excellent 35th-minute save to turn over Barnett's header from the edge of the box after the centre-half ventured upfield for a set-piece.

The 'keeper showed his athleticism to turn over Adam Boyd's 20-yard chip as Luton enjoyed their best spell of possession.

It was Bywater's time, and a couple of minutes before the break he was down smartly to his right to push away Boyd's shot from the edge of the box.

Two minutes after the break Derby were the width of a post away from scoring as Stead turned on the edge of the box, only to see his low effort rebound off the upright.

Luton failed to clear their lines, and when the Rams forced a corner Bisgaard could only stab the ball straight at Beresford from close range.

Giles Barnes was the next to threaten, cutting in from the left before firing a low right-footer from just outside the box that went narrowly past the post with Beresford beaten.

From a free-kick Derby came close as Stead's shot from Oakley's low cross was deflected over. And when the ball came out to Stead wide on the left, with 71 minutes on the clock, Luton couldn't have predicted what was to come.

Stead had a lot to do but cut in from the touchline, past a couple of

Luton challenges, and when space opened up in front of him he cracked a bullet-like right-footed shot that beat Beresford at his near post to open the scoring.

Two minutes later, the lead was doubled from a training-ground free-kick. Oakley dummied and then picked up Johnson's clever pass to drive the ball low across goal, where Bisgaard got a touch to it.

The Dane's effort bounced back off a post and one man was there first to ram it home – Howard, against his former club.

Luton broke quickly through Edwards, who forced Bywater to push away his powerful drive from the edge of the box.

Feeney's glance towards goal was headed off the line by Oakley with Luton pushing for a goal to make the late stages of the game interesting, and they were close again as Boyd curled a shot just wide of the far post.

Giles Barnes.

REACTION

First-team coach Julian Darby admitted that the on-form Rams had overcome a potential banana skin in the shape of Luton Town. Derby went into the Kenilworth Stadium encounter on the back of three straight wins, while the hosts had lost their last five matches.

The Rams left Bedfordshire having extended their own run to four wins and the Hatters' form to six defeats thanks to second-half goals from Jon Stead and Steve Howard.

'It definitely was,' Darby replied when asked if the Luton game could have proved a stumbling block. 'A few weeks ago we played Birmingham and they came into it on the back of a few defeats but rather fortunately did us at home.

'This was another one, but the lads showed great concentration, and the back five came out with a clean sheet, which they haven't done for a while.

'The front two scored again, which is also nice. Consistency sums us up at the moment. In our last 12 League games we have won eight, drawn two and only lost two. It shows that, when you're sometimes not playing well, it's important you grind the results out.'

New signing David Jones reckons he has arrived at a club that is 'pushing for the Premiership'.

Jones arrived on Friday as an emergency loan from Manchester United and was immediately thrust into the squad for the game at Luton Town. And he admitted that there were a number of factors that influenced his decision to move down from Old Trafford and join the Rams.

'Derby are a massive club with a great history, plus I also know the staff here from when I was at Preston,' he said. 'I spoke to the board; they seem like they're pushing for the Premiership. It looks to me like Derby is a club moving forward with great prospects.

'I'm trying to push my career forward and if I'm not getting the chance at Old Trafford then I have to look elsewhere. I have been there for 12 years so leaving is sad, but you've got to look forward and I'm glad to be at Derby.'

Paul Boertien says he has a double aim now that he is back in a Derby County shirt.

Saturday's 2–0 victory at Luton Town was the Rams' fourth on the spin – and it was also the first time that Boertien had played two successive games since April 2004.

Matt Oakley, who set up the first goal at Kenilworth Road.

Oakley says the fans could have a crucial role to play as Derby go in search of a fifth successive victory.

'The fans can really help us on Saturday,' he said. 'If it isn't a pretty game and they stick with us, they keep going, then I am sure we will come good in that last half-hour and give them the result that they need.

'It is probably not going to be a pretty game, we know that, and if the fans can understand that for this game then it is certainly going to help us.

'The fans have to go to work alongside these Leicester people and will get some stick if we are beaten. But we have come off the back of four straight wins, and Leicester were beaten last week.

'Let's take them while we're performing well and give the fans something to cheer about and go to work with on Monday morning.'

The left-back has had a nightmare couple of years through injury but took his chance last week at Coventry when he was called in to replace the suspended Mo Camara.

And after keeping his place for the trip to the Kenilworth Stadium, Boertien wants to continue performing well in boss Billy Davies's line up – as well as helping the Rams to continue their fine recent form.

'I have played two and we have won two,' the 27-year-old revealed. 'All I can do is keep going, keep trying to play my best, and if we keep winning then hopefully I will stay in.

'The last couple of years have been a nightmare for me so I don't get too carried away when I'm playing and not too down when I'm not playing. Obviously I'm pleased to be back playing and the more games the better for me.

'The fact that we are winning games gives you confidence and everyone is playing well at the moment so that is good.'

Derby County go into Saturday's East Midlands clash at home to Leicester City on the back of four successive victories – two of which have come in front of their own fans.

In those Pride Park games, against Barnsley and West Bromwich Albion, Derby have trailed after a poor first half only to then go on and turn the game round with goals in the last 20 minutes.

'It is something we are very much conscious about, and we want to perform in the opening 45,' boss Billy Davies said. 'But winning the game of football over the 90 minutes is what it is all about, and that is what we have been doing.

'We haven't managed to put in a consistent 90 minutes at Pride Park yet, but our results have been very good. The spirit has been excellent, as has the discipline in the second half. I'll take another different performance again but certainly with the victory it would be very nice.'

The local derby occasion is something that team skipper Matt Oakley is looking forward to – and he is confident the Rams can give their biggest home crowd of the season something to cheer in Saturday's clash.

Almost 27,000 tickets have been sold for the Coca-Cola Championship game, and Pride Park will welcome its highest gate of the campaign when the Foxes make the short journey over.

REPORT – 25 NOVEMBER 2006
DERBY COUNTY 1
LEICESTER 0

Debut-boy David Jones was quickly into the action with a fine fifth-minute tackle inside his own half that sparked a move eventually ending with Giles Barnes shooting wide from the edge of the box.

The 22-year-old's early touches showed an air of calmness and quality in what was already shaping up to be a hard-fought, frantic affair.

Jon Stead came closest to opening the scoring in the 14th minute with a shot from Matt Oakley's low corner that flashed into the side-netting.

Leicester's first good opportunity came on 26 minutes after a poor Danny Tiatto free-kick that fell to the feet of Iain Hume inside the box, but

Dean Leacock was there with a fine tackle to block from close range. They won a free-kick some 25 yards out in the 38th minute, but a good shooting opportunity came to nothing as Paddy McCarthy blasted it straight at the wall.

Seth Johnson had the first effort of the second period, a rasping 20-yarder that was straight at Logan, as Leicester opened up penned inside their own half. And eventually the pressure told as Derby opened the scoring on 52 minutes.

Barnes did well to create space for himself down the right, and although his cross was headed out to just inside the box it fell to Stead who calmly picked his spot in the bottom-right corner for his third goal in three games.

Jones turned smartly inside the box, but his effort was deflected away for a left-wing corner, which almost produced a second goal as Howard's header was nodded off the line by Tiatto.

Leicester probed in wide areas with no joy, but Tiatto then warmed Bywater's hands with a powerful shot from outside the box.

McCarthy headed wide after Hughes played the ball in following a quick corner.

There was controversy with four to go later as Leicester broke away from the Derby back line after a long ball, Stearman knocked it past Bywater and Hammond stroked it into an empty net.

Bywater had caught Stearman, and it looked as though referee Andy D'Urso was waving play-on and would give the goal rather than a possible penalty, but he was alerted to a raised flag by one of his assistants – and a free-kick went Derby's way, after the alert assistant had spotted Stearman's handball in the build-up.

Derby should have sealed the game on 89 minutes when Lupoli showed great pace and trickery to break away from the centre-circle, but he put his shot wide of the post with only Logan to beat.

DERBY: Bywater, Edworthy, Leacock, M. Johnson, Boertien, Oakley (C) (Moore 84), S. Johnson (Bisgaard 70), Jones, Barnes, Howard, Stead (Lupoli 75). **UNUSED SUBS:** Jackson, Smith.

LEICESTER: Logan, Maybury (McAuley 79), Kisnorbo, McCarthy (C), Hughes, Hume, Tiatto, Fryatt (Hammond 56), Johansson, Stearman, Welsh (Porter 67). **UNUSED SUBS:** Henderson, McAuley, Wesolowski.

ATTENDANCE: 28,315.

Jon Stead strikes the winner after 52 minutes.

David Jones had a lively debut in a Rams shirt.

Leicester players appeal to the referee after their late goal is disallowed.

REACTION

It's feet back on the ground for Billy Davies and his team ahead of Ipswich Town's visit on Wednesday night – but the Rams boss is delighted with his fledgling side's progress.

Speaking after Saturday's 1–0 home win over Leicester City – his side's fifth consecutive victory – Davies said 'We are not the finished article yet and there's a lot of building still to be done, but when you take into account what this club has had to endure these past few years we're making real progress.

'I think the fans and the players are beginning to understand Billy Davies's work ethic. From my point of view I look at the top six teams in this Division, and bearing in mind the amount of time other clubs have had to gel together it's remarkable where we are sitting right now.

'It's huge credit to the players and staff at the club for getting us there. The fans hopefully recognise all the hard work that's being done – but nothing has been won yet and it's feet back on the ground for everyone tomorrow.'

Winning the game and keeping a clean sheet at the same time – Dean Leacock won't ask for much more from a football match.

Leacock put in a fine performance at the heart of the Rams defence in the hard-fought 1–0 win over Leicester City.

It was Derby's fifth successive victory and a second clean sheet on the bounce, two facts that give Leacock as much pleasure as each other.

'As a defence we thrive on keeping clean sheets,' the 22-year-old said. 'Hopefully then the strikers can do their job and score the goals. They are doing that at the moment so it was a very good result for us today.

'We knew it was going to be a battle, and we would have to be up for it, which we were. Keeping a clean sheet too makes it an even better result for us.'

Rams boss Billy Davies has been preparing for Wednesday's game against Ipswich Town by making sure his players keep their feet on the ground.

Derby go into the Coca-Cola Championship encounter fourth in the table and on the back of five successive wins. But Davies is not getting carried away with his side's recent form and is making sure they stay fully focused on the challenge of Ipswich.

'The lads have done tremendously well so far, but our feet are now firmly back on the ground again and we look forward to the match against Ipswich,' he said. 'Again that will be a very tough match because of the way that they play, and on the night they will be a very capable side.

'We have to be on our guard again, be ready for them and go in with the right approach. If we can do that then I am sure we can cause them plenty of problems.'

One man looking to make the most of a good run in the team is defender Paul Boertien. His 100 percent record this season has continued in recent weeks and he'll be hoping to help the Rams to a sixth successive victory.

So is he Derby's lucky charm this season?

'I don't know about that, I'm not sure I have much luck in me!' he said.

'We'll just see how everything goes. It's not going too bad at the moment so hopefully that will continue.'

Billy Davies celebrates the win with the home crowd.

REPORT – 29 NOVEMBER 2006
DERBY COUNTY 2
IPSWICH TOWN 1

It was a slow opening to the game, though Derby had the first opportunity on eight minutes. Paul Boertien's free-kick from out on the left was nodded on by Steve Howard, but Michael Johnson – on the stretch – could only turn the ball over the bar.

A 14th-minute free-kick at the other end, from Town's Matt Richards, met the head of Billy Clarke, though the teenager could only glance it well wide rather than threaten the goal.

Jon Stead curled the game's first shot on target into the arms of Lewis Price, though his 29th-minute effort from a narrow angle on the left never really threatened to open the scoring.

Derby broke with pace on 38 minutes and had the ball in the back of the net, though the decision went against them. Boertien's fine cross from the left had been met powerfully by the head of Howard, whose effort beat Price but was ruled out for a push.

And within seconds the Rams found themselves behind. Matt Richards's cross was only half-cleared to Gary Roberts, who rifled home a volley from 20 yards into Stephen Bywater's bottom-right corner.

David Jones curled a free-kick just over the bar as the Rams looked to

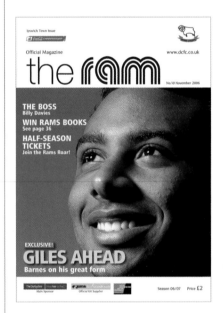

DERBY: Bywater, Edworthy, Leacock, M. Johnson (C), Boertien, Barnes, S. Johnson (Lupoli 59), Jones, Bisgaard, Howard, Stead (Moore 90).
UNUSED SUBS: Bolder, Grant, Jackson.

IPSWICH: Price, Bruce, Naylor, De Vos, Harding, Roberts (Sito 77), Garvan, Walton, Richards, Lee, Clarke (Williams 63).
UNUSED SUBS: Macken, Haynes, Supple.

ATTENDANCE: 22,606.

Steve Howard is foiled by the Ipswich 'keeper.

Steve Howard's goal celebration after scoring Derby's equaliser.

find a way back level before half-time, but all that went their way was the visitors' Simon Walton picking up a booking for kicking the ball away.

The Rams should have been level on 51 minutes, but Stead, so deadly in recent games, fired his shot wide of the near post from the edge of the six-yard box after fine work down the left by Barnes.

But just 60 seconds later they did level matters with as simple a goal as you are likely to see. Bisgaard lifted a corner beautifully over from the left where it was met superbly by the head of Howard, who this time wheeled away in celebration knowing his goal had been given.

The goal lifted the Pride Park crowd, and Derby were given another boost just six minutes later when Walton picked up his second yellow card of the night for a late challenge on Michael Johnson, reducing the visitors to 10 men.

Substitute Arturo Lupoli's first action was to stretch out a left leg superbly at the far post to divert Bisgaard's cross goalwards, only to be denied by a fine Price save.

Both Lupoli and Howard were inches away from getting a touch to Stead's fine low cross as the Rams began to open the play up and spread the ball around.

Derby were stepping up the pressure, and Lupoli almost created a second goal out of nothing with quick feet inside the box, but his shot flashed right the way across goal and just past the far post when only the slightest of touches would have turned it in.

Frustrations grew around Pride Park as time ticked down, but they were all released two minutes into stoppage time.

The Rams won a corner on the left, and Boertien swung it over to the head of Michael Johnson, who couldn't go for goal, but he could nod it into a dangerous area. And in that dangerous area lurked Lupoli, who headed powerfully past Price to earn Derby's sixth win on the spin in the most dramatic fashion.

REACTION

Despite six wins in a row and fourth place in the Championship, the Rams are far from the finished article.

That's the view of boss Billy Davies, who said after Wednesday night's 2–1 home victory over Ipswich Town 'One or two people have to remember we have a long way to go, and I for one am not fooled. The current group of players are giving their best and sometimes we want more, but we can't fault their attitude and effort.

'I think some people have forgotten the type of squad we have taken over and the state it was in this summer. It can take years to get it right. I want to talk about the long-term plan we have in place – there is no short-term fix.

'We want to become a fluent passing side, but when you look at where we've come from and the building that is taking place then some people in the crowd need to understand this is a long-term plan.'

Arturo Lupoli has revealed that he celebrated his stoppage time winner against Ipswich Town as a nod to his girlfriend.

The on-loan Italian struck late in the day to take Derby's winning run to six matches after they came from behind and eventually beat off a dogged resistance from the visitors.

And he ran off with his hand to his ear in the shape of a telephone – suggesting he was ringing her to say: 'I've scored!'

Lupoli said 'It was something I had planned with my girlfriend

Lupoli heads in Derby's late winner.

Letizia. I said to her that when I score, after not scoring for a while, I will celebrate by doing the phone movements. It was so that I could pretend to speak to her, tell her that finally I had scored, because she was joking with me about not scoring for a few games. She saw me do that so it was great to make the joke between us, and finally I got the opportunity to do it.'

Lupoli's goal celebration.

TABLE

	P	W	D	L	F	A	Pts
Preston	20	10	8	2	31	17	38
Cardiff	20	11	4	5	31	20	37
Birmingham	20	11	4	5	29	21	37
Derby	**20**	**11**	**4**	**5**	**31**	**24**	**37**
Burnley	20	10	4	6	29	21	34
Stoke	20	9	6	5	29	15	33
Southampton	20	9	6	5	30	22	33
Colchester	20	9	3	8	33	25	30
Plymouth	20	7	9	4	27	22	30
West Brom	20	8	5	7	32	23	29
Coventry	20	9	2	9	20	18	29
Norwich	20	8	5	7	28	32	29
Wolves	20	8	5	7	18	23	29
Sunderland	20	8	3	9	27	27	27
Sheffield W	20	7	6	7	24	26	27
Ipswich	20	7	3	10	30	30	24
QPR	20	6	6	8	31	33	24
C Palace	20	6	5	9	22	26	23
Leicester	20	5	7	8	19	24	22
Luton	20	6	4	10	26	36	22
Barnsley	20	6	3	11	25	36	21
Leeds	20	6	1	13	22	39	19
Hull	20	4	5	11	16	29	17
Southend	20	2	6	12	16	37	12

December

So that Giles Barnes effort did prove a spark after all – and what a response by the Rams with six wins from six in November.

The table is starting to take shape, though not necessarily the shape expected with some of the fancied sides struggling and the not-so-fancied sides in the upper reaches.

Leeds United, beaten Play-off finalists in 2005–06, find themselves in the bottom three, while West Bromwich Albion are hovering in mid-table.

Derby travel to both in the first two weeks of December.

Rams Academy midfielder Matt Richards will celebrate his 17th birthday by signing a two-and-a-half year professional contract with the club.

The first year scholar and England Under-17 international has penned a deal that keeps him with the club until the summer of 2009.

The Derby-born player said 'To sign professional forms is a dream come true. And to do it at my home-town club, on my birthday, makes it extra special.'

Rams manager Billy Davies insists his side's recent home win over West Bromwich Albion will have no bearing on the outcome of Saturday afternoon's game.

Derby travel to The Hawthorns on the back of six straight successes in the Coca-Cola Championship and one of those came against the Baggies less than a month ago.

But Davies says that that game is consigned to the history books and expects another stern challenge from Tony Mowbray's 10th-placed team.

'I don't think that game matters as we know how good a squad they have got and how good a team they are,' the boss said.

'I've said before that I do think they have got the best squad in the Division, and I do feel they are one of the more fancied teams because of the quality they have. But it is up to us to go down there and continue our good run of form, and hopefully cause one or two problems. We are on a good run so we have got to continue the hard work and belief.

'Our intention is to go there and ask questions of West Brom, who have got to come out of the traps and put pressure on us. That may help our game slightly so we are looking forward to the challenge.'

Meanwhile, Marc Edworthy has warned that the Rams should be ready for a backlash from a West Bromwich Albion side beaten in its last two games.

The Baggies go into Saturday's encounter having lost on the road to Sheffield Wednesday and Coventry City, so they are determined to put things right in front of their own fans.

And full-back Edworthy knows exactly how much danger they pose – particularly as they were beaten 2–1 at Pride Park just a few weeks ago.

Marc Edworthy.

'They are very organised and a quality side on their day as they have got some quality players, having just come down from the Premiership,' the 33-year-old said. 'They will want to do something for their fans as they have had a few defeats of late.

'It is a tough place to go, like everywhere is in this Division, and a big crowd is expected so we have got to be ready for that.

'We walked the tightrope a bit in the first half when we played them at our place, and they had a few chances. But I am sure Saturday will be another good game.'

WBA: Hoult, Robinson, Davies (C), Quashie, Greening, Gera, Albrechtsen, Kamara (Hartson 63), Koumas (Clement 90), McShane, Phillips.
UNUSED SUBS: Ellington, Steele, Hodgkiss.

DERBY: Bywater, Edworthy, Boertien, Leacock, M. Johnson (C) (Moore 16), Bolder, Barnes, Jones, Howard, Stead (Bisgaard 64), Lupoli (Peschisolido 81).

UNUSED SUBS: Grant, S. Johnson.

REPORT – 2 DECEMBER 2006
WEST BROMWICH ALBION 1
DERBY COUNTY 0

Koumas's cross from the left on four minutes was handled in the air by Bywater, who couldn't keep hold of the ball. It fell for Boertien to half clear, only for Kamara to squander a chance by heading wide from close range.

On eight minutes a Jones free-kick into the box from the left was headed wide by Leacock.

Kamara's first-time volley flew over Bywater's crossbar from Koumas's cross from the left on 13 minutes.

Within seconds a last-ditch Johnson tackle thwarted Kamara as he teed up to shoot from inside the area. The challenge left Jonno on the deck needing medical attention, and on 15 minutes he was replaced by Darren Moore, who received a standing ovation from the fans of his former club.

Robinson's header from Albrechtsen's cross trickled inches wide of Bywater's left-hand post on 18 minutes.

Koumas's deep free-kick was headed back across goal by Phillips and McShane's goalward header was cleared by Howard on 24 minutes.

Howard's strong run through the middle two minutes later deserved more than his weak shot on the turn that was easy for Hoult to gather.

A superb save from Bywater one-on-one with Phillips kept the Rams in the game on 30 minutes.

Robinson's through ball found Phillips with just the Rams 'keeper to beat – Bywater's brave dive to Phillips's feet clearing the ball to safety.

Howard met Barnes's low cross from the right in the centre of the area but fired tamely over Hoult's crossbar on 41 minutes.

A scrappy opening first 15 minutes of the second half saw little

Lupoli's running helped to release the constant Albion pressure.

opportunity for either side until, on 59 minutes, the Rams were momentarily down to 10 men while Boertien received treatment to a head injury.

As the bandage-clad full-back returned to the pitch, he could only watch as Kamara exposed the space left to fire high at Bywater's net – the 'keeper reacted quickly to tip on to the crossbar for a corner.

West Brom breached the Rams back line again on 75 with Gera's clever pass releasing Albrechtsen whose drilled pass across the goal was a certain goal for Phillips – but the ball squirmed harmlessly away as the striker found himself in a tangle.

As the game started to open up the Rams had the right man to help relieve the pressure. Lupoli jinked his way from the halfway line into the area only to see his angled shot parried to safety on 77 minutes.

As the game moved into the final five minutes all the pressure was being put on the Derby goal, and as Phillips wriggled clear in a packed box Moore was there to make a last-ditch block to concede a corner that Bywater gathered comfortably.

With two minutes to go Derby could withstand no more pressure as Hartson piled his way through a ragged back line to fire past Bywater with the aid of a Boertien deflection.

REACTION

Derby's run of victories was ended in the cruellest of fashions – with a deflected goal in the dying seconds – but boss Billy Davies was philosophical in defeat.

'There are always going to be peaks and troughs, and we were never going to win every game until the end of the season,' he said after the 1–0 defeat at The Hawthorns that ended a string of seven undefeated games – six of them wins.

'I was aware the law of averages may have been against us today, with us on a good run and West Brom going through a bad spell.

'Their squad is the strongest in this Division and they were always going to recover sooner or later. But it took a late deflected goal for them to get past us – a bit of luck, if you like.

'We can't really complain as we've had our own luck in recent weeks and it all evens itself out over a season.'

Darren Moore admitted to a day of mixed emotions after skippering the Rams against his former club at The Hawthorns. The big defender put in an outstanding performance after joining the action from the subs bench following injury to Michael Johnson.

However, he was powerless to prevent the 89th-minute winner that took a cruel deflection off Paul Boertien and brought a halt to a run of six straight wins.

'I had a great rapport with the fans during my time with West Brom, and it was really touching to get a warm reception from them,' said Moore. 'As chuffed as I was with the welcome, I was gutted we couldn't at least hold out for a draw against them to keep our unbeaten run going.

'You know what you're going to get when you play West Brom, and we needed every player fully committed, which was the case.

'This was a great learning curve for us, especially the younger players. We were turning out against a great squad, packed full of Premiership experience, and we were a couple of minutes away from picking up a point.

'We're all disappointed for the fans who, again, were brilliant.'

Morten Bisgaard.

Dejected Derby players leave the field after losing to a deflected Hartson shot.

Billy Davies with the Coca-Cola Championship Manager of the Month award for November, after Derby won six from six.

Rams boss Billy Davies gave his reaction to his side's home tie against League Two outfit Wrexham in the FA Cup third round.

Derby have been paired with the Welsh club for the first time in a Cup competition and will be looking to avoid an upset at Pride Park.

And minutes after the draw was made, Davies said 'I've always said that I think in Cup football a home draw is important, and we have got that this time.

'Obviously we are disappointed not to have got one of the big guns as we would have liked the challenge of a game like that, but it was not to be.

'What we have to do now is focus on beating Wrexham, and that is what we will be telling the players.

'For them it will be a wonderful occasion to come and play at Pride Park, but for us it is all about putting ourselves into the draw for the fourth round.

'We know it is all about what happens on the day, anything in possible in the Cup as it is a great leveller.

'We have got to be really up for the fight on the day, and that is exactly what we will be working on with the players.'

Derby boss Billy Davies is the Coca-Cola Championship Manager of the Month for November.

Davies was announced as the top man by Chris Kamara on Sky Sports News – making him the first Rams boss to win the award since Jim Smith exactly a decade ago.

His side won all six of their matches during November to lift themselves up to fourth in the Championship.

Davies said 'It is obviously a great achievement and honour, but as far as I'm concerned I am picking it up on behalf of the players and staff at Derby County. It is a great thing to get, especially with the run we have been on.

'To get it in such a short space of time when we are trying to rebuild and do what we're doing is excellent.

'We are delighted to have it, we are delighted to have gone on the run we have done, but we also know that there is a long way to go and a lot of hard work to be done.

'I won three at Motherwell and two at Preston so I am very proud and delighted to pick up one at Derby County, especially so early on.

'I am very proud of the players and the staff for all of the hard work they have put in – it is down to them as far as I am concerned.'

And the newly-crowned top boss told his Rams players to forget about their League position and 'get back on the bike again' following last week's first defeat in eight matches.

Now they travel to Leeds United on Saturday, and Davies says the priority is to return from Elland Road having got back to winning ways.

'It is a very difficult away match for us,' Davies said. 'What we have got to do is get back on the bike as quick as we can and get back to winning ways.

'It will be tough, we know it will be a physical encounter and we will have to work very hard to get something from the game. But we are very capable of doing that.

'I have said to the players to forget about the League position and situation because I think between now and the end of January there will be lots of strange results and movement up and down the Division.

'We have got to look to the next match, continue to grind away and if we can do that I'm sure we are capable of picking up the points.'

Davies will welcome Michael Johnson and Matt Oakley back into his squad. Johnson limped off during the defeat at West Brom with a hamstring problem but is fit to face Leeds, as is Oakley, who has missed the last two games with a calf strain.

REPORT – 9 DECEMBER 2006
LEEDS UNITED 0
DERBY COUNTY 1

Foxe's right-hand cross to the near post was knocked wide of Bywater by Healy under pressure from Moore on six minutes. But within seconds Giles Barnes had begun and ended a move that resulted in the goal.

His ball across the face of the area from the right was met by Stead – his ball back into the box saw Howard and Barnes both rise, the young midfielder's clean header beating Stack at the far post to take his goal tally for the campaign to five.

On 13 minutes, Blake's solo run deserved more than his weak shot from just inside the area that trickled into Bywater's arms.

Foxe's low shot from outside the box on 17 was easy for Bywater, and from the break Oakley had a gilt-edged chance to make it two for Derby – another dangerous ball into the box from the left by Stead was met by the captain rampaging into the box – but he fired over.

Seth Johnson faced the wrath of the home fans after a pretty crude but legal challenge on Douglas, on the edge of the Rams' box, eight minutes after the restart, and within a minute the half had sparked into life and Lewis fired low and wide of Bywater on 55.

Moore's challenge from behind on Healy on the hour mark saw a Leeds free-kick from 25 yards out rattle the side netting.

The best move of the afternoon by Leeds saw Healy squander a great

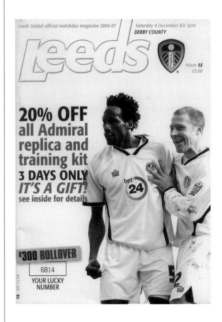

LEEDS: Stack, Crainey, Douglas, Ehiogu, Healy (Moore 67), Lewis (Carole 90), Heath, Foxe, Derry (C), Kandol, Blake.
UNUSED SUBS: Warner, Richardson, Howson.

DERBY: Bywater, Edworthy, Leacock, Jones, Howard, Stead (Lupoli 90), Boertien, S. Johnson (Bisgaard 68), Oakley (C), Moore, Barnes (M. Johnson 85).
UNUSED SUBS: Grant, Peschisolido.

ATTENDANCE: 20,087.

Barnes began and ended a move that resulted in his fifth goal of the season.

Barnes celebrates his goal with teammate Dean Leacock.

Barnes limps from the field late on in the game.

chance from inside the box with just Bywater to beat on 67 – his shot flew over the bar.

Bisgaard fired over the upright on 80 minutes, but the match had lost much of its early excitement – both sides appearing to have settled on the scoreline. Leacock then headed just over at a tight angle from a Jones free-kick on 83.

Jones almost settled the match with a shot that rattled the inside of Stack's crossbar, but landed the wrong side of the goal line.

Darren Moore was booked a minute later for delaying a Leeds free-kick by keeping hold of the ball.

The set-piece was headed goalwards, forcing a diving save from Bywater.

The cheers of delight from the Rams crowd almost drowned out the jeers of dissent from the Leeds stands on the final whistle as Derby celebrated this historic, long-awaited victory.

REACTION

Billy Davies is keeping his feet on the ground despite leading his side to the dizzy heights of second in the Championship. He's calling on fans to celebrate Derby's first victory at Elland Road since the Championship-winning 1974–75 season but insists it will be business as usual at Moor Farm next week as his squad prepares for a home match with Crystal Palace.

'I was delighted with our first-half performance,' he reflected, 'although we should have scored more than once and finished off the job. We passed and moved very well and defended brilliantly to limit Leeds.

'I was a little concerned at half-time because we should have been out of sight, but we showed spirit and determination to keep the lead.

'We were a little twitchy in the second half but remained disciplined, and Bywater made a first-class save at the death to ensure the points – it would have been rough justice for us not to have won.

'It was a wonderful three points at a difficult ground, one where we've had little success in recent times.'

Midfielder Seth Johnson was thrilled to be on the winning side against his former club. He faced the wrath of an element of the Elland Road crowd but was buoyed by the cheers and chants of the travelling Rams supporters.

'I played my first game against Leeds last season, and we lost, so it was great to pick up three points today and get ourselves back on track after last weekend's disappointment,' said Johnson.

'We played some great stuff in the first half, and they were struggling to get near us. Matt Oakley had a chance and to have gone in 2–0 up would have sealed it for us. But you will always end up defending for large periods, and we did that exceptionally well today.

'It would be terrific to remain in the automatic promotion places heading into Christmas, but we're not getting carried away. There's a hectic Christmas fixture list to consider and we're going to take it one game at a time.

'As the manager says, it's where you are in May that counts.'

Ever-present striker Steve Howard will sit out his first game of the season next weekend after landing his fifth booking of the campaign at Elland Road. But Billy Davies insists his absence will open the door for another player to make his mark.

'It's obviously a blow to lose Stevie, but the break will do him good and it will give another lad the chance to make a point,' said the gaffer. 'He's been terrific for us, and he'll return refreshed and ready to pick up where he left off.

'Now there's a chance for someone else to come in and do a job for us because we need as many players as possible weighing in with good performances and goals as we head into the busy Christmas period.'

As well as the absence of Howard, Derby will have to cope with the pressure of being the Division's form side when they host Crystal Palace on Saturday.

The fantastic recent run has taken them to second in the table and with that comes extra expectation. And midfielder David Jones admits it is a good situation to be in.

'It is nice to look at the table but with that comes the added pressure to win every week, demands from supporters and the media that you should be putting on good performances,' the 22-year-old said. 'But that's what you want, you'd prefer to be there than at the bottom of the League.

'It is really positive around the club at the moment. Coming in to training is a pleasure, everyone is looking at the table and thinking we've got a good chance.'

REPORT – 16 DECEMBER 2006
DERBY COUNTY 1
CRYSTAL PALACE 0

The Rams had a scare in the first minute when Stephen Bywater dropped Mark Hudson's header when under no pressure, but fortunately for them the ball rolled to safety.

Skipper Matt Oakley had the game's first shot on target, a 19th-minute volley from just outside the box that Speroni had no difficulty in claiming. David Jones then flashed one just over the bar after another slick midfield move. But the on-loan midfielder was on target from close range three minutes later to give Derby a deserved lead.

Lupoli showed great trickery on the left to jink his way past Matt Lawrence and pull back a fine low cross that Jones gleefully cracked home from six yards. Stead forced Speroni into a low save with his 20-yard effort, but it never really looked likely to beat the visiting custodian.

Shefki Kuqi headed over the bar from Kennedy's long cross at the other end with a chance he may well have done better from.

DERBY: Bywater, Edworthy, Leacock, Moore, Boertien, Oakley (C) (Malcolm 57), S. Johnson (M. Johnson 84), Jones, Barnes, Stead, Lupoli (Smith 70).
UNUSED SUBS: Peschisolido, Jackson.

PALACE: Speroni, Lawrence, Granville, Ward, Hudson, McAnuff (Scowcroft 74), Morrison, Watson (Fletcher HT), Kennedy (C), Soares, Kuqi (Green 74).
UNUSED SUBS: Flinders, Borrowdale.

ATTENDANCE: 23,875.

David Jones scores his first goal for Derby.

David Jones celebrates his first goal for the Rams with captain Matt Oakley.

The visitors opened the second half brightly, but Derby relieved some of the pressure when they broke quickly down the left and good work by Jones and Paul Boertien eventually led to Lupoli shooting over from the edge of the box.

Palace were certainly having the better of things and were controlling possession with Derby struggling to get out of their own half, though the visitors were not offering anything by way of an end product.

It needed someone to wrestle back control of midfield for the Rams and substitute Bob Malcolm immediately set about the task with three powerful tackles in quick succession to try and disrupt the Eagles.

But the visitors were far quicker to every ball, and when Derby did get the chance to attack Billy Davies's frustrations were clear as he could be heard shouting 'too slow' several times.

However Palace were still behind and struggling to threaten Stephen Bywater's goal, so a 74th-minute double substitution was their last throw of the dice.

Bywater did well to grab Kennedy's deflected effort before Derby finally broke the shackles and had a brief foray forwards, but they failed to make the most of it as Smith got to the by-line but tamely pulled the ball back into the arms of Speroni.

Derby won a corner on 84 minutes and Smith's delivery was only half-cleared out to Malcolm just outside the box, who had time to measure his shot – but unfortunately it dipped over the crossbar.

There was a nervous gasp around the Pride Park crowd as the board went up to signal four minutes of stoppage time.

Derby survived a scare when head tennis inside the box saw Green nod over from close range, though if there's one thing that can be said about this side it's that they know how to hold on to a lead once they have it.

REACTION

Despite another home win – the Rams' fifth in a row – Billy Davies remained frustrated at the final whistle by his side's inconsistency.

'We know we have character and that's vital – but I was disappointed by the second-half display,' the Derby boss said after Saturday's 1–0 Pride Park victory over Palace.

'For a long time at home we haven't performed as well in the second half as the first, but we had the courage and character to keep a clean sheet.

'Palace have a lot of good players yet we dominated the first half – we just couldn't get a second goal.

'We are organised and disciplined and those qualities can carry you a long way, but we have to improve the quality and create more competition for places.

'We looked leggy after the break, but David Jones scored the goal and had a great game. He has real quality and the fans are beginning to see he is something special.

'A lot of credit has to go to Palace after the break because they upped the tempo while we took our foot off the pedal, but it's a great three points.'

David Jones hopes his winning goal against Crystal Palace will be the first of many in Derby County colours. The 22-year-old struck from close range during the first half of Saturday's Coca-Cola Championship encounter to earn the Rams their eighth win in nine games. And Jones was delighted with the strike – but equally pleased that Derby picked up three points to further consolidate second spot.

'It was good to get off the mark today, but it was more important to get the three points,' Jones said. 'I've had a few starts now, and it was nice to get the goal, but I'm not looking to settle at that.

'I want to get a few goals and help the team to push on if possible. I know I am capable of scoring goals, and I feel I was a bit more of a goal threat today. That is what I'm looking to do each game – get more opportunities and more goals.'

Giles Barnes is injured in a challenge.

The Rams will welcome leading scorer Steve Howard back into their squad for Saturday's Coca-Cola Championship clash at Burnley.

Howard missed last week's win over Crystal Palace through a one-match suspension and took the opportunity to take in a couple of days away.

He is now back, refreshed and raring to go, having played in every minute of the season so far before his ban.

Derby boss Billy Davies is delighted to welcome the nine-goal hit-man back into the fold, and he is also expecting Matt Oakley to be fit after the skipper limped off against Palace with an ankle injury.

'Matt has had a couple of good days of training and running so he should be OK,' the gaffer said. 'Marc Edworthy is suspended but it is nice to welcome back a refreshed Steve Howard from a couple of days' break in the sunshine. He has looked very good in training so it is nice to have him back.

'Everyone is fit and well and all ready for the very tough fixtures ahead.'

BURNLEY: Coyne (Jensen 17), Foster, Thomas, Duff, Harley, Elliott, J. O'Connor, McCann, Jones, Noel-Williams, Lafferty.
UNUSED SUBS: Mahon, G. O'Connor, Branch, Spicer.

DERBY: Bywater, Jackson, Leacock, Moore, Boertien, Jones, S. Johnson, Oakley (Bisgaard 72), Barnes (M. Johnson 89), Howard, Stead (Lupoli 86).
UNUSED SUBS: Malcolm, Camara.

ATTENDANCE: 12,825.

Jon Stead battles for the ball with Jon Harley.

REPORT – 23 DECEMBER 2006
BURNLEY 0
DERBY COUNTY 0

Derby showed their attacking intent inside the first minute of the game, the returning Steve Howard firing over from 20 yards following a neat move down the right.

The hosts were trying to make an impression and Seth Johnson was forced into belting a clearance downfield eight yards out from his own goal, and then Darren Moore had to force the ball out for a corner under pressure.

Wade Elliott caused chaos from the resulting set-piece and there was an almighty scramble in the Derby penalty area before the Rams finally cleared.

Play then moved to the other end of the field, and skipper Matt Oakley found himself in space and bearing down on goal. He opted to shoot from 20 yards and his low left-footer squirted across the surface and into the arms of Coyne, who had to dive full-stretch to his left to save.

The Rams' best opportunity of the early spell came on the quarter-hour mark, and they were only denied by more brilliant Coyne goalkeeping.

Howard and Jon Stead linked up well, with the latter playing a ball from the left across the six-yard box for Oakley, who, after making an angled run to evade his marker, turned and placed a low shot on target at the near post. Sadly, though, Coyne matched the great move with an equally good save, stopping the ball instinctively with his feet.

Burnley really should have been in front a minute later. Elliott out-paced Paul Boertien on the right and delivered a perfect cross for the unmarked Gifton Noel-Williams, who headed feebly at Stephen Bywater from six yards.

Having had an exciting opening, the game then hit a bit of a lull as both sides tried hard to unlock the opposition's defence.

After the break the Rams again started at a lively pace, but it was the home side who caused the first scare on 50 minutes when James O'Connor hammered in a shot from range that Bywater did well to hold.

With 58 minutes played, Elliott went surging down the right and squared the ball to the onrushing McCann, who should have done better with his effort at the near post but instead shot wide.

On 80 minutes sub Bisgaard showed great skill down the right to chest down a sweeping Johnson ball and delivered a pass to the waiting Jones on the edge of the area, but unfortunately his shot flew wide.

Arturo Lupoli then came on for Derby and within seconds of entering the fray he very nearly grabbed the winner. Howard nodded the ball into the path of the Italian, but the striker couldn't quite reach with his outstretched right leg.

REACTION

Billy Davies wished Rams fans a very happy Christmas after seeing his side pick up a point at Turf Moor.

Having watched his team earn a hard-fought 0–0 draw against Burnley, the gaffer once again praised the Derby fans for their support.

And he called on the Rams faithful to enjoy Christmas Day, before he and his team see over 30,000 at Pride Park Stadium for the Boxing Day clash with Wolves.

Davies said 'I'd like to wish everyone connected with Derby County a very happy Christmas, and I hope you all enjoy yourselves on Christmas Day.

'Your support, particularly on our travels, has been fantastic, and I look forward to seeing the bumper crowd at Pride Park on Boxing Day.

'It's a real sign of how far we have come that we can command crowds of that sort of size at Pride Park, and the atmosphere should be tremendous.

'We've got two very big home games coming up now – against Wolves and Plymouth – and I would urge the fans to get right behind us on both occasions because I know how much the team appreciate the support.'

REPORT – 26 DECEMBER 2006
DERBY COUNTY 0
WOLVERHAMPTON WANDERERS 2

The early football was coming from Wolves, and they created a good opening on the right for Michael Kightly, who cut in to fire straight at Stephen Bywater from the edge of the box.

Derby began to find their feet and with 19 minutes on the clock they came close through Jon Stead, who curled his shot just wide from 25 yards with Matt Murray beaten.

They were given a second chance from the same incident as Stead was tugged back while shooting, and from the resulting free-kick David Jones saw his effort deflected on to the crossbar and out for a corner.

Bywater dived bravely at the feet of Kightly, but Derby broke once more in the 27th minute and were again inches away from opening the scoring, but Steve Howard's pile driver flashed just wide from the edge of the box.

Neither goalkeeper had been tested by a serious shot, though both were showing their ability to read the game and dive at the feet of opposition attackers on a regular basis.

A McIndoe corner for Wolves almost produced the opening goal three minutes before the interval, but after a scramble inside the Derby six-yard box the ball rolled inches wide.

Wolves opened up the second half with a strong penalty claim as they argued that Edworthy had handled a long ball, but referee Trevor Kettle and his assistant – who had a perfect view of the incident – were un-moved.

Derby were denied by the woodwork again seconds later as a good move down the left released Matt Oakley, whose low cross was slid against the post by Howard. Somehow the ball rebounded along the line and out, with Murray once again a spectator.

The Rams really should have opened the scoring on 62 minutes with the best chance of the game. Giles Barnes and Oakley combined to find Howard in the inside-right channel, and he in turn crossed well to find Stead some eight yards out.

The striker turned but somehow planted his shot wide of Murray's post when it looked so much easier to score.

DERBY: Bywater, Edworthy, Leacock, Moore, Boertien (M. Johnson 28), Oakley (C) (Peschisolido 84), S. Johnson (Lupoli 72), Jones, Barnes, Howard, Stead.
UNUSED SUBS: Bisgaard, Malcolm.

WOLVES: Murray, Collins, Olofinjana, Breen, McNamara, Henry (C), Potter, Clarke (Davies 76), Little, McIndoe, Kightly.
UNUSED SUBS: Hennessy, Clapham, Edwards, Ricketts.

ATTENDANCE: 31,920.

Giles Barnes and Darren Moore both go up for a header.

Steve Howard.

And the Rams were made to pay for their profligacy four minutes later.

McIndoe's square free-kick was chipped into the box from the right by Mark Little to the far post, where Seyi Olofinjana rose highest to power his header down and past Bywater.

Pride Park's highest attendance of the season was subdued, though it was then sparked into life once more as Stead raced on to a long ball, only to be denied by a fine Murray save.

Lupoli slipped his marker just inside the Wolves half and strode forward before feeding Howard, who could only weakly shoot into the arms of Murray when he had the time and space to have done much better.

Wolves sealed the game in stoppage time when a long ball sent Kightly clear down the right, and he out-paced Michael Johnson before showing plenty of composure to lob Bywater from just inside the box.

REACTION

Billy Davies called the Boxing Day home defeat at the hands of Wolves 'a reality check' for his side.

'It's a blip,' Davies said after Derby's first reversal at Pride Park in two months, adding 'It's the kick we need right now because maybe some people think we are bigger and better than we are. We now have to get our feet back on the ground and work harder.

'It was a disappointing opening 45 minutes because we didn't get started and never played the ball quickly enough.

'The second half we were better, hitting bar and post, and their 'keeper pulled off a couple of great saves.

'The ball into the box for their first was hugely disappointing, but when you look at the chances we had in the second half we were a little unlucky. We just needed one to go in for us.'

Defender Paul Boertien is facing further tests to determine how long he will be out of action after it was confirmed that he has suffered medial knee ligament damage.

Boertien was forced off 28 minutes into the Boxing Day defeat by Wolverhampton Wanderers after developing a problem in his right knee. Scans on Wednesday confirmed medial damage – but Rams boss Billy Davies says it is too early to say how long the 27-year-old would be out for.

'He will be going for further scans and x-rays to find out the full extent of the damage,' Davies said. 'It is a blow for the lad and we are keeping our fingers crossed that the timescale is not too lengthy.'

Boertien was establishing himself in the Derby side again and his appearance against Wolves was his ninth consecutive start, on the back of only three games in the previous 30 months.

He originally damaged cruciate ligaments in his left knee in April 2004 before coming back the following January, only to suffer cartilage damage to his right knee.

That kept him out until the end of the year, when he looked to be working his way back to fitness, only for a calf injury to rule him out for the remainder of 2005–06.

Boertien's appearance in the 2–1 win at Hull City on 12 August this season was his first League outing since the problems first began – his only other games came in the FA Cup.

Billy Davies's major selection headache for Saturday's game against

Plymouth Argyle surrounds the left-back slot – but he is considering 'freshening up' his side.

Paul Boertien had established himself on the left of the back four but is facing a spell on the sidelines after picking up a medial ligament injury in the defeat to Wolverhampton Wanderers on Boxing Day.

Davies says Mo Camara and Richard Jackson are the two main candidates to replace him, but the gaffer also admitted that changes are in the pipeline as Derby prepare for two games in three days.

'They are the two we have got, and Boets being out gives the opportunity for someone else to come in,' he said. 'I have said before that when a team goes on a run of two defeats in 12 games it is difficult for good players to be patient.

'But there is a door opening and it is up to someone to come in and do the best they can to keep the place for the rest of the season.'

The visit of Plymouth will be Derby's third game in a week, and it comes just 48 hours before they travel to Deepdale to face Preston North End on New Year's Day.

It is a busy time in the life of a footballer, and Davies acknowledges that some of his players could do with a break.

'Freshening things up on Saturday was always in my head as I think it is very important to do that over a tough period like this,' he said. 'You've got to look at the squad of players you have got and the type of personnel available.

'We certainly do have one or two in our team who could do with a rest so that is definitely in my thoughts. I'm sure that we will see one or two fresh faces for Saturday.'

Giles Barnes tries to get away from his marker.

REPORT – 30 DECEMBER 2006
DERBY COUNTY 1
PLYMOUTH ARGYLE 0

It was Plymouth who had the first chance seven minutes in after Darren Moore misplaced a headed clearance. The ball fell to David Norris, just outside the box, who took time to tee up his shot but placed the ball wide of Stephen Bywater's post.

Steve Howard's low cross almost forced Marcel Seip to put the ball into his own goal, but Romain Larrieu got back to grab it on the line.

Substitute Cherno Samba almost opened the scoring three minutes later after Derby failed to clear their lines from a throw-in. The ball bypassed several attempted boots away before Samba nodded it goalwards, only to be denied by a fine Bywater tip-over.

The game needed something to spark it into life, and it almost arrived when David Jones picked up the ball in the 37th minute. He drove forward only to see his shot deflected wide, and from his own corner Malcolm rose six yards out but headed well past the post.

Derby started the second period brightly and secured their first real shot on target after some good link-up play between Bisgaard and Oakley ended with the Dane being denied by Larrieu's block.

From the corner, Plymouth failed to clear the danger and the ball fell to Moore inside the area, who turned smartly and smashed a ferocious drive that was scrambled off the line.

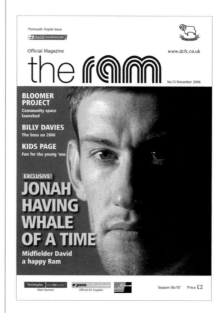

DERBY: Bywater, Edworthy, Leacock, Moore, Camara, Oakley (C), Malcolm (Lupoli 61), Jones (Barnes HT), Bisgaard, Howard, Stead (M. Johnson 89).
UNUSED SUBS: Peschisolido, S. Johnson.

PLYMOUTH: Larrieu, Nalis, Aljofree, Norris, Buszaky (Summerfield 89), Ebanks-Blake (Samba 12), Hayles (C), Doumbe, Capaldi, Seip, Connolly (Dickson 89).
UNUSED SUBS: McCormick, Sawyer.

ATTENDANCE: 25,775.

Bisgaard celebrates his 80th-minute winner.

Plymouth came back strongly and kept the pressure on after a right-wing corner, but Lilian Nalis could only shoot straight at Bywater from 20 yards.

Rain poured down from the skies to really slicken up the Pride Park turf, but the ball wasn't spending enough time on it.

When Derby did get the chance to play the ball around they almost created an opening as Camara, Oakley and Edworthy combined to find Bisgaard, whose cross was headed away from in front of goal.

But with 10 minutes to go Derby were in front.

Stead did break clear down the left and slipped a clever inside pass through to Lupoli, who got to the by-line before pulling the ball back for Bisgaard to drive it home from six yards.

A flurry of late cautions and substitutions interrupted the game's flow – much to Derby's delight as they saw out the win.

REACTION

Patience was the virtue Billy Davies demanded of his players on Saturday – and the strategy was rewarded with all three points at Pride Park against a dogged Plymouth side.

Morten Bisgaard's 80th-minute goal sealed a 1–0 win over the Pilgrims, and Davies said 'They slowed the game down and were compact so it was difficult, but I told the players beforehand it might take a 70th or 80th minute goal and that's the way it turned out.

'It's difficult at this stage of the season to create chances against teams like Plymouth, but we were disciplined and recorded another clean sheet.

'The players handled it well in the circumstances because you are always worried about a breakaway goal, but we got what we deserved in the end.'

Morten Bisgaard admitted to a 'fantastic feeling' after bringing 2006 to a close with the winning goal against Plymouth Argyle.

The Dane struck 10 minutes from time to earn Derby a 1–0 success that keeps them third in the Coca-Cola Championship, level on points with second-placed Preston North End – who they face on Monday.

Bisgaard was back in the team for his first start since November's win against Ipswich Town and responded by neatly tucking home his second goal of the campaign.

'It was a fantastic feeling as it seemed like we couldn't break them down,' he said. 'But Lupo [Arturo Lupoli] made a great pass in, and I was lucky that it came to my deadly left foot!

'I had missed some chances in previous games so that gives me great confidence.

'It was so important for me to get the goal and because it was the winning goal it makes things even better.'

Jon Stead is challenged by two Plymouth players.

TABLE

	P	W	D	L	F	A	Pts
Birmingham	26	16	5	5	46	25	53
Preston	26	13	8	5	39	26	47
Derby	**26**	**14**	**5**	**7**	**34**	**27**	**47**
Southampton	26	12	8	6	43	31	44
West Brom	26	12	7	7	47	28	43
Colchester	26	13	4	9	45	29	43
Stoke	26	12	7	7	35	21	43
Cardiff	26	11	9	6	36	28	42
Sheffield W	26	11	7	8	38	35	40
Wolves	26	11	6	9	26	29	39
Burnley	26	10	7	9	32	28	37
Sunderland	26	11	4	11	34	32	37
Plymouth	26	8	11	7	32	33	35
Coventry	26	10	4	12	24	29	34
Norwich	26	9	7	10	33	39	34
Ipswich	26	9	5	12	36	37	32
Leicester	26	8	8	10	26	32	32
C Palace	26	8	7	11	28	31	31
Luton	26	8	6	12	35	45	30
QPR	26	7	6	13	33	41	27
Barnsley	26	7	5	14	29	45	26
Hull	26	6	6	14	25	37	24
Leeds	26	6	3	17	25	48	21
Southend	26	3	9	14	19	44	18

January

A packed Pride Park over the Christmas period.

The turn of the year sees Derby right in among the chasing pack at the top of the table. The progress has come quicker than expected, but boss Billy Davies isn't getting carried away and has spoken about the need to continually develop his squad.

And with the transfer window re-opening the time couldn't be better to do so – but first there's another significant fixture on the horizon.

After refusing to comment on the big clash against former club Preston until it was next-up on the fixture list, Rams boss Billy Davies now concedes it's a 'tasty' game.

On New Year's Day, Derby County, in third place, travel to Preston, one place higher on goal difference, for the biggest game in the Championship.

'With the amount of preparation that had gone in at Preston, as club a and group of players over the past number of years, at the start of this season they had a ready-made side, and I expected them to be where they are,' Davies said. 'But for us to be sitting there with the same

number of points at the top of the table is remarkable.

'I'm looking forward to it – it's the type of game you have to enjoy.

'I'm going back proud of what I left in terms of the condition of the club when I went away and the young players who have come through.

'I'm very proud of what I achieved at Deepdale, but I'm going there as Derby County manager, looking forward to a good match and looking forward to a good reception from the Preston fans.'

Billy Davies's former club Preston North End's Deepdale stadium.

REPORT – 1 JANUARY 2007
PRESTON NORTH END 1
DERBY COUNTY 2

The Rams enjoyed some good possession in the early stages and twice Jon Stead played lovely threaded through balls in behind the defence to try and carve the Preston back line open.

On six minutes the home side themselves threatened. Matt Oakley was dispossessed in midfield and after a series of passes the ball fell to Callum Davidson, but he could only fire high over Stephen Bywater's goal from 25 yards out.

With 22 minutes played Derby were desperately close to taking the lead after Matt Hill fouled Morten Bisgaard 25 yards out from goal. Jones curled in a free-kick that Nash fumbled up into the air and Michael Johnson headed against the underside of the bar. Chaos then ensued inside the area as Bisgaard and then Stead saw efforts blocked by some last-gasp defending.

The Rams then counter-attacked, and Stead wasted the opportunity by dragging a shot wide from range when he had Howard bursting through on his left and Bisgaard making advances down the right.

On the half-hour mark Brett Ormerod missed a glaring opportunity to put the hosts in front. David Nugent got past Jonno and squared the ball to the advancing Ormerod, who took a touch and then belted over when it looked easier to score.

There was drama deep in first-half injury time when Dean Leacock brought down Ormerod and received a booking; however, the Preston man did appear to go down extremely easily. From the resulting set-piece Stead got a head on the cross and diverted it in the general direction of his own goal, but thankfully only into the side netting.

Three minutes after the break the Rams took the lead with a typical poacher's goal by striker Howard.

Derby hit Preston on the counter attack down the right and Bisgaard whipped in a shot that Nash could only palm into the path of Howard, who prodded the ball home from six yards.

Just minutes after taking the lead, it was 2–0 when Stead was up-ended in the box by Liam Chilvers and Howard stepped up to thump the resulting penalty past a despairing Nash.

Jones then curled a left-footed free-kick narrowly over Nash's goal as the Rams picked up a head of steam.

A great block from Johnson on 66 minutes kept Miller's shot from causing too many problems as the Rams were forced into a brief period of defending.

However, the visitors were soon back on the attack and, following a Camara throw-in on the left, Jones sent a fizzing right-footed volley just wide from an angle 18 yards out.

On 76 minutes Danny Pugh flung himself at a Graham Alexander cross and was heartbroken to see his volley fly back off the crossbar. Three minutes

PRESTON: Nash, Alexander, Davidson (McKenna 61), Pugh, Sedgwick (Whaley 61), Nugent, St Ledger, Chilvers, Ormerod, Hill, Miller (Neal 75).
UNUSED SUBS: Lonergan, Wilson.

DERBY: Bywater, Edworthy, Leacock, M. Johnson, Camara, Barnes (Malcolm 84) Bisgaard (Lupoli 69), Oakley, Jones, Stead (Moore 89), Howard.
UNUSED SUBS: Grant, S. Johnson.

ATTENDANCE: 19,204.

Steve Howard celebrates on the pitch after scoring two goals for Derby.

Steve Howard celebrates after scoring his, and Derby's, second.

Steve Howard is booked by the referee.

later Preston were back in the game, and once again the provider was Alexander.

He charged down the right and played a low curled ball perfectly into the path of Nugent, who slotted calmly past Bywater from six yards. Howard had to clear a header off the line and then Jones was booked for dissent after the referee had awarded Preston a free-kick. Sub McKenna then wastefully lifted a shot over the bar as time ticked away.

Lupoli almost made it an even more emphatic win when he bore down on the Preston goal in injury time and forced a save from Nash.

REACTION

The manager was extremely happy but keen for everyone around Derby County to stay calm after seeing his side tear Preston's 31-match unbeaten home run to shreds.

Talking after the deserved 2–1 win over his former club, Davies said it was an excellent three points but stressed there was still a lot of hard work to do if the Rams are to keep moving forward.

Having experienced a hostile reception from the home fans – a little unfair after bringing them some of the greatest days in their history in the form of back-to-back Play-offs – Davies watched as a Steve Howard brace earned the win.

The gaffer said 'We are very pleased with what is a very good result, but at the end of the day it's just another three points. It keeps us moving along in the right direction, but there's still a lot of hard work to be done. We are not going to get carried away.

'I'm delighted for the Rams fans, who once again were fantastic and truly deserve the victory. To see so many of them make the journey up to Deepdale on New Year's Day once again sums up how magnificent our travelling supporters are.

'It was a bit disappointing to receive the response I did from the home fans, especially as I made a point of applauding them before the game to thank them for their support when I was Preston manager, but the fact we had such great backing from the Rams supporters more than made up for that.

'The game was a little bit flat for most of the first half, but I was very satisfied with the way we came out and attacked them in the second period.

'I was a bit worried we'd scored a bit too early because, even at 2–0 up, when there's nearly 40 minutes still to go there's still going to be some defending to do. But we kept our organisation and discipline and, other than conceding a goal to a very good striker in David Nugent, defended well to pick up the points.'

Derby County have completed the signing of Manchester United midfielder David Jones for a fee of £1m plus appearances. The 22-year-old has put pen to paper on a three-and-a-half year deal with the Rams after initially arriving on loan in November.

Derby boss Billy Davies said 'I'm delighted to have secured the services of such a talented young player. I'm sure from what he's shown for the Rams so far that the Derby fans will know we've signed a first-class footballer.

'David has settled in really well at the club and shown signs of his quality. I'm sure he will get better and better the more games he plays.

'As I've said so many times, we've got a long-term plan at this football club, so with his age, potential and ability I see no reason why a player like David can't be a major influence in a Derby shirt.'

Jones, meanwhile, knew the time had come for a move away from Manchester United – and he is delighted with life at Derby County.

'I had been trying for years to get into United's first team, that was my number-one aim, but it got to the stage that maybe that opportunity wasn't going to come,' he revealed.

'I had to look elsewhere, and I am delighted to have signed for Derby as I have really enjoyed my time here, and I'm looking forward to a good career with the club.

'We are doing really well as a team and are full of confidence, looking forward to each game at the moment. Looking at the League table and seeing that we are in a good position makes it a pleasure to come into training. It is a brilliant set-up here at Derby and everything is going really well.'

Davies also confirmed that talks were ongoing with Sunderland regarding Jon Stead and Lewin Nyatanga, as well as with Bradford City over possible loan-deal extensions for Nathan Doyle and Lee Holmes.

Defender Theo Streete, who had been on loan at Doncaster Rovers, has been released after the expiry of his short-term professional deal with the Rams since he graduated from the Academy last summer.

Fellow Academy product Tom Cumberworth, meanwhile, will stay with the club for another six months in a bid to earn himself a longer deal. The midfielder's scholarship was disrupted by injury, and he signed professional at the same time as Streete, only to again pick up a serious knee injury that has kept him out of action since August.

Rams midfielder Paul Thirlwell has joined Carlisle United for an undisclosed fee. The 27-year-old has signed for the League One side on a permanent deal after spending three months on loan with them earlier this season.

Thirlwell was an August 2005 capture from Sheffield United, but he struggled to establish himself in the side and made only 17 starts, with six further substitute appearances.

Carlisle moved in for the former England Under-21 man in September last year, and he appeared 16 times for the Brunton Park club during his loan spell.

Defender Michael Johnson reckons a good Cup run would sit nicely alongside the Rams' excellent Coca-Cola Championship form. Derby host League Two side Wrexham in Saturday's third-round clash at Pride Park.

'I've always said that there is no better competition in the land than the FA Cup – so many memories, great games, great goals,' he said. 'For us it is a welcome break from the League, but we still want to do the right things and win the game.

'It would be nice to coincide a run in the Cup with the good League position we are in.

'A good Cup run is always welcome as it brings good revenue for the club, so it would be good for us to progress.'

Meanwhile, Nathan Doyle will celebrate his 20th birthday next week back at Bradford City after the Rams agreed to an emergency loan arrangement until 3 February.

The Academy product, on loan at the League One outfit from the start of the current campaign until the end of 2006, is on a 24-hour recall after the first seven days.

David Jones's loan deal became permanent at the beginning of January.

Mo Camara in action against Preston.

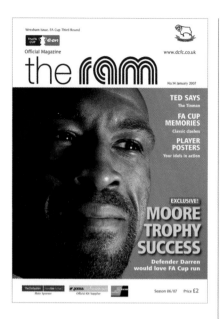

DERBY: Bywater, Edworthy, Moore, M. Johnson, Camara, Oakley (C) (Peschisolido 90), Malcolm (Smith 70), Jones, Bisgaard (Barnes 75), Howard, Lupoli.
UNUSED SUBS: Jackson, S. Johnson.

WREXHAM: Ingham, Valentine, Pejic, S. Evans, D. Williams, McEvilly, Ferguson (C), Llewellyn, Crowell (J. Johnson 57), Mike Williams, Done.
UNUSED SUBS: Jones, Spender, Marc Williams, G. Evans.

ATTENDANCE: 15,609.

REPORT – 6 JANUARY 2007
DERBY COUNTY 3
WREXHAM 1
FA CUP THIRD ROUND

The visitors – backed by almost 3,000 travelling fans – had the first shot of the game, but Chris Lewellyn drove safely wide after being fed by Lee McEvilly's clever header.

McEvilly came closer still in the seventh minute as he latched on to a long ball and out-muscled Moore, only to be denied by a fine Stephen Bywater save.

Wrexham were working hard, but Derby's football was bright, though they failed to craft an effort on goal until the 23rd minute when Morten Bisgaard turned and got his head down but fired well over from 25 yards.

Seconds later came their first shot on target, but Mo Camara's right-footer was no danger to Michael Ingham.

And by the 32nd minute they were in front. Michael Johnson strongly cleared with his head and the ball fell to Bisgaard inside the centre circle.

The Dane turned well and shrugged off a challenge before neatly feeding Lupoli, who took a touch before steadying himself inside the penalty area and smashing the ball emphatically past Ingham.

Ingham dropped David Jones's bobbling 30-yarder, but no Rams players were alert enough to follow in and snap up the rebound; however, Ingham did better later from the same player's effort, although chances were few and far between at either end of the field.

Wrexham came out for the second half fired up, though again they weren't making the most of their possession, and they could have gone two behind when Derby broke quickly only for Jones's shot to be deflected out for a 55th-minute corner. But, from that flag-kick, the lead was indeed doubled.

Bisgaard floated the ball into the six-yard box where Lupoli had the simplest of tasks to nod it downwards and into the back of the net.

Wrexham found themselves back in the game on the hour thanks to a goal that was all Derby's own fault.

A low cross was deflected out to the edge of the box where Malcolm attempted to nod it back to Bywater. But the midfielder didn't spot McEvilly lurking and the visiting number nine poked the ball around Bywater and stabbed it over the line from a couple of yards out.

And they were almost level two minutes later after Darren Ferguson's free-kick was headed goalwards by Shaun Pejic but dropped just the wrong side of the post.

The visiting fans were in raptures on 68 minutes as the ball was in the back of the Derby net again, but although Steve Evans had rammed it home from close range after a free-kick the flag had already gone up for offside.

McEvilly saw a header cleared from in front of goal before volleying straight at Bywater from the edge of the box – the chances were falling at one end, and it was the wrong end from a Derby perspective.

The number nine was proving a handful, and

Giles Barnes runs at the Wrexham midfield.

Lupoli has the simplest of headers for his third goal.

when Michael Johnson hauled him down Ferguson's free-kick led to another good chance that Evans could only head at Bywater.

Smith broke clear down the left with six minutes to go and showed what he could do with a fine cross that ultimately led to one of Derby's longest-running hoodoos being broken.

Howard's header was tipped on to the bar by Ingham but dropped down in front of goal, where Lupoli was waiting and headed it home for his hat-trick.

It was the first Derby County hat-trick since Paul Simpson's treble in a 6–2 win over Tranmere Rovers in April 1996, well over a decade ago.

REACTION

Billy Davies praised the goalscoring prowess of hat-trick hero Arturo Lupoli after Saturday's 3–1 Cup win over Wrexham – but stressed the on-loan youngster needs to remain patient for his starting chances.

'Arturo showed today what he is capable of,' said the Rams boss. 'I'm very aware of the good points of all the young players at this club, but I'm also aware of the bad points, and they have to understand they still have a lot to learn.

'He got a wonderful hat-trick today, but next week will be a different type of game.

'Arturo is a natural finisher who puts himself in the right areas at the right time.

'We have young players, like Arturo, who can be lacking in patience at times, and they must realise if they are to have long and successful careers they won't start every game and they have to approach the decisions I make with professionalism.'

Arturo Lupoli clutched the man-of-the-match champagne and the matchball for his hat-trick when he spoke after the 3–1 FA Cup win over Wrexham.

The Rams players congratulate Lupoli on his hat-trick.

Lupoli celebrates his hat-trick.

The beginning of January means a busy time in the transfer market. Firstly, Craig Fagan joins the Rams from Hull.

Nothing too significant about the matchball, you might think, except that the on-loan Italian was only eight-years-old the last time a Derby County player netted three times in the same match.

Lupoli, now 19, scored all the goals as League Two side Wrexham were eliminated after a tough third-round battle at Pride Park.

And after the match he revealed his delight at becoming the first hat-trick hero since Paul Simpson way back in April 1996.

'Today was fantastic for me,' the on-loan star said. 'It was a great game, we won through to the next round and I scored a hat-trick, so it has been unbelievable. I felt I played quite well so I am very proud of this. I knew that it was a long time since the last hat-trick as when I scored twice against Southend, people told me I was close.

'So I said that I will do it the next time; today I did and that was fantastic.'

Billy Davies's Rams will entertain League Two opposition in Bristol Rovers at Pride Park Stadium in the FA Cup fourth round to be played on the weekend of 27 and 28 January.

First-team coach of Rovers, currently 10th in League Two, is former Rams player Paul Trollope.

He said of the draw, 'It's a good draw for us – an away tie against a big club. It's a great stadium to go to against a team that's going great guns with a good manager.

'We go up there full of confidence and will take a lot of fans, and it's a one-off game so we have a chance. I had a fantastic few years up there and it will be good to go back.'

Another former Ram, centre-back Steve Elliott, is also on Rovers' books.

Five years ago Rovers came to Pride Park for a third-round FA Cup tie and knocked out the Rams, Fabrizio Ravanelli scoring for Derby in a 3–1 defeat.

And Derby gaffer Davies said 'You can ask for no more than a home draw, so we're pleased with it. It's a good opportunity for us to progress into the next round.

'Recent history has seen Bristol Rovers come to Pride Park and win in the FA Cup, so it will be a difficult game, that's for sure.

'There are no easy matches in the FA Cup, but we're pleased to be playing a fourth-round tie at Pride Park and we're looking to progress as far as we can in the competition.'

The Rams have completed their second signing of the transfer window – Hull City forward Craig Fagan.

Fagan is young, hungry, has been a success at this level already and can play in a variety of positions.

'I'm delighted with the signing,' boss Billy Davies said. 'Craig is just the sort of player I want in my squad – determined, pacy, versatile and with that all-important ability to score goals.

'I've been watching him for some time, and he's a very welcome addition to the ranks here at Derby County. I'm not saying he's going to walk straight into the team, but he adds quality to the squad and that's so important right now.

'We remain hopeful of adding more new faces during this transfer window, and it's great that the board has recognised the need to bring new impetus to the squad as we continue our push.'

Fagan believes he is arriving at a club full of confidence. After swapping the bottom of the Coca-Cola Championship for the top, he can't wait to get cracking in his Derby County career.

'There isn't too much difference in terms of potential of the two clubs, but the big difference is that Derby is a team high on confidence,' he said.

'When you're in a team like that maybe you can play better yourself and ride on the crest of a wave for the rest of the season.

'At the start of the season at Hull we lost quite a few games and were on a downhill slope, which they've only just started to pick up.

'I hope we can go all the way this season at Derby. Knowing how the manager is – very determined – then if it's not this season I'm sure it will be the following year.

'For me, my target for the rest of the season is more goals, and maybe promotion at the end of it.'

And two signings have very quickly become four with the arrivals of two Scottish internationals. Midfielders Stephen Pearson and Gary Teale have joined Derby from Celtic and Wigan Athletic respectively.

Davies said 'We said from the very beginning last summer that there would be no short-term fix – it's a long-term plan which will take three or four transfer windows because there was a massive job in hand.

'The board has recognised the position we are in and the opportunity we have to progress, and that's reflected in the four new signings in the past week.'

Of 24-year-old Pearson, signed for £750,000 from Celtic, and 28-year-old Teale, captured from Wigan Athletic for £600,000, Davies joked 'They are both Scottish, which is good! But more important than that, they are good players.

'I know their characters, and I know what they bring to the dressing room. They have been welcomed by the other players, and they have settled very quickly.'

Pearson has immediately set his sights on winning promotion to the Premiership.

He said 'I'm looking forward to the challenge, and I definitely don't see this move as a step down because the Championship is a tough League and in any case we are aiming for the Premiership.

'I've had a good day today. I trained with the lads this morning and enjoyed it.

'I already know Bob Malcolm and Mo Camara from their time in Scotland, so that makes it easier to settle in.'

Pearson played previously under Billy Davies's management at Motherwell and added 'I'm looking forward to working with him again because he's always been a winner.

'Billy was a big factor in my decision to come here, but so were the impressive facilities and the fan base.'

And Teale had no doubts about signing for Derby after speaking to Davies.

'When you get here you see the stadium and the training facilities, but the manager's enthusiasm and ambition to take this club to the Premiership in the next few months stands out,' the 28-year-old revealed.

'If anyone was to spend time with him you would see how driven he is about taking this club forward. Looking from the outside of the club you would think it should be in the Premiership anyway, and that is the way Billy sees it.'

Then Stephen Pearson comes in from Celtic.

Finally Gary Teale joins from Wigan.

DERBY: Bywater, Edworthy, Leacock, Moore (C), Camara, Barnes (Fagan 62), S. Johnson (Pearson 63), Jones, Teale (Bisgaard 71), Howard, Lupoli.
UNUSED SUBS: M. Johnson, Malcolm.

WEDNESDAY: Crossley, Bullen (C), Lunt, Whelan, Tudgay, MacLean (Graham 89), Burton, Brunt (Small 68), Simek, Bougherra, Spurr.
UNUSED SUBS: Adamson, Coughlan, Folly.

ATTENDANCE: 28,936.

Both Pearson (above) and Fagan (below) make their debuts for the Rams.

REPORT – 13 JANUARY 2007
DERBY COUNTY 1
SHEFFIELD WEDNESDAY 0

New-boy Gary Teale's first involvement came five minutes in when he was fed by Marc Edworthy and embarked on a jinking run down the right that led to Derby's first corner of the game.

David Jones swung the ball over from the right wing, and it was met at the far post by Arturo Lupoli, but he was denied by Kenny Lunt's clearance off the line.

Scotsman Teale's early touches showed plenty of promise, and every time he escaped down the right he looked likely to create something. One cross was cleared out to Seth Johnson, who volleyed wide, while on 16 minutes another was headed over his own bar by Lee Bullen.

Chris Brunt's 20-yard fizzer was Wednesday's first real threat, but the ball zipped just the wrong side of Stephen Bywater's left-hand post.

Teale escaped to the by-line again on 20 minutes and once more delivered a beautiful ball to the far post, but Steve Howard could only head it wide of the target.

At the other end Marcus Tudgay volleyed wide when in plenty of space after being fed by Steve MacLean.

Lupoli wasted a good chance to build on his FA Cup treble eight minutes before the break. Jones played a fine ball over the top of the visiting defence that the Italian ran on to, but, with more time than perhaps he realised, Lupoli snatched at his shot from the edge of the box and never threatened to trouble the scorers.

Wednesday broke after getting the game going again and the ball fell to Lunt on the edge of the box, who forced Bywater into a fine sprawling save to his left.

Derby had their own spell of pressure just before the hour mark, sparked by more Teale trickery down the right, and again they were denied by a clearance off the line after Darren Moore headed down a corner.

A fine move involving Pearson and Fagan – now on as substitutes – ultimately saw Mark Crossley turn away Lupoli's low shot for a corner.

Ten minutes remained when Morten Bisgaard had a good opportunity to open the scoring after good work from Howard and Pearson, but the Dane was denied by a fine Bullen block.

Crossley picked up a late caution for time-wasting, and Tommy Spurr was cautioned for a tug on Fagan to give the Rams a free-kick with seconds of stoppage time remaining. Then, from a very narrow angle out on the right, Jones crashed it into the back of the net – a goal out of nothing, and no better time to score.

REACTION

Billy Davies wants to see more of the dead ball strikes from David Jones that won the Rams all three points against Sheffield Wednesday.

After his last-gasp free-kick fizzed past Mark Crossley to break the deadlock at Pride Park on Saturday, Davies said 'David is sometimes too nice and steps aside when others demand the ball in that situation. But because of what he is capable of doing from dead-ball situations it's silly he doesn't take more of them.

'David has a football brain – he sees spaces, gaps and he's a wonderful young talent who still has a lot to do in this game.

'It's another game gone and now only 18 left and the more points we can pick up the better.

'These players recognise the opportunity we have and we must continue to get at the opposition at Pride Park. No one could deny us the three points today.'

David Jones lined up a stoppage time free-kick in a position where most players would have crossed – but one man inside Pride Park Stadium knew a shot was on the cards.

It looked like Derby would have to settle for a Coca-Cola Championship point at home to Sheffield Wednesday after a tight game that saw neither goalkeeper seriously tested.

But Jones had other ideas and made it three with an outrageous effort from a right-wing position that crashed past visiting custodian Mark Crossley.

'I know I'm capable of scoring from there – I've done it before,' the 22-year-old said.

'I thought that if I could get a good contact on it and whip it in with pace, get it in the top corner, the 'keeper wouldn't get across. I had a look at the 'keeper and saw a bit of a gap at the near post so I knew I had a chance.

'It was probably going to be the last chance of the game so I took my time, composed myself, and if you do that then the results can speak for themselves.'

Billy Davies is refusing to take his eye off the ball – despite ongoing transfer speculation involving Derby County.

'There's every possibility there will be more business in this transfer window because lots can happen between now and the end of the month, so we are prepared for anything,' the boss said.

'We are still looking and asking questions, but we have to concentrate on winning games of football.

'So far this week there have been no transfer dealings but plenty of activity.

Teale had an impressive debut; here he is finding space down the right to deliver a cross.

Gary Teale.

That doesn't take our focus away from a difficult away game on Saturday and we've had another week training hard on the training ground.'

While the Rams and Southend are at different ends of the Championship table, Billy says the Roots Hall outfit will be treated with respect.

'It makes no difference to us where a club is sitting in the League because we will treat them with the utmost respect, especially the likes of Southend, as they've not lost in six,' he said.

'We have to go down there and be on our own game to pick up three points.'

With skipper Matt Oakley and winger Ryan Smith reporting fit again after a virus, Paul Boertien is the only notable absentee from the Rams squad that travels to Southend.

Saturday's game at Roots Hall will be the first League encounter there between the two sides for over a decade.

The Essex club's ground is a tightly-packed venue with fans crammed in close to the pitch. And that's just the kind of environment that goalkeeper Stephen Bywater relishes.

'That's alright, I like that and get a buzz off it – that means our supporters who travel down there will be close in too,' he said.

'It should be a good atmosphere as they are fighting for their lives and we want to win the game, so hopefully it should be a good day.

'There is never an easy game in this League though, everyone can and does beat everyone.

'Southend know what it is like in the division below, and they won't want that again. But we are going there to win the game, to put on a good performance and to come back with the three points.

'I hate the long journey back when we've not won a game so that is going to make me even more determined.'

REPORT – 20 JANUARY 2007
SOUTHEND UNITED 0
DERBY COUNTY 1

The Rams are three points clear at the top of the Championship after Steve Howard's 32nd-minute header gave Billy Davies's side all the points at Roots Hall.

It's the first time since the early months of 1996 that Derby County have headed the table, but it wasn't all one-way traffic against a sparky Southend United.

The ball was in the Derby net within seconds of the kick-off, but an offside flag was up from an assistant referee wearing a baseball cap against the strong sun.

On four minutes Gary Teale, starting wide on the left, spurned a great chance. Howard and Craig Fagan exchanged passes before Teale ran in on goal with only Flahavan to beat, but his tame shot from 16 yards was easily held by the 'keeper. Malcolm's long-range effort was saved by Flahavan diving to his left on 17.

For the umpteenth time this season Howard hit the woodwork when on 27 minutes Bywater's clearance was knocked back on the edge of the visitors' area by Teale to the big striker who, from the D, struck a

SOUTHEND: Flahavan, Hunt, Barrett, Clarke, Hammell, Campbell-Ryce, Maher (C), McCormack, Gower, Eastwood (Harrold 83), Bradbury.
UNUSED SUBS: Guttridge, Sodje, Hooper, Welch.

DERBY: Bywater; Edworthy, Leacock, Moore (C), Camara, Jones, Malcolm (Oakley 55), Pearson, Fagan (M. Johnson 83), Howard, Teale (Bisgaard 65).
UNUSED SUBS: Lupoli, Barnes.

ATTENDANCE: 10,745.

powerful shot that beat Flahavan but rebounded back into play off the 'keeper's left post.

Camara's persistence down the Derby left saw Hunt concede a corner on 32 and Teale's low near-post corner found Howard diving in to head home his 12th goal of the campaign.

Southend penalty claims after Moore jostled Eastwood off the ball were waved aside by Iain Williamson, and six minutes before the break Pearson's strength created a chance for Fagan who, from the edge of the area, curled his shot wide of Flahavan's left post.

A foul on Fagan down the right side of the Southend defence saw Jones curl in a free-kick which was headed down by Howard for Moore to fire narrowly wide from 18 yards with the goal at his mercy.

Seconds after the restart Malcolm hit in a shot that was comfortable for Flahavan, but Howard should have doubled Derby's lead shortly afterwards when Teale's pass released Fagan down the right.

His cross found Howard with time and space, but from 12 yards the striker smashed his effort over the top.

With Derby under pressure at the other end, Davies introduced Oakley for Malcolm on 55 minutes and during the substitution an argument developed between the Rams boss and the fourth official, leading to the gaffer being sent to an already crowded directors' box.

A strong run out of midfield by Pearson saw Fagan run clear on the right on 62 minutes. His ball into the box found Pearson stretching at the far post and Flahavan saved, though conceded a corner that he contested.

On 68 minutes Howard was a whisker away from scoring again when Fagan's low cross from the left ran tantalisingly across the box and past Howard's out-stretched right leg as he lunged in four yards out.

Edworthy was the hero when he dived in to deny Eastwood after Bywater had saved McCormack's shot. Then the same player miraculously headed Clarke's effort off the line as the Shrimpers centre-half connected from a corner.

At the other end it was suddenly four-on-one in Derby's favour as Pearson ran in on Flahavan to settle the game, but the 'keeper saved as the midfielder tried to squeeze a right-footer under his body.

Another curler from Fagan was saved, and then Edworthy went into the book for bringing down Shrimpers flyer Campbell-Ryce.

Michael Johnson came on for Fagan on 83 to bolster the Derby defence, and he made a crucial tackle as Eastwood powered through on 87 minutes.

And it was Derby's day as they kept it tight at the back to ensure they hit the top of the table.

REACTION

Billy Davies is not a manager who is likely to sit back and enjoy the fact that his side is three points clear at the top of the League. After Saturday's battling 1–0 victory at Roots Hall, the Rams boss was more concerned about the chances his side had missed.

'We made it difficult for ourselves

Steve Howard being congratulated by teammate Craig Fagan after scoring his 12th goal of the season for Derby.

Michael Johnson's tackle to deny Freddy Eastwood.

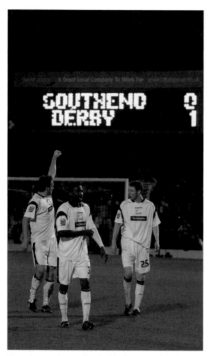

The players leave the field after another hard-fought win.

with the chances we missed,' Davies said. 'We knew Southend would scrap well on this ground because they've made it difficult here in the past for some very good sides – so we're happy with the points.'

'You get nothing for being shy in this game' – that was the verdict of striker Steve Howard after he dived in among defenders' boots to net his 12th goal of the season.

The striker's 32nd-minute header was enough to take all three points from the tricky trip to Essex on Saturday and take the Rams three points clear of Birmingham City at the top of the Championship table.

'That's what I've been successful with during my football career,' Howard said.

'You get stuck in and you get the rewards. It was a good ball in from Tealey and I dived in.'

Defender Dean Leacock will sit out Saturday's FA Cup fourth-round tie with Bristol Rovers after picking up his fifth booking of the season.

Leacock was cautioned in Saturday's 1–0 win at Southend United – a result that took the Rams three points clear at the top of the Coca-Cola Championship. It took the 22-year-old over the threshold and earned him a one-match ban.

Young striker Lionel Ainsworth has gone out on loan to Conference side Halifax Town until 18 February. The 19-year-old England Youth international, a local product of the Rams Academy, signed professional forms with Derby County in August 2005, but his chances have been restricted by injuries.

Ainsworth had a spell on loan at the end of last year with League One side Bournemouth.

Derby County manager Billy Davies has been charged with using abusive and/or insulting words towards a match official.

The charge relates to Davies's conduct during Derby's match against Southend United on Saturday 20 January. He has until 6 February to respond.

Big defender Darren Moore is amazed by the turnaround in the fortunes of Derby County over the last 12 months. He moved from West Bromwich Albion on 26 January 2006 with the club struggling at the bottom end of the Coca-Cola Championship.

Phil Brown was the manager, Murdo Mackay the director of football, while the boardroom was headed up by chairman John Sleightholme and the club's financial situation was worsening.

Now the Rams sit top of the table, Billy Davies is in charge, chairman Peter Gadsby and his colleagues have boardroom control and they have secured the finances.

It's a situation that Moore is excited by, and he believes it is down to the hard work of everyone at the club.

'It's amazing – right through the whole structure of the club things have changed, from the board and the chairman to the youth level staff and players,' Moore said.

'To see the team and the club as a whole, sitting where it is, is a great testament to everyone, from the chairman to the behind-the-scenes staff. It has been a big effort from

The travelling faithful in full voice.

everyone for the club to be in the position we are now, and it is going to take a huge effort from everyone for it to remain and get better.

'It has been a huge transitional period but it has been great to see that – with so many changes at the club – the hard work is paying off. That has been the most pleasing thing and long may it continue.'

Michael Johnson admits the prospect of Paul Trollope and Steve Elliott returning to Derby County is an 'interesting' one.

Trollope is in charge at Bristol Rovers and brings his side to Pride Park on Saturday for an FA Cup fourth-round clash.

Rovers' defence is likely to be marshalled by Derby-born Elliott, a lifelong Rams fan and product of the club's Academy. And Jonno is looking forward to the challenge.

'I don't know too much about Paul, but I know of him and probably played against him when I was at Notts County,' he revealed. 'I know more about Steve Elliott as he was here when I first signed for the club under George Burley.

'It will be interesting for the two guys to come back, and they will want to do well, but hopefully – from our point of view – not too well.'

He wasn't involved in the game, but Richard Jackson remembers the Rams' last FA Cup tie with Bristol Rovers very well.

Rovers visited Pride Park in January 2002 while they were in the League's bottom tier to take on a Derby side bereft of confidence and in deep Premiership trouble. And they left having caused a major upset and heaped even more pressure on then-boss Colin Todd.

'It was a bad day for the club,' Jackson recalled.

'We got beat 3–1 and Fabrizio Ravanelli scored for us, but Nathan Ellington got a hat-trick for them. That's all in the past now though and we're looking forward to Saturday's game.

'With the way that we are playing in the League we will hopefully put in another good performance and get through to the next round.

'It's a banana skin as we're top of the Championship, and they're doing quite well in League Two, and it's the FA Cup so anything can happen. But we'll be on our toes and take our recent performances into this game.'

REPORT – 27 JANUARY 2007
DERBY COUNTY 1
BRISTOL ROVERS 0
FA CUP FOURTH ROUND

Rovers had the first chance of the game two minutes in after forcing a corner. It was played short then whipped over by skipper Stuart Campbell to the far post where Steve Elliott got up well but could only direct his header into the arms of Stephen Bywater.

And it was almost disaster for the Rams on 17 minutes as they were a couple of inches away from falling behind.

A breakdown in communications saw Jackson's back-pass roll dangerously towards goal with Bywater seemingly helpless, but the goalkeeper raced back to clear it off the line with Richard Walker waiting to pounce.

That lifted Rovers and their near-6,000 travelling support, who

DERBY: Bywater, Jackson, Moore, M. Johnson (C), Camara, Malcolm (Smith 80), Barnes, S. Johnson, Fagan (Bisgaard 84), Howard, Lupoli (Peschisolido 73).
UNUSED SUBS: Edworthy, Oakley.

ROVERS: Phillips, Igoe (Rigg 82), Hinton, Elliott, Campbell (C), Lambert, Walker (Green 71), Carruthers, Sandell (Haldane 76), Disley, Lescott.
UNUSED SUBS: Lines, Parrinello.

ATTENDANCE: 25,033.

Steve Howard heads the ball clear of the area as Rovers have the best of the first half.

thought that Chris Carruthers's 20-yarder had found the back of the net, only to be disappointed upon realising it had gone just wide.

Bywater produced the game's first real save of note on 31 minutes when Rickie Lambert escaped from the attentions of Mo Camara down the Rovers right and crossed for Walker to power a 12-yard header goalwards that Bywater turned over the bar.

Again Rovers were lifted and again Bywater saved Derby once more with a tremendous block on the line from Campbell's forceful downward header after Carruthers crossed.

Steve Phillips pushed away Barnes's driven effort from the edge of the box a couple of minutes later as both sides looked to be stepping things up. From the save, Rovers broke quickly and fed Lambert inside the box, who really should have put his side in front but totally missed his kick from 12 yards.

Rovers had the ball in the back of the net five minutes before half-time through Andy Sandell's header from Campbell's corner, but it was ruled out for a foul on Bywater.

As for the Rams, the best they could muster before half-time was a scramble inside the six-yard box that led to Phillips gleefully diving on the loose ball.

Derby forced a couple of corners early in the second half but failed to make them count, though they did come close in the 50th minute when Steve Howard drove narrowly wide from the edge of the box.

On 70 minutes Rovers suffered a blow when they were reduced to 10 men. Lescott was pulled up for a tackle on Lupoli out on the touchline that was certainly late and looked a little high, but referee Andy D'Urso had no hesitation in pulling out his red card immediately.

Howard then rose to meet Seth Johnson's in-swinging corner from the right but couldn't direct his header on target.

And the frustration was eased with nine minutes to go as Derby took the lead. Bywater cleared long and substitute Ryan Smith had an immediate impact with a neat through ball to Peschisolido in behind the Rovers defence.

The Canadian did what he does best with a composed finish past Phillips from 14 yards.

Haldane saw an 89th-minute effort comfortably saved by Bywater with Rovers pushing for a late equaliser.

Smith saw a shot well-saved by Phillips, who also went up for a corner deep into stoppage time, but the Rams defended it solidly to seal their passage into the fifth round.

Lupoli lies injured on the touchline.

REACTION

Billy Davies was giving away nothing about his half-time team talk as his side recovered from a disappointing first 45 minutes to march into the fifth round of the FA Cup with a 1–0 victory over Bristol Rovers.

'We didn't get a grip of the ball or the game in the first half,' the Rams boss said. 'We have to be better than that and the players knew that at half-time.

'Rovers came and enjoyed the stadium and the occasion, and they certainly made life difficult for us, but what you can't afford to do is give the opposition the ball as often as we did in the first half.

'Our goalkeeper had to make some good saves, but it's another clean sheet and a fantastic result for us.'

Paul Peschisolido was off the bench and on the spot yet again – and says another late victory showed how consistent the Rams have become. The Canadian came on in the 73rd minute of the FA Cup fourth-round tie against Bristol Rovers and took Derby into the last 16 thanks to his strike with nine minutes to go.

It meant a sixth straight win in all competitions, with three of them coming via goals after the 80-minute mark.

'It shows how resilient we are at the moment,' Pesch said. 'We're winning games late consistently, which is not luck – it's hard work paying off and that's why we're in the position we're in.

'We know that today would be difficult as Bristol Rovers are a team who work hard and have a lot of energy.

'It was a Cup Final for them, with 6,000 supporters cheering them, and they came and performed as we expected them to. But thankfully we are through and into the next round.'

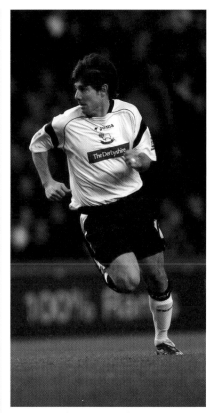

Paul Peschisolido comes on for Lupoli and is soon celebrating scoring the winner with nine minutes to go.

Derby County midfielder Adam Bolder has joined Coca-Cola Championship side Queen's Park Rangers. The 26-year-old has agreed personal terms at Loftus Road and will put pen to paper on a permanent move to West London for an undisclosed fee.

He will be re-united with former Derby boss John Gregory, who saw Bolder as an integral part of his team during the 2002–03 season following relegation from the Premiership.

Bolder joined the Rams from Hull City – who had also expressed an interest in re-signing him – in March 2000 and has made more appearances for Derby than any other member of the current squad.

In all competitions Bolder made 121 starts, 60 substitute appearances and scored 11 goals.

Derby County will travel to Plymouth Argyle in the fifth round of the FA Cup – and boss Billy Davies says the draw has provided his side with a tough test.

The Rams sit top of the Coca-Cola Championship and earned their place in the last 16 thanks to a 1–0 win over Bristol Rovers, while the Pilgrims got through with a victory at Barnet.

'Obviously we were looking for a big Premiership club, as everyone was, but you've got to take what comes out of the hat and do the job,' Davies said. 'It doesn't really matter who you get though – if you're going to progress in the Cup then you have got to do the job regardless.

'It is a tough match, but we will be looking forward to it.'

Derby County have completed the signing of Blackburn Rovers defender Jay McEveley for a fee of £600,000 plus add-ons.

The 21-year-old has put pen to paper on a three-and-a-half-year deal with the Rams after agreeing personal terms and passing a medical.

Jay McEveley.

McEveley will add further options to Derby's defensive ranks and becomes the club's fifth permanent signing of the January transfer window – following on from Gary Teale, Stephen Pearson, Craig Fagan and David Jones.

Of the latest addition to the Derby squad, Jay McEveley, Rams boss Billy Davies said 'We are delighted to have Jay. He is an excellent young player who gives us great competition and we're looking forward to working with him.

'The people we are bringing in have good pace, good presence, a lot of good ability is coming into the squad and, of course, they are raising the bar in terms of quality.

'We are delighted to bring in another quality player.'

Derby County will welcome back several senior figures into their squad for Tuesday's Coca-Cola Championship match with Burnley.

Dean Leacock (suspension) and Gary Teale (cup-tied) were absent from Saturday's FA Cup win, but they will be welcomed back into the fold for the Pride Park clash.

They will be joined by the likes of David Jones, Stephen Pearson, Matt Oakley and Marc Edworthy, who were all given a rest against the Pirates.

'We rested a few legs at the weekend so we'll be bringing players back on Tuesday,' Billy Davies said. 'But I've said before that it doesn't matter who plays, whether it's League or Cup, it will be horses for courses between now and the end of the season. Every single member of our staff needs to be ready for every battle we face.'

And Gary Teale can't wait to get back into the swing of things again after an enforced hold-up to the start of his Derby County career.

The winger has been in the side for both Coca-Cola Championship games since his arrival from Wigan Athletic but was ruled out of Saturday's FA Cup win over Bristol Rovers having already appeared for the Latics in this season's competition.

But he is back in the frame for the Pride Park clash with Burnley for what he knows is an important game.

'I was obviously disappointed to be Cup-tied because as a player you want to play in all the games,' the 28-year-old revealed. 'But if you can pick then you'd probably want to be involved against Burnley as the League is important for us this season.

'Training when you know you've got nothing at the end of the week is difficult, but I trained at the weekend, then at the start of this week.

'It's just great to be back involved and getting back in among the games, and hopefully we can get the three points.'

REPORT – 30 JANUARY 2007
DERBY COUNTY 1
BURNLEY 0

Only three minutes were on the clock when Derby took the lead. They won a free-kick in midfield and Jones delivered it superbly from left to right, where Steve Howard dived home to head emphatically past Mike Pollitt.

It was almost two a couple of minutes later as Edworthy's throw was flicked on by Howard, but Jones couldn't quite steer it goalwards from close range. Pollitt did well to scramble a deflected Gary Teale cross from in front of goal as Howard closed in with a second in his sights.

A wonderful Pearson pass from midfield on 19 minutes split the Burnley defence open and sent Craig Fagan away, but from a narrow angle to the left he saw his shot rebound off the post.

The Derby dominance continued as Fagan curled a cross over from the left that Jones met with his head and Pollitt clawed away spectacularly.

Burnley's first shot on target came 28 minutes in as a training-ground move ended with Joey Gudjonsson firing straight at Stephen Bywater from 25 yards.

FIFA-list official Mike Riley was hardly endearing himself to either set of fans with his constant whistle-blowing and breaking up of play, just when a move looked to be developing.

He endeared himself even less to the home faithful with a 43rd-minute yellow card for Fagan, after the slightest of touches on Wayne Thomas.

Burnley started the second half brightly and peppered the Derby box with crosses, but again they failed to seriously threaten.

Derby's patience with Riley wore even thinner on 54 minutes when – after Fagan was pulled up for another nothing challenge – boss Billy Davies was sent to the stands after expressing his dismay with the decision.

Jon Harley then hacked down Teale, who was on a flying run down the right, but amazingly wasn't cautioned for the challenge. But Burnley were still having more of the ball, if little by way of chances, though Kyle Lafferty did force Bywater to make a comfortable save with a low 20-yarder.

Bywater produced another sprawling save to keep out another low Lafferty effort on 78 minutes, but this stop was more impressive as the Derby man couldn't have seen the edge-of-the-box shot until very late.

Eric Djemba-Djemba saw yellow with nine minutes to go for sliding through Jones from behind, but the tension was growing around Pride Park.

Burnley collected four yellow cards in a short space of time and two went to Djemba-Djemba, who picked up a second for a late challenge on Howard and became the second visiting player sent off at Pride Park in a matter of days.

Visiting boss Steve Cotterill was also sent from the touchline in stoppage time.

REACTION

With goals in each of his last three games, striker Steve Howard is showing determination that rubs off on his teammates and the Derby crowd.

That was the view of first-team coach Julian Darby, who took over

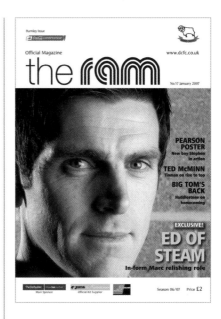

DERBY: Bywater, Edworthy, Moore, Leacock, Camara, Teale (Bisgaard 60), Oakley (C), Jones, Pearson, Fagan, Howard.
UNUSED SUBS: M. Johnson, Peschisolido, Lupoli, Malcolm.

BURNLEY: Pollitt, Thomas (C) (Foster 43), Harley (McCann 87), McGreal, Duff, J. O'Connor, Elliott (Mahon 69), Lafferty, Djemba-Djemba, Akinbiyi, Gudjonsson.
UNUSED SUBS: Coyne, G. O'Connor.

ATTENDANCE: 23,122.

Goalscorer Steve Howard has a word with the referee, Mike Riley.

The players celebrate Howard's early goal.

media duties from boss Billy Davies after Tuesday night's 1–0 home win over Burnley took the Rams six points clear at the top of the Championship table.

'Steve Howard's goal return is terrific – three in three games,' Darby said.

'He's now getting better service with more balls into the box and the delivery from set-pieces is better. David Jones's cross in for the goal was terrific.

'Steve will always put his head on the line and it's great for him that he's up there with the leading goalscorers in the Division.

'His determination rubs off on everyone in the team and the crowd joins in.'

Steve Howard scored the goal that put Derby six points clear at the top of the Coca-Cola Championship – then admitted to having the easy task.

David Jones's beautiful free-kick cross in the fourth minute was finished off by the Rams' number nine for his 13th goal of the season.

'It was a great ball in from Jonah – he just put it in there and said "head that," which I've done,' Howard said.

'I've had my fair share of goals like that, but it was a good ball in and all I had to do was direct it.

'It gave Burnley the kick up the backside they needed though, and they lifted their game and came at us. But we did well and our defence was outstanding.'

David Jones in action against Burnley.

The January transfer deadline has passed with two players joining the Rams and one heading out.

The departure is 20-year-old midfielder Nathan Doyle, who has joined Coca-Cola Championship side Hull City. He had been on loan at League One club Bradford City but has made a permanent switch to the KC Stadium for an undisclosed fee.

Coming in are striker Jon Macken — on a free transfer from Crystal Palace — along with defender Tyrone Mears on loan from West Ham United. They join Blackburn Rovers defender Jay McEveley, who signed earlier in the week.

'We are delighted to have all three on board, and I'm sure they will contribute greatly to this club,' boss Billy Davies revealed.

'We find ourselves in a wonderful position, and we don't want to mend something that isn't broken, but we do have to prepare for injuries and suspensions and have that competition in the squad.'

Of McEveley, Davies said 'He has great quality and a lovely left foot. Jay brings excellent quality into the squad and will add extra competition as he can play at centre-half or full-back.

'He is another one I feel will come in and improve over time, like Dean Leacock and one or two others.'

Mears is a player well-known to Davies, who worked with the 23-year-old at Preston North End until the pair left Deepdale in the summer. The full-back's career has stalled a bit this season after a difficult few months at West Ham, but Davies is a big admirer of his talents.

'We watched the young lad develop, and he did a wonderful job at Preston before getting his big move to West Ham,' the gaffer said.

'Tye is a very quick full-back who can play in several positions, he is an excellent professional and again is a very young man.

'We are delighted to have him on board, and I'm sure he will be looking forward to the challenge here.'

At 29, striker Macken is the most experienced of the week's captures. He also made his name at Preston – though left Deepdale before Davies arrived – and brings knowledge of the Championship as well as backup for Steve Howard.

'We looked around the market as the concern was always cover for Steve Howard; adding to the front area was important to us,' Davies said. 'We have asked Steve to do an awful lot since the start of the season so we are delighted to have signed an experienced striker who has been there before, and who was sold on for big money earlier in his career.

'Once we get working with him and get him fully fit, he will be a great addition.

'I would describe Jon as a Mark Hughes-style player – he is great with his back to the game, he is very clever at picking up positions and can link play very well, and he can put the ball in the back of the net.'

McEveley cited Davies's influence as a key reason for his move.

'I'm really excited about what lies ahead,' he said. 'I'm looking forward to the next three and a half years, and hope I can help take this club to where it belongs – the Premiership.

'When I sat down with Billy to talk to him he made me feel wanted. He said I was a good young player and that he wanted to make me stronger and fitter.

'In short, he wants to make me a better player, and I want that too. His enthusiasm was everything really. It made my mind up for me that I wanted to come and play for Derby County.'

For Mears, it was also an easy decision to make.

'I couldn't turn this chance down at all,' he revealed. 'There were a few clubs interested in me, but this was the team I wanted to come to.

'Billy always wants the best out of his players, and I don't know why, but my first training session was a bit of a shock with the intensity of it!

'He is very hungry and wants his team to be the best, he gets the best out of his players, he wants to get to the Premiership and win things.

'When you've worked with Billy you realise that and it makes you respect him so much and want to work hard.'

Macken, meanwhile, reckons he's joined 'a club on the move'.

'I'm obviously delighted as this is a great club that is going places – we are top of the League, on a fantastic run, and I'm over the moon to be here,' he said. 'I can see already that I'm joining a club on the move.

'Billy has got the boys playing some great football, we're at the top of the table and everything is geared up at the club for the Premiership.

'I'm delighted to be coming here, and I'll be looking to improve myself, to play football, to help the team be successful and win promotion.'

New signings Tyrone Mears, Jay McEveley and Jon Macken.

TABLE

	P	W	D	L	F	A	Pts
Derby	**30**	**18**	**5**	**7**	**39**	**28**	**59**
Birmingham	28	16	5	7	47	29	53
Preston	30	15	8	7	44	31	53
West Brom	30	15	7	8	56	36	52
Southampton	30	14	10	6	48	33	52
Cardiff	30	13	10	7	41	32	49
Stoke	30	13	9	8	39	25	48
Colchester	20	14	5	11	49	34	47
Sunderland	30	14	5	11	41	34	47
Wolves	30	13	7	10	31	32	46
Plymouth	30	10	12	8	40	39	42
Sheffield W	30	11	7	12	42	44	40
C Palace	30	10	9	11	36	35	39
Ipswich	30	11	6	13	40	40	39
Burnley	29	10	8	11	32	30	38
Coventry	30	11	4	15	30	38	37
Norwich	29	9	7	13	35	46	34
Leicester	29	8	9	12	29	38	33
Barnsley	30	9	5	16	33	48	32
Hull	30	8	7	15	31	42	31
Luton	30	8	7	15	37	51	31
QPR	30	8	6	16	35	47	30
Southend	30	6	9	15	26	47	27
Leeds	29	8	3	18	31	53	27

February

Another 100 percent month and a six-point gap opened up at the top of the table – not a bad way for the Rams to begin 2007. Add to that progress to the fifth round of the FA Cup for the first time since 1999 and it's not hard to see why excitement levels are rising around the city.

But with that comes increased expectation and a continuing run of crucial games.

A last–16 tie at Plymouth Argyle awaits in the FA Cup, but first it's a trip to fifth-placed Southampton.

The FA have confirmed that Billy Davies will not be charged after being sent to the stands by referee Mike Riley during Tuesday night's home victory over Burnley.

Davies now has a few more days to decide whether to appeal against being charged by the FA after being sent to the stands at Roots Hall during the victory at Southend on 20 January.

Billy Davies, whose passion on the touchline got him in trouble at the end of January.

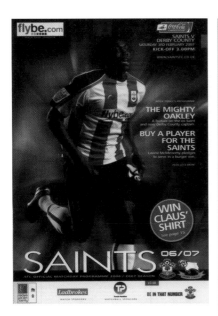

SOUTHAMPTON: Davis, Baird, Lundekvam (C), Pele, Bale, Wright, Idiakez, Viafara, Skacel (McGoldrick 54), Rasiak (Dyer 77), Saganowski (Wright-Phillips 53).
UNUSED SUBS: Bialkowski, Ostlund.

RAMS: Bywater, Edworthy, Leacock, Moore, Camara, Oakley (C) (Mears 84), Pearson, Jones, Malcolm (Teale 35), Fagan (Barnes 53), Howard.
UNUSED SUBS: M. Johnson, Lupoli.

ATTENDANCE: 27,656.

After early pressure, a tactical change saw Gary Teale come on for Bob Malcolm in the first half.

REPORT – 3 FEBRUARY 2007
SOUTHAMPTON 0
DERBY COUNTY 1

Southampton broke quickly after kick-off with Rudi Skacel finding space down the left, and his low cross was sliced goalwards by Marek Saganowski from 16 yards – forcing Stephen Bywater into a fine save.

Gareth Bale's storming run down the left earned the game's first corner, and as the Saints forced a second they almost opened the scoring. Skacel whipped it back in across goal, where both Saganowski and Rasiak just needed to get a touch to poke it home. Even then, the ball bounced off the far post and along the line before being cleared to safety.

Rasiak again came close in the 14th minute when he capitalised on a loose ball just outside the Derby box and took a touch to steady himself, but he fired wide of the target with only Bywater to beat.

Saints rattled the frame of the goal just after the half-hour mark when Jhon Viafara smashed one goalwards that Bywater pushed onto the woodwork. The ball then came back across for Saganowski, who headed wide from six yards when it looked easier to score.

Derby made their first change of the afternoon with 35 minutes gone as Teale came on for Malcolm, though there looked to be no obvious injury to the former Rangers man.

The Rams were beginning to get more of a foothold in the game, though with five minutes to go before half-time home 'keeper Kelvin Davis was still to be tested.

Bywater produced another good block to deny Rasiak as half-time approached, and the whistle blew with Derby relieved to still be on level terms. And having improved towards the end of the first half the Rams showed more in the early stages of the second, culminating in Fagan shooting wide after a good move.

Pearson was beginning to show his class for Derby with a number of surging runs from the centre circle as the game looked to be opening up.

The visitors had a good chance in the 69th minute after some trickery down the left to Barnes.

His cross was cleared out to Pearson, who headed the ball back towards the danger area, only for it to return to him once more, and this time he went for a deft chip that sailed safely over.

Then Pearson should have opened the scoring on 71 minutes.

Barnes and Jones combined on the right for Jones to float a lovely ball over that Howard rose and headed back across goal, but Pearson could only nod over from seven yards.

But with nine minutes to go Howard rammed home what proved to be the winning goal.

Barnes, impressive since coming on, showed great awareness on the left to beat two men and cut the ball back to the on-rushing Jones.

Jones's initial shot was blocked on the edge of the six-yard box, but it rolled out to Derby's leading scorer, who showed typical ruthlessness to lash it into the roof of the net.

Not surprisingly, Southampton threw everything forward in the latter stages in a bid to try and rescue the game.

The ball spent a lot of time travelling towards the Derby box, but each time it was met by some sturdy resistance from those in Rams shirts.

REACTION

Billy Davies pointed to the introduction of Gary Teale after half an hour as a turning point in the Rams' vital Coca-Cola Championship win at Southampton.

The Saints had been in control of the game from the first whistle, but Davies changed his tactics around by throwing on winger Teale in place of defensive midfielder Bob Malcolm.

'I got it wrong at the start – we decided to play a certain way and unfortunately one or two didn't quite understand what we wanted,' the boss said.

'We caused problems for ourselves early in the game as we knew they would come out quickly, but we helped them with the way we started.

'We made the changes, and in the last 15 minutes of the first half we threw one or two punches back, and after the break we fully deserved it.

'I will take responsibility for the start, and I will certainly take responsibility for the change I felt won us the game: bringing on Gary Teale.

'At times we rode our luck slightly, but we showed great courage and determination to get all three points.'

Darren Moore always felt one goal would settle the clash between the fifth and top-placed teams in the Coca-Cola Championship – and says the Rams deserved their three points.

'It was great for us to get another 1–0 win today, and again we showed great spirit and determination to come away with the points,' Moore said.

'Southampton are a very good team and tough to beat at home, and in the first half they put us under pressure.

'The tactical switch of Gary Teale coming on changed the game for us, and we finished the first half well, and the second half was there for all to see.

'For us to come here and get the three points is magnificent.

'The run we are on keeps confidence up and gives us that momentum.

Pearson's runs in midfield help relieve the pressure on Derby's defence.

David Jones's shot was blocked, but Howard was there to score from the loose ball.

The players celebrate the late winner.

Billy Davies has picked up his second Coca-Cola Championship Manager of the Month award of the season.

'Obviously I'm delighted on behalf of everyone at Derby County – the players, staff, everyone connected with the club,' he said.

'I'm picking up this award on behalf of them, and we are delighted with what was a tremendous achievement in January.

'Hopefully we can continue this from now until the end of the season.'

DERBY: Bywater, Edworthy, Moore, Leacock, McEveley, Teale (Macken 73), Oakley (C) (Bisgaard 84), Pearson, Jones, Barnes (Lupoli 89), Howard.
UNUSED SUBS: M. Johnson, Mears.

HULL: Myhill, Dawson, Coles (C), Turner, Forster, McPhee, Parkin (Windass 61), Delaney, Welsh (Parlour 61), Ricketts, Livermore.
UNUSED: Duke, Elliott, Duffy.

ATTENDANCE: 28,140.

'We were disciplined in the second half today, and it was always going to be one goal that settled the game.

'I'm very pleased that it came to us, and we were able to close the game out.'

The Rams cemented their six-point advantage at the top of the Coca-Cola Championship by seeing off one of their rivals at the right end of the table last weekend.

Now struggling Hull City – third from bottom and in danger of relegation – head to Pride Park with their own battle to fight.

'We've gone unbeaten through January and now into February, so we want to continue that,' Oakley revealed. 'Hull is as big a game as Southampton now.

'The home fans are going to be expecting us to win the game, but if we were to slip up it would only be like beating Hull and losing to Southampton.

'We've got to keep rolling on, getting the points, and pushing the teams further and further away from us.'

Forward Craig Fagan will miss the next two matches after picking up his 10th yellow card of the season in Saturday's 1–0 win at Southampton.

The 24-year-old has been booked in his last two Rams outings, taking him over the threshold for a second ban of the campaign. He was booked eight times for Hull City before joining Derby in January for £750,000 and had already served a one-match suspension while at the KC Stadium.

He will be suspended for Saturday's visit of the Tigers to Pride Park, and he will be ruled out of the FA Cup fifth-round clash at Plymouth Argyle on 17 February.

The Football Association has confirmed that Billy Davies has denied a charge of abusive and/or insulting words towards a match official. The charge relates to the Rams manager's conduct during the match at Southend United on 20 January. Davies has requested a personal hearing.

REPORT – 10 FEBRUARY 2007
DERBY COUNTY 2
HULL CITY 2

The best move of the early stages came nine minutes in when Matt Oakley started things in the middle and fed David Jones, who in turn played McEveley away down the left. The former Blackburn man's cross was inviting, but Steve Howard couldn't get a vital touch to it at the far post.

Howard was closer on 18 minutes from Teale's delicious right-wing cross with a flicked effort that Myhill spectacularly dived to grab.

The visitors could have taken the lead just before the half-hour mark with an almighty scramble in front of goal that saw no less than three efforts cleared off the line. But from that, Derby showed why they are top of the table.

They immediately broke away down the left through Stephen Pearson, who ran some 60 yards before showing great vision to pick out a low cross along the edge of the box that found Teale.

The Scotsman had time to take a touch and compose himself before firing the ball low past Myhill for his first Derby County goal.

But the joy was short-lived as on 32 minutes the visitors were level.

Darren Moore was pulled up for a foul on Jon Parkin just outside the box, and up stepped Andy Dawson to curl a lovely effort over the wall and past Bywater's out-stretched arms.

It was the first goal Derby had conceded since the New Year's Day win at Preston.

Derby broke at pace once more on 41 minutes and another fine move should have seen them go back in front.

Barnes, Teale and Jones were all involved, before McEveley crossed from the left and Pearson met it with a powerful downward header, but his effort was saved by the feet of Myhill. Either side of the goalkeeper and it would have undoubtedly been in the back of the net.

And in stoppage time they were back in front.

Jones swung over a corner from the left, and Moore met it with a downward header that looked to be going wide, but was watched into the back of the net.

Hull forced a couple of corners to open the second half up, but Derby defended them well, and then the home side forced Myhill into a low save when Barnes drove goalwards from 20 yards.

Myhill grabbed Pearson's low effort on 69 minutes, but Hull were battling for everything and there was a sense that Derby needed a third goal to make things more secure.

Myhill looked less assured than he had done all afternoon as Barnes turned inside the box to hit a weak shot that the goalkeeper could only fumble around the post for a corner.

Jones's free-kick from 25 yards was blocked by the Hull wall, but Derby kept up the pressure and forced a corner on the left – again taken by Jones – but it came to nothing.

Teale celebrates scoring his first goal for Derby.

The rest of the team arrive to join the celebration.

Bisgaard has a shot as Derby look for a winner.

Nothing, that was, apart from a Hull break that led to their equaliser.

Sam Ricketts found space down the right with two minutes left and pulled a fine low ball back for David Livermore to drive home from 10 yards.

REACTION

Billy Davies pledged his side would stay 'calm and focused' after picking up a point against Hull City that the boss believes could be crucial at the end of the campaign.

'We've let in a late goal today, and it means we picked up an important point that could have been three,' Davies said after the 2–2 home draw.

'That said, other teams would have taken a point today.

'We've increased our lead at the top of the table from six points to seven, and a return of seven points from the last three games has to be good.

'There will be plenty of twists and turns between now and the end of the season, but we have 63 points and with only 14 games left there is no reason not to be upbeat and positive.

'We just have to keep ticking the games off.'

Goalscorer Gary Teale admitted that the Rams paid the price for not killing off Hull City after the visitors fought back to equalise late and earn a 2–2 draw at Pride Park.

Teale had put Derby in front after 29 minutes of an important Coca-Cola Championship encounter for both sides.

Andy Dawson equalised quickly, but Darren Moore restored the lead and it looked as though Derby would hold on until David Livermore earned the visitors a point at the death.

'I think over the course of the game we probably deserved to win,' Teale said. 'But teams will fight all the way at this stage of the season, and a point is worth a lot to them as they want to stay in the League.

'Fair play to Hull as they kept going and got their equaliser, but we should have put the game to bed well before then.

'We need to take our chances, but the good thing is we're creating them, but at the moment we're not killing teams off.'

Skipper Matt Oakley will miss the FA Cup fifth-round tie at Plymouth Argyle after picking up his fifth booking of the season in Saturday's 2–2 Coca-Cola Championship draw with Hull City.

Marc Edworthy.

The 29-year-old was cautioned for unsporting behaviour nine minutes before the end of the game against the Tigers, earning him a one-match ban.

Defender Lewin Nyatanga has joined Coca-Cola Championship side Barnsley on loan until 6 May. The 18-year-old is heading to Oakwell for a spell with the Championship relegation-battlers in a bid to get more first-team football under his belt.

Nyatanga is a product of Derby's Academy and was a regular in the starting line up last season but has found opportunities hard to come by this time around. He was loaned to Sunderland for the last three months of 2006 and will hope to gain plenty of experience with Simon Davey's men.

Rams boss Billy Davies has said he is willing to let some of his players head out on loan to get first-team football, and Nyatanga is the second departure this week, following goalkeeper Lee Camp's move to Queen's Park Rangers.

The Rams will break another record when they take on Plymouth at Home Park on Saturday – by chartering a plane to a domestic match for the first time in the club's history.

Table-topping Derby's fifth-round FA Cup tie is the first time the club have got to that stage of the prestigious competition since 1999, and the side will be literally flying high as they bid to reach the quarter-finals.

A 31-seater Scotairways Dorner 328 aircraft, complete with captain, first officer and cabin crew member, has been arranged to take Billy Davies and his squad from East Midlands Airport to Plymouth Airport – a journey that would take around five hours by coach.

At a stage of the season when the fixtures are piling up thick and fast – the Rams take on Stoke City in the Coca-Cola Championship at Pride Park Stadium just four days after – the flight should help aid player recovery.

Rams managing director Mike Horton explained 'As far as I know this is the first time this has been done in the club's history.

'The management, coaching staff and medical team feel a one-hour plane flight will be much more beneficial to the players' recovery than a five-hour coach journey, especially in light of the Stoke game coming so soon after Plymouth.'

Davies added 'The club have recognised the need to do all we possibly can to prepare the players for the remaining matches of the season.

'It's very important that, with the Stoke game on the Wednesday night, we recover from our efforts at Plymouth as quickly as we can, and we believe a short flight will help us do that.

'As we enter the business end of the season that extra little one percent we're able to get out of the players here and there could be very helpful in achieving our aims.'

Billy Davies wants the Rams to seize the opportunity to put themselves into the quarter-final of the FA Cup when they head to Plymouth Argyle.

Saturday's fifth-round tie against the Pilgrims gives Derby the chance to reach the last eight of the competition for the first time since 1999.

Home Park is a tough place to go at the best of times, and the Rams have already been beaten there in the Coca-Cola Championship this season, but Davies is looking forward to the task.

'It would be first class if we can put ourselves into the next round, and that is our intention,' Davies said. 'We want to go as far as we can and keep that winning mentality going through the club.'

Stephen Pearson.

David Jones.

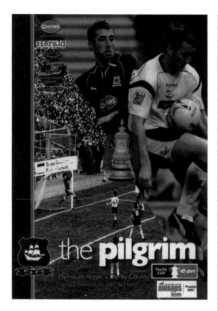

PLYMOUTH: McCormick, Nalis, Timar, Norris, Ebanks-Blake, Gallen, Sawyer, Seip, Connolly, Sinclair, Gosling (Halmosi 77).
UNUSED SUBS: Hodges, Clapham, Summerfield, Djordjic.

DERBY: Bywater, Mears, Leacock, Moore, Camara, Bisgaard, Pearson, Jones (Barnes 45), S. Johnson (M. Johnson 69), Smith (Macken 45), Howard.
UNUSED SUBS: Peschisolido, Lupoli.

ATTENDANCE: 18,026.

Dean Leacock is shown the yellow card after the challenge which gave away the first penalty.

REPORT – 17 FEBRUARY 2007
PLYMOUTH ARGYLE 2
DERBY COUNTY 0
FA CUP FIFTH ROUND

The home side started brightly and would have gone ahead in the fourth minute had it not been for a brilliant Bywater stop. Sylvan Ebanks-Blake spread the ball out to the left where it was picked up by the livewire Scott Sinclair, who cut inside and unleashed a curler from 20 yards that Bywater dived full-stretch to his left to save.

The first sign of real drama came in the 12th minute when Gallen bore down on goal, chased by Dean Leacock.

Gallen twisted and turned into the box before going down under what appeared to be little contact. However, the referee thought differently and instantly awarded a penalty, as well as booking the Rams defender.

Up stepped Gallen to score past Bywater to his left, although the Rams stopper did guess the direction correctly and was unlucky not to push the ball round the post.

With 17 minutes played, Krisztian Timar felled Steve Howard 25 yards out from goal in a central position and up stepped David Jones to take the resulting set-piece, one which he curled just over the bar with Luke McCormick at full stretch.

On 28 minutes Bywater pulled another outstanding save out of the bag.

Dan Gosling cut in on the right of the box and curled a left-footer in towards the back post, and it was only the fingertips of the Derby man that took it inches round the woodwork. And as the ball came over from a corner, Moore was adjudged to have been pushing Timar inside the box – in what looked like another soft decision – and a penalty was awarded.

However, this time justice was served as Gallen opted to shoot to Bywater's right and the 'keeper flung himself the very same way to palm the ball to safety.

It was the Rams who were attempting to finish the half strongest and put the memory of those two contentious spot-kicks behind them, and both Bisgaard and Pearson saw shots blocked as the interval approached.

On 54 minutes Sinclair sent a ball in at the near post from the Plymouth right that was meant as a cross, but it drifted towards the goal and Bywater was forced to tip it over.

Soon after, Derby came mightily close to levelling, following a hefty ball forward by centre-half Leacock.

The perfect pass found its intended target, Macken, and he took a touch before unleashing a fierce curler from just inside the box that McCormick was forced to tip over.

In what was a pulsating Cup tie followed even more drama with 25 minutes to go when Moore saw red for a second bookable offence.

On 70 minutes Howard, so often a Rams scorer himself, turned provider when he looped a ball over the Pilgrims defence to Macken, his strike partner's shot deflecting over off Timar.

Macken himself got on the end of the resulting Bisgaard header but could only put it over.

Plymouth then broke to the other end and Nalis's cross cut open the

Derby defence and found the head of Gallen, who should have done better than simply heading the ball into the arms of Bywater.

A neat moved saw Howard play in Pearson on the left, and he rolled it back to Bisgaard, whose shot from the edge of the area was deflected behind.

However, the corner that followed was wasted. And almost immediately the Rams were made to pay the price.

The Pilgrims counter-attacked and, after beating the off-side trap, David Norris crossed from the right and Sinclair, standing virtually on the penalty spot, rose superbly to head past Bywater and in off the post.

REACTION

Derby manager Billy Davies is keen to get his hands on the match video so he can watch again the controversial incidents that saw his side knocked out of the FA Cup at Plymouth.

The Rams boss refused to level any criticism at the match officials following the 2–0 defeat at Home Park, but he did say that he had 'raised eyebrows' during the game at some of the decisions made.

The visitors saw two penalties awarded against them – one scored and one missed by Kevin Gallen – and also had Darren Moore sent off in the 65th minute, something which bemused many onlookers.

But Derby were denied a penalty themselves in the second half when sub Jon Macken's shot hit the arm of a Plymouth player inside their area.

All of this will make interesting viewing for Davies when he watches it again.

He said 'We are bitterly disappointed to be out of the Cup as we were very keen to progress.

'We didn't battle as well as Plymouth in the first 45 minutes and our style of play didn't suit the spongy conditions as much as theirs did, but we were a lot better after the break.

'We were denied a penalty at 1–0 down which did seem a bit odd

Darren Moore is furious with referee Mike Dean after a challenge that left Kevin Gallen on the ground.

Seth Johnson.

The Derby players leave the field at the end of the game.

David Jones runs with the ball.

because as far as I know the rules say that if a player raises an arm to block a ball in the box it is a penalty.

'But as for the decisions against us, all I would say is that I really do need to see them again before making any further comment. I had raised eyebrows when they were made, but would like to take another look.'

Teenage defender James Meredith has joined Coca-Cola League One side Chesterfield on a one-month emergency loan. The 18-year-old will make the move to Saltergate, where his temporary boss will be Rams legend Roy McFarland.

Meredith is an Academy product who was born in Albury, Australia, and he signed a two-year professional deal with the club in the summer of 2006. He has yet to make a first-team appearance for the Rams and has also been out on loan to Conference National side Cambridge United this season.

Big defender Darren Moore will miss Wednesday evening's Coca-Cola Championship clash with Stoke City with a one-match ban.

The centre-half was sent off in Saturday's FA Cup exit at Plymouth Argyle after collecting two yellow cards in a short space of time during the second half.

But clear of suspension will be skipper Matt Oakley and forward Craig Fagan, who will be available again after one and two-match absences respectively.

All eyes are focusing firmly on the Coca-Cola Championship campaign, with the Rams into the 'business end' of their season.

That's the verdict of boss Billy Davies as he takes his table-toppers into the final 14 games of what has already been an exciting first season in charge. And he is prepared for Derby to give as good as they get in what promises to be a thrilling run-in.

'We now focus firmly on the League campaign and the last 14 matches,' he said. 'We know exactly what needs to be done but there will be plenty of very difficult games for Derby and everyone else in the League.

'There will be blips, there will be changes, so it is time for calm heads between now and the end of the season.

'We could be fighting against relegation, we could be mid-table with nowhere to go, but instead we have given ourselves a great opportunity.

'There are some great games to look forward to and we know how difficult it will be, but at the same time we are very pleased to take on the challenge.'

Derby's next task is the clash on Wednesday night with Stoke City, as the Potters travel to Pride Park shorn of a number of key players, but Tony Pulis's side will provide a typically tough test.

'There are no easy games, whether you're at the top or the bottom of the table,' Davies said. 'We know that along the way there will be plenty of tough matches for us, but that's the same for everyone at the business end of the League.

'We are looking forward to the challenge.'

REPORT – 21 FEBRUARY 2007
DERBY COUNTY 0
STOKE CITY 2

Steve Howard had the game's first shot on target, a safe 30-yarder that Steve Simonsen dealt with, but Derby were in trouble on nine minutes when Mamady Sidibe ran away on a long ball and was tugged back by Dean Leacock.

It was only a yellow card for the centre-half, but the visitors had a free-kick in a dangerous left-wing position that ultimately came to nothing.

Then the visitors were given the chance to go in front from the penalty spot. Darel Russell's corner found Leacock's arm some 10 yards out and up stepped Higginbotham, who drove the ball low into the bottom-left corner.

Derby pressed for an immediate equaliser and a good move saw Oakley drive goalwards, only for his 25-yarder to curl safely over.

On 21 minutes Howard headed over a fine David Jones free-kick when well placed just outside the six-yard box.

Hendrie's free-kick was deflected away for a left-wing corner, which he took himself, and that led to the lead being doubled when Dominic Matteo ghosted in to head powerfully home from close range.

After half an hour a low Oakley half-volley forced Simonsen into a sharp save after a good move ended with Mears's clever cross, but the visiting custodian was never really in danger.

Indeed, the visitors should have extended their advantage further before the break, but Russell shot wide when in space on the edge of the box.

Derby needed to start the second half well, and they did so by getting plenty of possession in and around the Stoke box, although they failed to make anything of their efforts.

They came close on 53 minutes when Oakley's deflected effort from well outside the box forced Simonsen to scramble across his goal and turn the ball away for a corner.

DERBY: Bywater, Edworthy, Leacock (Mears 15), M. Johnson, McEveley, Teale, Oakley (C), Jones (Pearson 68), Fagan, Howard, Macken (Lupoli 60).
UNUSED SUBS: Peschisolido, Grant.

STOKE: Simonsen, Hoefkens, Sidibe (Rooney 88), Higginbottom (C), Hendrie (Dickinson 83), Russell, Diao, Matteo (Eustace 62), Griffin, Lawrence, Zakuani.
UNUSED SUBS: Martin, Hoult.

ATTENDANCE: 24,897.

Lupoli started to celebrate his goal before finding out it had been disallowed.

Pearson's shot is saved as Derby try to score.

Gary Teale heads clear.

Stoke failed to clear properly after Jones's weak delivery, and McEveley whipped a cross back in, only for Howard to head straight at Simonsen.

A spell of pressure two minutes later resulted in Howard somehow heading Teale's perfect right-wing cross straight at Simonsen – either side of the custodian and it would surely have been a goal.

Jones cracked a 20-yarder just past the post on 66 minutes, but for all their efforts Derby were still in desperate need of a goal from somewhere.

Lupoli had the ball in the back of the net on 73 minutes, but the whistle had already blown to pull him back for offside, though the Italian hadn't heard it and looked crest-fallen to discover his finish had been chalked off. Howard was then denied again as Simonsen turned away his close-range effort after McEveley's free-kick had been deflected his way.

The game ended with a bit of a ruck involving some two thirds of the players on the pitch, but referee Keith Stroud issued just the one yellow card – to Derby's McEveley.

REACTION

Billy Davies had no complaints with the officials about the two goals conceded against Stoke City on Wednesday night – but he was disappointed with his side's display in the first half.

'I think it was a clear handball for the penalty, and we can't complain about that, but I really did feel that Lupoli was onside for his goal in the second half and so did he, so that was disappointing,' the Rams boss said.

'The first goal is always crucial against Stoke because of the way they play. It was a very poor goal to give away, and then we had to work hard to get back into the game.

'We showed great effort, energy and wonderful spirit after the break, but we couldn't get the ball in the back of the net.

'This was a lost opportunity, but I've just said to the players that with 13 matches remaining we are still sitting at the top of the League.

'We gave away two sloppy goals tonight, but I can't fault the players in the second half. We just didn't get the breaks.'

Matt Oakley admitted the Rams were always up against it after going two goals down in a short space of time as they fell to their first League defeat since Boxing Day.

Goals on 12 and 25 minutes gave visitors Stoke City all three points as Derby struggled to recover from a sluggish start and missed a chance to extend their advantage at the top of the Coca-Cola Championship.

'They came here with a plan, and I thought we started the game well, then the penalty changed the way the game was going to go,' skipper Oakley said.

'It was a definite penalty, and then they hit us with another one soon afterwards. That goal killed us a bit because we then found ourselves two goals down quickly.

'The referee's decision for the penalty was right, but I think he made quite a few late in the game that were wrong.

'I felt Lupoli's goal was onside, and I think that would have changed the game if it had have stood.'

Youngster Lionel Ainsworth has joined Coca-Cola League Two side Wycombe Wanderers on loan until the end of the season. The 19-year-old Academy product has made only two substitute appearances for the Rams since signing professional forms and is joining Paul Lambert's promotion-chasers in a bid to get some first-team football under his belt.

Learn the lessons of seasons past – that's the message from Billy Davies to his Rams players as the Coca-Cola Championship rumbles excitingly on.

Davies has seen his side go as far as seven points clear at the top of the table in recent weeks, only for that advantage to be whittled down to just one.

Derby missed a good chance to extend their lead on Wednesday night when they were beaten 2–0 at home to Stoke City, and the gaffer wants his players to take heed from what has happened to other clubs in similar positions over the years.

'We reminded the players last night that being first in February and then maybe dropping down a place or two would not be a reason to panic,' he said. 'It is where we are at the end of the season that counts.'

'Experience over the years tells you that Ipswich, who were clear at the top a couple of years ago and ended up losing out in a Play-off semi-final to West Ham, who went on and won promotion from nowhere, is a good lesson for us all.

'We need to keep calm and be ready for the remaining matches.

'It will fluctuate between now and the end of the season, there will be dips and disappointments, but the most important thing to know is that there will always be another opportunity coming up.'

Derby's next opportunity to get back on the winning run comes on Saturday, in the shape of a visit to Sunderland – the Championship's in-form team.

Jay McEveley is predicting a 'proper football match' when the Rams travel to Sunderland on Saturday. The Black Cats are in great form as they are unbeaten in the Coca-Cola Championship this year, and Roy Keane has got them playing some excellent stuff.

'We have got to go up there and match them first and foremost, and then hopefully we can play a bit of football,' the defender said.

'They will like to get the ball down and play so it could be a proper football match, which the lads will like.'

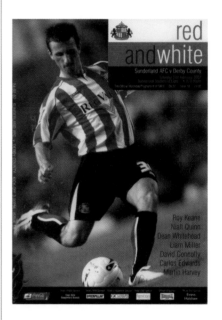

REPORT – 24 FEBRUARY 2007
SUNDERLAND 2
DERBY COUNTY 1

The home side had the first chance of the afternoon on 11 minutes through Tobias Hysen, who tricked his way into space inside the Derby box but fired across goal from a narrow angle.

Derby's midfield – with skipper Matt Oakley sitting between Pearson and David Jones – looked more compact in the early stages of the game than it had done in recent weeks.

Sunderland were awarded a controversial penalty on 27 minutes for what looked to be the most trivial of offences. Edwards crossed low, and as David Connolly tried to turn referee Martin Atkinson blew his whistle to pull up Edworthy for an apparent tug on the striker's shirt.

Connolly himself stepped up to fire the penalty past Stephen Bywater – bizarrely, it was Sunderland's first penalty in any game since November 2005.

SUNDERLAND: Ward, Simpson, Evans, Edwards, Nosworthy, Collins, Hysen (Leadbitter 68), John (Murphy 57), Connolly, Yorke (C), L. Miller.
UNUSED SUBS: T. Miller, Varga, Fulop.

DERBY: Bywater, Mears, Edworthy, Moore, McEveley, Oakley (C), Jones, Pearson (M. Johnson 85), Teale (Barnes HT), Howard, Fagan (Peschisolido 70).
UNUSED SUBS: Macken, Grant.

ATTENDANCE: 36,049.

Craig Fagan takes on Sunderland's Danny Simpson.

Howard celebrates Giles Barnes's equaliser.

Giles Barnes is mobbed by the Rams players.

They almost doubled their lead two minutes later as Danny Simpson skipped down the right and crossed for Stern John to volley wide.

Sunderland were getting up a head of steam and came close again as Hysen found space, though his shot was deflected into the arms of Bywater. John then volleyed straight at Bywater from inside the six-yard box when it looked easier to score.

On 41 minutes Derby won their first corner as Ward turned away Gary Teale's crossed free-kick, but it was only blocked out for a throw-in that the Rams failed to make the most of.

Their first effort on target came with 90 seconds remaining of the first half as Howard flicked on McEveley's long throw from the left, but Teale's header was comfortable for Ward.

Derby threw on Giles Barnes in place of Gary Teale at half-time, and the teenager had an immediate chance to level matters as Jones fed Fagan down the right, who crossed to the far post, where Barnes rose unchallenged but headed over from eight yards.

The visiting pressure continued as McEveley's low cross was prodded goalwards by Howard, who forced Ward to turn it over the bar. Jones's corner was then deflected out to Oakley, who cracked one in from 25 yards that Ward again tipped over the woodwork.

From the resulting corner, Howard's header was cleared off the line by Danny Collins. Then just before the hour the Rams were level thanks to a goal right out of the top drawer.

McEveley played the ball up to Howard, who flicked it on to Barnes with his back to goal on the edge of the box, with three players around him.

Barnes showed a turn that no less a player than Ronaldinho would have been proud of before steadying himself and smashing a low shot firmly past Ward.

Murphy struck a post from 18 yards after turning well on the edge of the box, with Sunderland beginning to enjoy a spell of pressure on 76 minutes.

Bywater then dived bravely at the feet of Dwight Yorke, who had advanced from midfield.

The players' heads drop as Liam Miller scores the late winner for Sunderland.

Barnes shows his appreciation to the travelling contingent.

The Rams broke in stoppage time and won a corner on the left, but failed to make the most of it. And they were made to pay right at the death. Leadbitter whipped over a cross from the left, and Miller got the slightest of touches to glance it home from six yards.

REACTION

Rams boss Billy Davies felt his side suffered an undeserved defeat at the hands of Sunderland after being beaten in stoppage time following a stirring second-half performance.

Derby trailed at the interval thanks to David Connolly's 26th-minute penalty but came out fighting after the break and warranted Giles Barnes's superb equaliser just before the hour.

It looked as though they would take home a superb point from the Stadium of Light until Liam Miller had the last word with a glancing header deep into stoppage time.

'In the first half there was another controversial penalty against us, but after the break only one team was going to win the game,' Davies said. 'We had chance after chance and deserved to be two or three goals ahead – the game should have been dead and buried, but then we lost a disappointing goal at the end.

'Today we deserved an awful lot more than what we got after coming to a very big club and having a right good go in the second half.'

Marc Edworthy felt that the Rams were dealt a bad decision for the penalty that put them behind at Sunderland.

David Connolly struck it home on 26 minutes after Edworthy himself was harshly adjudged to have been tugging the striker's shirt.

'We've been hard done by on penalties lately, we've not had many ourselves and it seems as if everything is going against us,' he said.

'I spoke to the referee and the linesman at half-time – the linesman didn't flag, and he said he didn't see anything.

'What the referee didn't see is that there's a lot of pushing and shoving going on inside the box; Connolly is tugging my shirt and maybe I've got my hand on his back.

'There's a lot of pulling and shoving going on in there, but he's given the penalty this time.'

TABLE

	P	W	D	L	F	A	Pts
Birmingham	34	19	7	8	52	33	64
West Brom	35	18	9	8	62	39	63
Derby	**34**	**19**	**6**	**9**	**43**	**34**	**63**
Sunderland	35	18	6	11	52	36	60
Southampton	35	16	11	8	56	39	59
Cardiff	35	16	11	8	50	36	59
Preston	34	17	8	9	50	38	59
Wolves	35	17	8	10	38	35	59
Stoke	35	14	11	10	42	28	53
Colchester	35	15	7	13	54	40	52
C Palace	35	13	9	13	42	39	48
Plymouth	34	11	14	9	46	44	47
Leicester	34	11	11	12	37	40	44
Sheffield W	34	12	8	14	49	53	44
Coventry	35	12	6	17	35	47	42
Norwich	33	11	8	14	42	52	41
Burnley	34	10	10	14	35	37	40
Ipswich	34	11	6	17	40	46	39
Barnsley	35	11	5	19	39	58	38
Luton	35	9	9	17	44	59	36
Hull	34	9	8	17	35	48	35
QPR	34	9	8	17	39	54	35
Southend	35	7	10	18	34	56	31
Leeds	35	9	4	22	34	59	31

March

Derby came close to slowing down the Sunderland steam train – and it could be the Black Cats who prove a major threat in the closing weeks of the season. Roy Keane's side are yet to be beaten since the turn of the year but know they got a bit lucky against the Rams.

Birmingham City have taken over the top spot, and they host Derby at St Andrews later this month.

But first it's a televised Friday night encounter at Pride Park with Colchester United – looking to spring a surprise themselves and sneak into the Play-offs.

Having depth in his squad has given Rams boss Billy Davies plenty of choices as he looks to counter the likely absence of Stephen Pearson and Dean Leacock from his side on Friday night.

Pearson and Leacock are struggling to be ready in time to face Colchester United at Pride Park with foot and hand injuries respectively.

However, Davies has options at his disposal and says that whoever comes in will be itching to take their chance as the Coca-Cola Championship season continues to move excitingly forward.

'That's why you need a squad as you know there will be injuries and suspensions at this time of year, and you've got to be ready for that,' Davies revealed.

'It is important we do have that depth and freshness so there will be one or two I'm sure who will be looking forward to starting on Friday, and one or two looking forward to getting a goal or two.

'Stephen and Dean are both very doubtful for Friday, and we also have Paul Boertien and Richard Jackson struggling with injuries. But other than that everyone is OK.'

Goalkeeper Stephen Bywater wants to use Friday's game against Colchester United to send out a message to the rest of the Division. The Coca-Cola Championship encounter is being broadcast live on Sky Sports and will give Derby the chance to return to the top of the table ahead of the rest of the weekend's fixtures.

And Bywater says putting on a good display in front of the cameras will remind their rivals that the Rams are a force to be reckoned with.

'We have lost a few, and we're going to rectify that situation, starting on Friday when we play Colchester,' the shot-stopper said.

'Especially with it being on Sky as well, because other clubs will be watching, so we want them to think "Derby have got a team here".

'I was watching Cardiff v Preston [a 4–1 victory for the home side] the other day, and I thought to myself that Preston have gone.

'I want to give the impression that Derby have a strong squad and are playing good football.

'It is good to be on Sky because it sends a message to other teams that we mean business – come and play us, be scared of playing Derby.'

DERBY: Bywater, Edworthy, Moore, M. Johnson (Mears 45), McEveley, Oakley (C) (Macken 81), Jones, Teale, Barnes, Lupoli (Fagan 68), Howard.
UNUSED SUBS: Bisgaard, Grant.

COLCHESTER: Gerken, White (Baldwin 72), Jackson, Brown, Watson (Ephraim 72), Duguid (C), Cureton (Iwelumo HT), Izzet, Garcia, Barker, Mills.
UNUSED SUBS: Davison, McLeod.

ATTENDANCE: 26,704.

Darren Moore is beaten by Richard Garcia.

REPORT – 2 MARCH 2007
DERBY COUNTY 5
COLCHESTER UNITED 1

The returning Giles Barnes had an immediate impact as the Rams came out of the blocks flying with a goal in the second minute. He broke from midfield and laid the ball off to Steve Howard in a right-wing position, who exchanged passes with Gary Teale before whipping over a beautiful ball to the far post. Howard's cross was just too high for Lupoli, but David Jones was on hand to smash it into the net from eight yards.

Visiting 'keeper Dean Gerken did well to punch away a deflected corner from under his own crossbar in the 12th minute as the Rams looked to capitalise on their lightning opening.

It was not hard to see why Colchester had settled well in their first season in the Championship, but on 19 minutes Derby cut through them like a knife through butter and doubled their lead.

Jones broke up play in midfield and played Barnes away down the right, who fired over a wonderful first-time cross that Lupoli met with a bullet-like volley from 10 yards out, but over to the left and from a narrow angle. The ball was past Gerken before he had chance to move and the back of the net was billowing.

And by 29 minutes the Rams were totally rampant.

Barnes found a bit of space on the left and made ground inside the box before, despite being closed down by three Colchester defenders, squeezing the ball past Gerken from the narrowest of angles for his second goal in as many games.

Matt Oakley then strode forward on 33 minutes but curled safely over with his left-footed effort from 25 yards as Derby went looking for more.

The Rams showcased some of their training-ground set-piece work with three minutes to go before half-time as Jones and Oakley combined to set up Barnes, who shot wide from 25 yards.

And they were almost four ahead on 50 minutes as McEveley's long ball sent Barnes away down the left, only for the teenager's shot to flash across goal.

The visitors pulled one back on 55 minutes – as they had threatened to do since the restart – when ex-Ram Johnnie Jackson headed home from close range after Duguid broke down the right.

More Barnes magic in the 61st minute won Derby a penalty. This time the teenager was in a tight space down in the left-corner but turned superbly before being hacked down by White inside the box.

There were no complaints from the Colchester players, and up stepped Howard to drive his shot low past Gerken for his 15th goal of the season.

Most of Pride Park thought it was five when Gary Teale went through and smashed his shot past Gerken, but it flew the wrong side of the post before running along the outside of the back of the net.

But it was five on 68 minutes. A long ball was picked up by Jones, who drove low across the box where it was turned past his own goalkeeper by the unfortunate Chris Barker.

It could have been six shortly after, but Gerken – who had stood no chance with any of the goals – produced a fine block to deny Jones from close range.

Jackson missed a sitter on 78 minutes after dragging his shot well wide when excellently placed, though Derby didn't make the most of a quick break.

Duguid forced a good stoppage time save from Bywater, though that was the 'keeper's only serious action all night.

REACTION

The 'crisis' at Derby County is officially over! That was the tongue-in-cheek comment of Billy Davies after Friday night's 5–1 win over Colchester put the Rams back on top of the Championship.

'I've said for weeks and weeks it was only a matter of time before someone got on the end of a few goals from us,' the Rams boss said.

'On playing performances and chances this was a result that was waiting to happen. It was a tremendous performance, and I'm delighted for the team and the fans.

'When we play at that tempo we know we have players who can cause all kinds of problems – but the important thing is the crisis at Derby County is officially over!

'Some people have been saying that the club has hit a brick wall, but they will be thinking twice about that after tonight.'

David Jones set the ball rolling with the opening goal inside two minutes – and he felt the Rams' five-star performance had been coming.

Colchester United were the unfortunate victims of a rampant Derby side looking to put three League games without a win behind them and return to the top of the table.

The 5–1 success was the Derby's biggest for over a year and sends a big message out to those who felt Billy Davies's side was stuttering.

'That's what happens when you've had a few defeats – they all start saying it's a crisis,' Jones said. 'We have had a few defeats lately but our performances, certainly the second halves, have been excellent.

'Tonight we put in a 90-minute performance and were enthusiastic from the word go, a real high-energy display.

'The quality of the finishes was excellent, and I think it was about time we gave someone a battering.'

Steve Howard's yellow card.

Arturo Lupoli celebrates with Steve Howard after Howard's penalty.

The Rams players celebrate the fifth goal.

Jones tries to get past a Colchester defender.

Matt Oakley argues with referee Mick Jones.

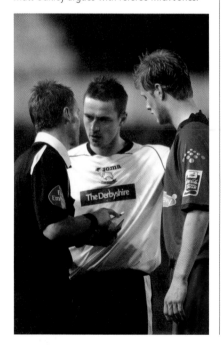

Dean Leacock is looking set for a return to the Derby County line up on Tuesday night. The centre-half has missed the last two games after injuring his hand during the 2–0 defeat at home to Stoke City a fortnight ago, but he is back in contention for a return to the side at Carrow Road tomorrow evening when the Rams take on Norwich City.

'I think Dean has got a good chance of making it,' boss Billy Davies revealed. 'He has trained for the last two days and is looking very sharp, so I'm delighted to say he has got a very good chance of being in the team.'

Leacock's anticipated return is countered by news that Michael Johnson is expected to be on the sidelines for six weeks.

Johnson suffered a hamstring injury during Friday night's 5–1 win over Colchester United – though it did appear at first that he had picked up a serious-looking knee problem.

'We have got cover there – Marc Edworthy, Tyrone Mears and Jay McEveley can all play there, and we've also got Steve Howard who's also claiming to be a very good centre-back!' Davies said.

'We do have one or two guys who can fill in at centre-half.

'It's a massive blow for us though because I thought Jonno and Mooro were excellent on Friday night, up until the injury. We are very disappointed to lose him.'

Derby County head to Norwich City looking to build on their biggest win of the season so far. Now they head to Carrow Road – where they haven't won since 1987 – with the chance to go back to the top of the Coca-Cola Championship.

But boss Billy Davies knows it won't be an easy ride in East Anglia.

'It will be another tough match, but any away game is a tough one,' the gaffer said.

'Again they have got lots to play for as they are fighting tooth and nail to try and drag themselves away from the bottom end.

'We have got to continue with this good run of form over the last number of weeks and hopefully continue picking up the points.'

A road trip to Norwich is a long and gruelling one, so Derby are taking alternative means of transport to and from the game.

The squad were flying down this morning and Davies says gaining extra recovery time ahead of Friday night's clash with Birmingham City is vital.

'We are very concerned about the recovery time between Tuesday and Friday,' he said. 'So the quicker we can get back the better it will be for us to get back on the training ground on Thursday, get the legs moving again, and get ready for the Friday match.'

REPORT – 6 MARCH 2007
NORWICH CITY 1
DERBY COUNTY 2

Inside four minutes Etuhu cut in from the Norwich right and hit a 25-yarder with his left foot which Bywater held.

The Canaries had a great chance to go in front when Martin released Croft, running at pace into the Derby area on six minutes. His angled drive from 10 yards was well parried by Bywater, diving to his right.

In the melee that followed Martin had penalty appeals turned down as Fotheringham fired in a low shot that was again saved by Bywater.

Hughes's powerful long-range drive was well blocked by Leacock on 12 minutes as the Rams struggled to get hold of the ball, though Barnes got in a low shot from the right angle of the Norwich box two minutes later that loanee 'keeper Warner held well.

Jones's through ball on 23 minutes set Fagan off down the middle, and he shrugged off the challenge of Shackell before hitting a low drive from 20 yards that didn't trouble Warner.

Howard's flick on from Fagan's touch from the right two minutes later found Barnes, and the teenager lashed in a left-footer from the right angle of the box that flew narrowly wide of Warner's left post.

On 31 minutes Leacock's foul on Martin presented Norwich with a free-kick, dead centre, 30 yards out, which Safri curled just wide of Bywater's right post with the 'keeper stranded.

Five minutes later Martin's low shot was parried by Bywater who just managed to scoop the ball clear at the second attempt as Etuhu charged in.

Two minutes into the half, Oakley's clever through ball saw Lupoli running in on goal, but Warner got his angles right to deny the Italian striker low down at his left post.

It was a bright start by the visitors, but Norwich took the lead on 51

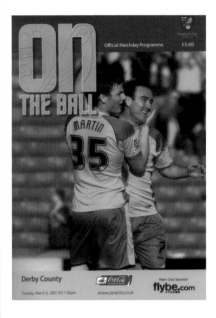

NORWICH: Warner, Shackell, Huckerby (C), Croft, Safri, Fotheringham, Hughes, Lappin, Etuhu, Doherty, Martin.
UNUSED SUBS: Lewis, Dublin, McVeigh, Colin, Eagle.

DERBY: Bywater, Edworthy (Mears 45), McEveley, Leacock, Moore, Oakley (C), Jones, Barnes, Lupoli (Macken 73), Fagan (Teale 60), Howard.
UNUSED SUBS: Grant, Malcolm.

ATTENDANCE: 23,462.

Giles Barnes takes the ball through the Norwich midfield.

Lupoli is down injured.

Steve Howard celebrates at full-time.

Steve Howard embraces David Jones after his second goal.

minutes when Martin, in too much space as Lappin found him on the left angle of Derby's 18 yard box, turned to hit home a low drive that evaded Bywater's grasp as it sneaked inside the 'keeper's right post.

Jones's 30-yard screamer on 55 minutes flew just over the top of Warner's bar, and a minute later Jones, fed by Barnes, jinked his way to the edge of the Norwich box before hitting his shot again just too high. It proved to be a sighter for what was to come.

On 62 minutes Jones latched on to Oakley's quick throw on the Derby right before cutting inside to hit a delicious left-foot curler from 22 yards that Warner – at full stretch – couldn't get anywhere near as it flew into the corner beyond the 'keeper's left glove.

Martin had the ball in the Derby net on 65 minutes but was flagged offside.

Jones then notched his second to put the Rams 2–1 up. Teale made ground on the Derby left before cutting inside to chip into Barnes in the area.

The youngster's audacious first-time back-heel found the ex-Manchester United man, who picked his spot – again just inside Warner's right post – from 12 yards.

Bywater pulled off a breathtaking reaction save after 75 minutes diving high to his right, after Fotheringham set up a perfect volley for Dublin.

Three minutes from time Howard was just too high with a header as he got up well for Teale's cross from the right.

Bywater, who had earlier received treatment after Huckerby challenged late, dived in bravely at Martin's feet after the striker had poleaxed Leacock as he turned in the area.

REACTION

First-team coach Julian Darby wasn't getting carried away after a hard-fought three points at Norwich City's Carrow Road put the Rams back on top of the Championship.

'We just keep going – we keep plugging away,' he said after his side had come back from a goal down to win 2–1 thanks to David Jones's brace.

'We were happy to come in at 0–0 to be fair, and then they got their first goal. Stephen Bywater was a bit unlucky with that one, but the lads got stuck in and Jonah got two great goals.

'He has that quality – he does it every day in training, and we know he has it in him and it can come at any time.'

Goal hero Jones conceded that the Rams hadn't started well.

'We didn't get out of the blocks, but we showed our character in the second and got the three points,' he said.

David Jones is congratulated at full-time by Gary Teale.

'The boss said at half-time we needed to up the tempo, and he wanted more. He thought we didn't match them for work rate in the first half and that wasn't acceptable.

'Obviously I love scoring goals. The first came from a quick throw in from Matty Oakley, and I had time and space to take one touch.

'I saw the gap and whipped it into the corner – I was happy with that. I'd had two chances just before the first goal, so I'd got my range. I fancied my chances tonight.'

Of his winner, Jonah said 'The second goal was a good team goal.'

It is second versus top in the Coca-Cola Championship – and Derby boss Billy Davies reckons the pressure is on the home side.

The Rams went back to the top of the table on Tuesday, thanks to their 2–1 win at Norwich City, and opened up a two-point gap ahead of Birmingham City.

Now they travel to St Andrews looking to extend that advantage over the Blues further and really put the onus on the chasing pack to get results.

'It's a big game, of course, for both clubs,' Davies said. 'But the pressure is on the home side because they can't afford to lose the game.

'We will certainly go down there knowing that if we win the match then the gap will be very good for us at this stage of the season.

'We will go down with confidence, to be positive, and certainly with the aim of picking up three points.'

Striker Steve Howard is relishing the prospect of the Coca-Cola Championship clash at Birmingham City. The Rams' leading scorer says occasions like St Andrews this evening are why he made a million-pound move to Derby last summer.

'Without a shadow of a doubt, if you don't enjoy these types of games then you're in the wrong business,' he said. 'We're looking forward to it, and hopefully we can get the result we need. It won't be for the faint-hearted, let's put it that way.'

The pitch at St Andrews has been the subject of much debate over recent months, and even though it was re-laid in January it is still causing problems.

Last Sunday's game against Cardiff City was affected by the playing surface, which won't have been helped by the weekend's torrential rain. But the weather has relented somewhat this week and hopes are high of an improvement ahead of kick-off.

David Jones.

BIRMINGHAM: Doyle, Muamba, Kelly, McSheffrey, Sadler, Clemence (C), Martin Taylor, Larsson (Johnson 89), Vine, N'Gotty, Bendtner (Jerome 78).
UNUSED SUBS: Maik Taylor, Nafti, Forssell.

DERBY: Bywater, Mears, Leacock, Moore, McEveley (Peschisolido 80), Teale, Barnes, Oakley (C) (Lupoli 69), Jones, Macken (Bisgaard 52), Howard.
UNUSED SUBS: Edworthy, Grant.

ATTENDANCE: 20,962.

Whatever is served up, Howard is looking forward to getting out and playing.

When asked whether it could be his type of game, the talismanic number nine replied 'Yes, it could be, it may be a balls-in-the-air type of game. Their pitch, by all accounts, is terrible, but it will be the same for both teams, so we'll just get on with it.'

REPORT – 9 MARCH 2007
BIRMINGHAM CITY 1
DERBY COUNTY 0

Before the game, Billy Davies lodged a complaint with match referee Steve Bennett over the state of the St Andrews turf. He felt that the playing surface was a danger to player safety and wanted to make his feelings known ahead of the game. But the official said that the pitch was fit to be played on.

Even in the early stages the lack of bounce was clear, though Giles Barnes tried to use the surface to his advantage with a bobbling 25-yard shot that Colin Doyle grabbed at the second attempt.

Birmingham broke straight back with Gary McSheffrey taking advantage of Mears's slip inside the box, only for Stephen Bywater to dive and turn the ball away for a corner.

Derby's first flag-kick wasn't the best of deliveries from David Jones, though it bounced up inside the area, but Steve Howard's looping header dropped safely on top of the bar.

Nicklas Bendtner then collected a long ball from Doyle and created a fine opportunity for himself that Bywater brilliantly turned away with his legs having looked as though he was beaten.

The corner was cleared away for another flag-kick, which resulted in Martin Taylor heading over from six yards.

Bendtner and Gary McSheffrey combined at one end for McSheffrey to curl safely over from 20 yards, and at the other end Howard was an inch away from opening the scoring with a similarly-distanced effort in the 19th minute.

But despite both sides playing some nice football on what was clearly a difficult surface, the chances dried up.

Teenager Giles Barnes broke on 38 minutes, but the ball got caught up

The Rams bench at the start of the game.

in his feet with Macken in space to his left. Doyle dived to save Jones's effort, but right on the whistle Birmingham went in front through Rowan Vine.

The striker collected Mat Sadler's pass and turned Dean Leacock on the edge of the box before sliding in his first goal for the Blues.

Derby's crisp passing of the first period had deserted them somewhat, but Birmingham were clearly afraid of Barnes's pace.

The possession was Birmingham's, but twice they failed to make the most of good situations with Derby caught upfield.

And on 66 minutes they could have paid as the Rams forced a flurry of corners, but they also didn't take advantage of their time in charge.

Bywater makes a save from a Birmingham attack.

There were claims for a Derby penalty just after as Bisgaard went down under challenge from Sadler, but referee Bennett was un-moved. And Derby's hopes were then raised again as McSheffrey lunged in two-footed on Leacock, in full view of Bennett. The official had no choice – or hesitation – in bringing out a straight red card, his decision further backed up by TV replays.

Howard should have done better with only 12 minutes to go when he volleyed Jones's cross over from 14 yards.

Jerome fired wide from 25 yards as Birmingham went on a rare break upfield, though the ball hadn't been spending much time inside their box.

Even in the four minutes of stoppage time Derby had the chance to lay siege on the Birmingham goal, but in truth Doyle was never seriously threatened.

REACTION

Billy Davies conceded, after Friday night's single-goal defeat at Birmingham, that the home side adapted better to the dodgy pitch. He said 'We were naive tonight because instead of banging balls into the box like they did we tried to play it.

'Teams who come to St Andrews are going to have to change their game to cope with the pitch, especially teams like Derby County who have a lot of ball players.

'It is a lesson to players like Jones who like to run with the ball. You simply have to play differently at places like this.

'Three games in a week was a big ask, and, with the pitch being as heavy as it was, two extra days' recovery from their last game for Birmingham was definitely a factor.'

Tyrone Mears believes the Rams' return of three points from two difficult away games this week has them ahead of schedule. He reckons two draws from the two games would have been a good return – and Derby are a point ahead of that.

'We would have taken a point at Norwich and a point here so I think we're a bit ahead of ourselves,' the full-back said.

'It was very disappointing to lose because we came here on a high after Tuesday and we expected to beat them, but it wasn't to be.

'I think it had 0–0 written all over it – the pitch was horrendous, but Birmingham used that to their advantage.

'We have got the quality players within our squad to get the goals, but it wasn't happening for us tonight.'

Birmingham goalkeeper Colin Doyle punches the ball away.

Steve Howard, Jon Macken and Giles Barnes are disappointed as they get ready to restart the game after Birmingham's goal.

Gary Teale applauds the crowd.

Billy Davies wants to see his Derby County side get at Queen's Park Rangers from the opening whistle on Tuesday night.

The Rams' last home outing was a 5–1 thrashing of Colchester United after they raced to a three-goal lead before 30 minutes had passed.

Davies was delighted by his team's performance that night and admits a repeat showing would be good.

'Yes, it would be nice, and that's the target now – we've got to go and really get at them as much as we can,' he said.

'We have got to cause them a lot of problems and continue the target of picking up as many points as we can.

'It will be a tough match for both sides, but it is one we're looking forward to.'

QPR are scrapping for points at the wrong end of the Coca-Cola Championship after a run of five games without a win that has dragged them into relegation trouble. But Davies expects 'no favours' from John Gregory's side.

The visitors will be without Lee Camp and Adam Bolder, who are prevented from playing against the Rams due to clauses in their respective loan and permanent transfers. But they will have in their ranks Spanish midfielder Inigo Idiakez, Derby's 2004–05 player of the year who joined the Londoners on loan from Southampton last week.

'We expect no favours, but that's the way it has always been,' Davies added.

'We have got to where we are because we have deserved it from the first day of the season.

'It doesn't matter who they have in their team, or on the bench, we know what we have got to do.

'We will continue to try and pick up the three points.'

Winger Gary Teale is hoping to draw on the experiences of Wigan Athletic's successful promotion campaign in 2005 as the Rams' season really hots up.

Derby sit second in the Coca-Cola Championship with a three-point advantage over the chasing pack and only nine games remaining.

Teale went through it all with the Latics two years ago and can see the similarities in the way the Rams' fortunes are unfolding.

'I think there are comparisons from when we went up with Wigan two years ago,' he said ahead of the visit of Queen's Park Rangers. We were riding high at the time but then hit a sticky patch and played West Ham and Sunderland, but lost both by the odd goal.

'The comparisons are a wee bit freaky, but we got there in the end – we had a few victories and ended up in second.

'Now we're hoping we can do the same at Derby.

'We have got two games coming up, and if we can get six points before the international break it will be a massive lift for everyone.'

Also this week, Billy Davies has been charged with using abusive and/or insulting words towards a Southend United FC steward. The FA charge relates to the Derby manager's conduct during the match at Roots Hall on 20 January, and Billy has until 22 March to respond to the charge.

He said 'The truth about the events of that day will come out in due course, but unfortunately I can't say anything more at this time.'

Davies has denied a separate charge of using abusive and/or insulting words towards a match official during the same match and requested a personal hearing, which has yet to be scheduled.

REPORT – 13 MARCH 2007
DERBY COUNTY 1
QUEEN'S PARK RANGERS 1

Marc Nygaard headed over in the 11th minute from Lee Cook's inviting left-wing cross with the visitors looking more settled in the early stages. But Rangers were in front seconds later as Derby were caught out by a long free-kick.

Paul Furlong turned the ball goalwards, and it was allowed to bounce off a post, where Martin Rowlands had time and space to dive in and head it home.

Cook then broke through midfield and squared the ball to Furlong, who was already proving a handful, but the experienced striker should have done better than roll a tame effort straight at Bywater.

It was all QPR as Rowlands threatened a second, only to drive wide from 20 yards after another visiting break. And the home side's first effort on goal followed shortly before the half-hour mark, though Giles Barnes's header never threatened the back of Simon Royce's net.

Derby came close to an equaliser on 36 minutes with an effort from a set-piece as Howard met Jones's corner with a powerful header, but Cook cleared it away from off the line.

The Rams were having their best spell of the game and were close to levelling it six minutes before the interval when Howard and Matt Oakley combined for Lupoli to cut in from the right and beat two defenders before driving low and against the outside of Royce's post.

Then Jay McEveley tried a snap-shot from all of 40 yards that Royce had to move sharply to gather, though he was never in any danger of being beaten.

Jones almost got lucky with an over-hit free-kick that Royce had to turn over the bar, though Derby failed to make the most of the resulting corner.

DERBY: Bywater, Edworthy, Leacock, Moore, McEveley, Teale (Fagan 65), Oakley (C), D. Jones (Peschisolido 76), Lupoli, Barnes, Howard.
UNUSED SUBS: Grant, S. Johnson, Mears.

QPR: Royce, Bignot (C), Cullip, Rowlands (Ainsworth 27), Lomas (Smith 90), Cook, Stewart, Idiakez, Furlong (R. Jones 83), Nygaard, Mancienne.
UNUSED SUBS: Cole, Kanyuka.

ATTENDANCE: 27,567.

Barnes is given some treatment for an injury.

Damion Stewart almost turned Jones's free-kick past his own 'keeper in the second period's first goalmouth incident, five minutes in. But with Derby pushing forward for an equaliser, gaps were opening up at the back for Rangers to exploit.

And in the 58th minute they almost did as Ainsworth found space on the right and pulled the ball back for Steve Lomas, whose 20-yard drive produced a marvellous save from Bywater.

Dean Leacock headed Jones's delivery back across the six-yard box, where it was controlled and turned goalwards by Moore, but straight into the arms of Royce.

Substitute Craig Fagan set up a chance for Lupoli with his second touch, and the Italian finished it off well, but once again the flag went up for offside – and, in fairness, he looked a yard ahead of the defence.

Fellow replacement Paul Peschisolido was straight into the action to feed Fagan inside the box, and the former Hull man went down under Stewart's challenge, but referee Tanner waved away the penalty appeals.

But the breakthrough eventually came with four minutes to go.

Howard did well to chase down an over-hit Fagan cross and pull the ball back to McEveley, who whipped over a lovely ball to the far post.

And in Howard's absence, the towering far-post header came from Moore, who powered his effort down and past Royce for a deserved equaliser.

Howard did get his head to a ball in the box as four minutes of stoppage time got under way when he rose to meet McEveley's corner, but the effort was off-target.

Matt Oakley.

REACTION

Billy Davies reckons the point won against QPR on Tuesday night could prove vital at the end of the 2006–07 campaign.

'Of course we would have been delighted with three points,' the Rams boss said. 'But if you look right across the country tonight teams are fighting for their lives and others have dropped points.

'What matters is that we continue to pick up points along the way.

'I have just told the players that tonight could be a very important point come the end of the season.

'Teams like Stoke and QPR scrap – that's the way they play – and it's a learning process for some of our players.'

Defender Darren Moore says the Rams will have to learn from their 1–1 draw against Queen's Park Rangers when they come up against similar tests before the season ends.

QPR came to Pride Park desperate for the points, after a run of five

Peschisolido is challenged by the QPR 'keeper.

games without a win saw them dragged right into the Coca-Cola Championship's relegation battle. And it looked as though they would leave with all three until Moore powered home an 87th-minute equaliser to earn Derby a draw.

'QPR came and made it hard for us, and we've got to realise that, such has been the efforts of everyone at the club this season, nobody will come up to Pride Park and play open football against us,' he said.

'Teams are going to make it hard, they'll make it difficult and frustrating for us, they'll slow the game down and every tactic in the book an away team can use against us they will do.

'But the players showed great resilience as it was a tough game out there tonight, and credit to QPR as they are scrapping for their lives.

'We have got a few more fixtures like that and all we can do is learn, and make sure that when we face these games we perform instead of dragging ourselves up from behind.'

Billy Davies reckons new-boy Darren Currie's experience makes him a strong addition to the Derby County squad.

Currie has joined on loan from Ipswich Town in a deal that will keep him at Pride Park until the end of the season. The 32-year-old winger brings with him experience of more than 600 senior games and arrives with the knowledge that will make him an important addition to Davies's set-up.

David Jones.

The players congratulate Darren Moore on his equaliser.

Darren Currie watching the Rams draw with QPR.

Darren Currie unveiled as a Rams player.

'Darren has vast experience, he is a wonderful talent with a great range of passing and excellent crossing ability,' the gaffer revealed.

'He is a first-class lad to have in the dressing room and this is a great opportunity for him.

'I'm delighted to have Darren here because I do feel that his experience and ability could be very crucial over the next eight games.'

Currie jetted back in from a two-week trial with American MLS side LA Galaxy – the club David Beckham is off to in the summer – after hearing of the Rams' interest.

Quite early into his time Stateside, the new Derby man had decided that soccer wasn't the next step for him and he still had a burning desire to play good, old-fashioned English football.

And it didn't take too long for the player, who has wracked up over 600 appearances for Shrewsbury, Leyton Orient, Plymouth, Barnet, Wycombe, Brighton and the Tractor Boys, to decide that Pride Park should be his next destination.

'To be honest, when I was out there and found out the Rams were interested I had a look to see if there was a direct flight from Los Angeles Airport to Derby Airport, and was a bit gutted when I found out Derby didn't have an airport,' he joked.

'By then I'd decided, in a mutual decision with LA Galaxy boss Frank Yallop, that the American game was not for me and that I wanted to keep playing in the English game.

'It's in my blood, and I would miss it if I wasn't playing in this country. In the States football seems to be the fourth or fifth thing on peoples' minds, but for me after my family it is the most important thing in my life.

'So when I heard about Derby's interest I was very keen, and it didn't take me long at all to decide to come here.

'Now I'm pleased and proud to be here for the last eight games and relishing the challenges ahead. It's a big eight matches for the club as a whole and for me as an individual.'

With eight vital games remaining in the Rams' Coca-Cola Championship campaign boss Billy Davies says: 'We need heroes.'

Davies is looking for his players to come to the fore and stamp their authority on every game between now and the end of the season.

The prize couldn't be bigger come May, and the gaffer says it's up to all of his squad to take the mantle when it matters.

'We need heroes, whether they're young or old,' he revealed. 'We need calm heads, and that's exactly what you get from the experienced boys.

'But at the same time it doesn't make it any easier for them – they've got to work as hard as they can, approach the games in the right way, they have got to fight the corner like everyone else.

'It is about getting that balance right and making sure that the one thing we do get is one or two heroes coming out of each match.'

Cardiff City are first-up in the Rams' remaining matches, and they too need the points to further fuel their own Premiership ambitions.

The Bluebirds sit seven points behind Derby and are seventh in the table, out of the Play-off places only on goal difference.

REPORT – 17 MARCH 2007
DERBY COUNTY 3
CARDIFF CITY 1

The visitors wasted a good early opportunity from 25 yards as Michael Chopra could only fire a dangerously-positioned free-kick into the Derby wall.

The game needed a lift after a scrappy opening and one arrived on 27 minutes as Derby were awarded a penalty. Giles Barnes dived in to head David Jones's corner but couldn't get a decent connection, though the ball flew on and struck Steven Thompson's arm.

Cardiff protested, but referee Martin Atkinson had no hesitation – and neither did Steve Howard, with a sweet spot-kick low to Alexander's right that opened the scoring.

But the Rams' joy was short-lived as on 31 the visitors were level. Derby failed to clear a ball up, and Paul Parry was given the simplest of tasks to nip in on the loose ball and calmly slide it past Stephen Bywater.

Seconds later Chopra, the Championship's leading scorer, struck the Derby crossbar with a fierce effort. But it was Chopra's last action as he injured himself while shooting and hobbled off to be replaced by Jason Byrne.

Derby were on the attack immediately after the break, and only a fine Alexander save with his feet denied Barnes after the visitors only half-cleared a cross.

At the other end, Bywater did well to block out Parry's shot.

But Barnes was on the mark three minutes after the interval with an excellent finish. McEveley cleared the ball up to halfway, where the teenager nipped in ahead of Kevin McNaughton.

He still had a lot to do but showed great pace to get away from his marker and plant an excellent finish past Alexander with the outside of his right foot.

And by the hour the Rams were in command.

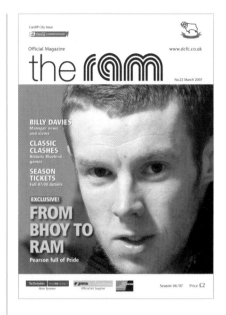

DERBY: Bywater, Mears, Leacock, Moore, McEveley, Fagan, Oakley (C), S. Johnson (Currie 74), Jones, Fagan, Howard.
UNUSED SUBS: Grant, Camara, Peschisolido, Teale.

CARDIFF: Alexander, Gunter, Ledley, McNaughton, R. Johnson, McPhail (C), Walton, Thompson, Chopra (Byrne 34 (Green 77)), Whittingham, Parry.
UNUSED SUBS: Forde, Purse, Blake.

ATTENDANCE: 27,689.

Steve Howard scores from the penalty spot.

Howard celebrates after scoring the penalty.

Darren Moore makes a point to referee Martin Atkinson.

Oakley did well to break up play in midfield and lift a lovely ball through to Howard, who was in behind the Cardiff defence.

Derby's leading scorer took a touch on his chest to steady himself before smashing a left-footed drive past Alexander for his second of the game.

It should have been 3–2 with 20 minutes to go as Thompson crossed low for Byrne, but the Irishman somehow completely missed his kick from inside the six-yard box.

Bywater then pushed over Simon Walton's 25-yard drive with the visitors enjoying a spell of pressure. He then grabbed a powerful, stoppage time Thompson effort but there was no real danger, and with Birmingham not playing until Sunday the win was enough to see Derby back to the top of the table.

REACTION

Billy Davies says he's looking forward to a break that will see his side at least joint top of the Championship for the next two weeks.

Talking after Saturday's 3–1 home win over Cardiff City, the Rams boss said 'I'm giving the players and staff a few days off because they fully deserve it – and I'm giving myself a few days off because I deserve it too!

'Seriously though, we will soon be back and getting our heads down.

'The break gives us time to get the likes of Stephen Pearson and Marc Edworthy back to fitness, so I'm delighted with the break.'

Two goals and the Rams back on top of the Coca-Cola Championship would have been enough for most men to celebrate – but not Steve Howard.

Derby's leading scorer netted a tremendous hat-trick over the weekend of a double in the 3–1 win over Cardiff City and the arrival of a new baby girl.

Howard's involvement against the Bluebirds was made even more remarkable with the thought in his mind that he was about to become a father for the second time, with his wife due to give birth at any moment. And after striking twice to put Derby back top of the table he dashed home ready for his new arrival.

The only blot on Howard's day was a first-half caution, his 10th of the campaign, that rules him out for two matches.

Boss Billy Davies joked that the 30-year-old had deliberately got himself disciplined so that he could spend more time bottle feeding his new addition to the family.

'I wouldn't get myself booked deliberately for that!' Was his response, before heading off to be with his wife for the birth. 'I'll take the booking on the chin though.

'It's a crucial time of the season, and I really wanted to play in all of the games, but it's one of those things I'll have to deal with.

'I took the penalty then got booked, so I thought I needed another one as I've now got two games off.'

Marc Edworthy says the Rams have got to be ready for teams trying to earn the scalp of the Coca-Cola Championship leaders.

Derby sit top of the pile with seven games remaining and have put themselves in a great position in the race for the Premiership.

But with that comes the added prize for their opponents who will want to have the glory of beating the table-toppers.

'Every game is a Cup Final, and with seven games to go you become the side everyone wants to beat because you're at the top,' Edworthy said.

'Teams won't come and lie down and let you play – they'll fight for everything and will want to upset the apple cart.

'We're one of the top teams so people want to beat us, and we've got to make sure we're committed and ready for that.'

Winger Ryan Smith has joined Coca-Cola League One side Millwall on loan for a month.

The 20-year-old arrived at Pride Park last summer after coming through the Academy ranks at Premiership giants Arsenal. But he hasn't cemented himself in the Derby side and is heading to the New Den until 21 April to get more first-team football under his belt.

Derby boss Billy Davies said 'The loan spell with Millwall will allow Ryan to get a couple of games under his belt and then come back for the last four or five games of the Coca-Cola Championship season and be available for selection.

'He is a young player who has always been very much a long-term signing for us. When a team finds themselves doing well in the League, as we are, inevitably certain young players find games restricted.

'That's been the case with Ryan so the month at Millwall should be very beneficial to both the player and Derby County.'

Smith has made seven starts for the Rams, with a further 13 appearances coming from the bench.

Darren Currie makes his debut.

Defender Paul Boertien has become the second Derby player to leave for a temporary move in the space of a couple of hours.

Boertien will join League One side Chesterfield for a month to get football and fitness under his belt after an injury-blighted season.

Davies said 'It's a chance for him to be involved in matches and to work on improving his match fitness.

'Boets has been very unlucky with injuries and this is an opportunity for him to get back into action and get some games for Chesterfield under his belt.'

Chesterfield have already raided the Rams once this season for one loan deal – Australian teenager James Meredith, who has just finished a month at Saltergate, during which time he made a single League One appearance.

Derby County won't rush Stephen Pearson back into action unless he is 100 percent ready for a return.

Steve Howard applauds the Rams fans at full-time.

The Scottish midfielder has been out of action since injuring a foot in the 2–1 defeat at Sunderland in February. He has been making good progress, but Rams boss Billy Davies will take no chances with the 24-year-old.

'Pearo is making good progress, but we don't want to rush him back and end up losing him for five or six weeks,' Davies said. 'The timing of his re-introduction is very important.

'I would probably say that if he's not back this weekend at Barnsley, it will be the following week at Leicester City.'

It's all to play for with seven games to go – and Darren Moore is urging the Rams to carry on as they have been performing.

Derby sit proudly on top of the Coca-Cola Championship and begin their final push with a trip to Barnsley on Saturday.

The home side will want the points to aid their relegation battle so it's sure to be a tough afternoon in South Yorkshire.

But Moore believes that the Rams have been on the right track lately and need to pick up where they left off before an enforced break for international fixtures.

'All I'm going to do is continue what I have been doing, and I'm saying that to the boys,' the big defender said. 'We shouldn't need to do anything different – if it's not broken then don't fix it.

'What I mean by that is that we should continue to show the same work rate, energy and endeavour that we have done since the start of the season. And from the fans, they should keep giving us the same support they have been doing.

'If anything we need to work even harder as everyone can see the finish line now.

'But even though we're delighted at the position the club is in now, we know that we have won nothing yet.

'We have got to continue what we've been doing and just concentrate on ourselves.'

REPORT – 31 MARCH 2007
BARNSLEY 1
DERBY COUNTY 2

Some 7,400 Derby supporters made the trip up to cheer on their team, and it was they who were noisiest in the early stages of this vital encounter for both sides. And the volume went up even higher on 11 minutes as the Rams went in front.

An excellent midfield move involving Macken, Matt Oakley and David Jones resulted in David Lucas saving Giles Barnes's shot.

But the ball rolled out to Jones, who smashed it hard and low into the back of the net.

Barnsley were offering very little in attack, despite their own need for the points, and almost got themselves in trouble again on 20 when Antony Kay's clearance hit Macken but was grabbed by Lucas.

At the other end the Rams broke quickly, but Oakley could only fire safely over from 25 yards after Barnsley failed to deal with Currie's cross.

Macken could have opened his account with seven minutes to go until half-time, but he headed over from Jones's fine centre after a corner.

Howard drove wide from 30 yards after breaking through midfield, but with stoppage time approaching it was still the home side's best effort.

Currie fired a 25-yard free-kick straight at Lucas to open up the second period, though it was never a serious contender to double Derby's lead.

But just seconds later it was two.

Bywater drove a free-kick long into the box and out came Lucas to punch clear, but under pressure from Barnes he could only get the ball to the edge of the box.

There waited Oakley, who smashed home a superb left-footed effort on

BARNSLEY: Lucas (Colgan 54), Hassell, Heckingbottom, P. Reid (C) (Austin 73), Togwell, Ferenczi, B. Howard, Rajczi, Kay, K. Reid, McCann (Hayes 54).
UNUSED SUBS: R. Jones, Nardiello.

DERBY: Bywater, Mears, Moore, Leacock, McEveley, Fagan (Peschisolido 90), Oakley (C), D. Jones (S Johnson 77), Currie (Teale 67), Barnes, Macken.
UNUSED SUBS: Grant, Edworthy.

ATTENDANCE: 17,059.

the half-volley that sent the mass ranks of Derby fans into raptures. Of concern, however, was the collision between Lucas and Barnes, which left both players on the floor for some time.

Barnes was up and able to continue after treatment, but Lucas looked in a bad way and left the field strapped to a stretcher, his neck in a brace.

He was unconscious for a time but came round and was taken to hospital.

Barnsley's first real shot on target came just before the hour, though Kyel Reid's free-kick was comfortably dealt with by Bywater.

They came close again on 66 minutes after a quick move forward, but Bywater was alert enough to dive on the ball inside his six-yard box with Istvan Ferenczi ready to pounce.

Ferenczi then turned and stroked a left-footer from just inside the box that gave Bywater no difficulties at all.

A Barnsley break on 78 minutes brought about Bywater's first real save when he diverted Kyel Reid's volley away with his feet.

It was largely cruise-control for the Rams in the last few minutes as they slowed the game down where necessary and kept hold of the ball, nullifying any home threat.

Sam Togwell pulled a goal back deep into stoppage time, but there was no danger to Derby's three points.

REACTION

Skipper Matt Oakley says the Rams can rightly feel proud of having equalled the club's record for number of away wins in a season.

The 2–1 victory over Barnsley at Oakwell signalled Derby's 12th success on the road in 2006–07 – and the record could be beaten as there are still three away fixtures to play.

Matt Oakley is congratulated by his teammates after scoring the Rams' second goal.

Giles Barnes is treated by the physiotherapist following a knock on the shin.

Kyel Reid shoots for goal – which Stephen Bywater saves superbly.

TABLE

	P	W	D	L	F	A	Pts
Derby	**40**	**23**	**7**	**10**	**56**	**40**	**76**
Sunderland	40	22	7	11	61	39	73
Birmingham	38	21	8	9	55	35	71
Preston	39	20	8	11	57	43	68
West Brom	40	19	10	11	68	47	67
Wolves	40	19	9	12	45	47	66
Southampton	40	17	12	11	67	48	63
Cardiff	40	17	12	11	54	43	63
Stoke	40	16	13	11	51	35	61
Colchester	40	17	8	15	60	48	59
Sheffield W	40	15	11	14	60	60	56
C Palace	40	15	10	15	49	45	55
Plymouth	39	12	16	11	51	53	52
Coventry	39	15	7	17	43	49	42
Ipswich	40	15	6	19	52	52	51
Norwich	39	14	8	17	48	59	50
Leicester	39	11	13	15	43	52	46
Hull	40	12	8	20	45	58	44
Burnley	38	10	12	16	36	41	42
Barnsley	40	12	5	23	46	71	41
QPR	39	10	10	19	46	61	40
Southend	40	9	12	19	40	63	39
Leeds	40	11	6	23	41	65	39
Luton	40	9	10	21	47	67	37

The Rams maintained their place at the top of the table after David Jones's early strike and made sure of the points when Oakley himself hammered into the roof of the net early in the second half.

Only a late Barnsley consolation goal denied Derby a clean sheet.

Oakley said 'It is a proud achievement, and we are very happy to have equalled the record, but we still have a job to do in the next six games so we won't be getting too carried away about the fact.

'When I arrived at this club the manager told me about how poor Derby's away form had been last season before he took over, so to have turned it around so quickly is credit to all of the lads and their hard work.'

Billy Davies was delighted his side managed to equal a club record 12 away wins – but at the same time frustrated the Rams gave away a late goal in the 2–1 win at Oakwell.

The Rams boss saw his team take an early lead through David Jones and seal the win in the second half courtesy of a Matt Oakley goal, to send the magnificent 7,400 travelling faithful home in raptures.

And it was that great band of supporters who Billy was keen to mention first of all in his post-match interviews.

He said 'The support was absolutely superb, seeing so many fans travel to back us once again was great.

'I'd like to thank the supporters once again for their loyalty, and I'm pleased we were able to send them back down the motorway celebrating another very important three points.'

The victory reaffirmed Derby's standing as the Coca-Cola Championship's leaders and came at the expense of a side fighting for survival.

It's the latter fact that pleased Billy most of all, but the late Tykes' consolation was clearly still on his mind.

'All of the games in this League are tough, but it's especially difficult when you take on sides who are fighting for their lives,' he said.

'Barnsley is never an easy place to go, particularly with the wind howling in between the stands, so it's satisfying to come away with the points. The only slight frustration is that we got a bit sloppy towards the end and conceded the late goal.

'We defended extremely well for the majority of the game, and it would have been nice to have earned a clean sheet too.'

April

It looks like any two from three for the automatic promotion places – and it's Derby in pole position as the final few weeks approach.

The Rams have a three-point advantage over Roy Keane's Sunderland, still unbeaten since the turn of the year, with Birmingham City a further two points back.

The top three have all played each other twice so it's now down to a straight battle to see who can pick up the most points and earn those automatic places in the Premiership.

Midfield duo Stephen Pearson and David Jones have both returned to training ahead of Friday's Coca-Cola Championship trip to Leicester City.

Pearson has been absent since the defeat at Sunderland at the end of February with a foot injury, while Jones left Saturday's win at Barnsley with a calf problem.

But the pair have come through well this week and are in Billy Davies's thoughts for the televised Walkers Stadium encounter.

'Both have trained and both have come on fine, though Pearo's slightly behind Jonah,' the gaffer said.

'We'll get them in on Friday morning, have a good check on both of them, and see how they are for the match.'

Davies is hopeful of getting Pearson back in action over the Easter weekend with two games in just three days.

Coventry City are the visitors to Pride Park Stadium on Monday, and it could well be a time for fresh legs.

The Rams will also be boosted by the return of Steve Howard after suspension for the clash with the Sky Blues.

'It will need to be a time for freshness, this is why we carry the squad and this is where the appearance of someone like Pearo, for example, and bringing back Steve Howard could be crucial for us,' Davies said.

'It's about the rotation, and getting the fresh legs in the team at the right time.

'But we will look at the first match, try to take care of it, and then we'll think ahead after that.'

REPORT – 6 APRIL 2007
LEICESTER CITY 1
DERBY COUNTY 1

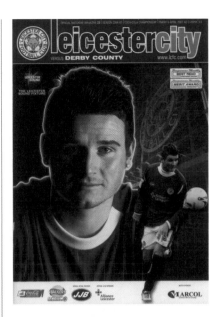

Leicester had the game's first chance after a bright opening, in which they forced a couple of corners.

From the second, on four minutes, Levi Porter and Iain Hume both saw efforts cleared away from in front of goal.

The Foxes had strong claims for a 22nd-minute penalty when Patrick Kisnorbo felt the full weight of Darren Moore on his back from a corner, but Webb was un-moved. And Derby took advantage to break straight up the other end of the field and open the scoring.

Barnes found space just inside the Leicester half and made ground through the middle before drawing the home defence towards him. The teenager slipped an excellent pass through to Fagan, who took a touch to steady himself before finishing superbly past Paul Henderson for his first Rams goal.

Giles Barnes was close with an eight-yard shot that flashed just over the bar after an excellent move.

There was a spring in the step of Hume on 47 minutes as he cut in from the right and fired a shot goalwards, though his 25-yarder was always dipping just over.

Tiatto was next to threaten from a similar distance, but again he couldn't find the target.

Leicester were presented with a good opportunity on 53 minutes as they were awarded a free-kick right on the edge of the D, just to the right of centre, after Tyrone Mears was harshly pulled up for a foul on Jason Jarrett.

Hume stepped forward and curled it over the wall, but Bywater hurled himself to his left to push the ball out for a corner.

It was Fagan who had Derby's first opportunity of the second period when, just after the hour, he capitalised on hesitation by Patrick Kisnorbo.

LEICESTER: Henderson, Stearman, Kenton, Kisnorbo (C), Maybury, Hughes (Yeates 65), Jarrett, Tiatto, Porter, Hume, Hammond (Fryatt 55).
UNUSED SUBS: Logan, Johansson, Horsfield.

DERBY: Bywater, Mears, Moore, Leacock, McEveley, Oakley (C), Barnes, Jones (Bisgaard 74), Fagan, Macken (Teale 57), Currie (Lupoli 80).
UNUSED SUBS: Grant, Edworthy.

ATTENDANCE: 24,704.

Fagan scores his first goal for Derby.

Tyrone Mears's header.

Craig Fagan's goal celebration said it all at Leicester on Good Friday.

'It's been a long time coming, and it was a great feeling to score my first goal for Derby,' he said after the 1–1 draw.

'Barnesy did the work to be honest because he attracted at least three defenders to him before playing the ball to me in space.'

Of his celebration, Fagan explained 'The manager has a saying about other teams – he asks, "Who's blinking?" which means who is cracking under the pressure. All the lads knew what I meant!

'But it's not really about me scoring – we're all just disappointed about not picking up three points.'

But he perhaps didn't realise how much time he had on his side and instead rushed his shot straight into the arms of Paul Henderson.

The Rams were a foot away from doubling their lead shortly afterwards. Good work by Currie on the left pulled the ball back for McEveley, who whipped over a fine cross that Jones could only nod past the post.

And Leicester made them pay by going straight up the other end of the field and levelling matters.

Jarrett managed to find enough space to squeeze the ball through to Fryatt, who turned inside Leacock before slotting the ball past Bywater.

Fryatt had his eyes on a second on 72 as he latched on to Alan Maybury's long pass, but this time his control let him down and Bywater dropped on the loose ball.

Substitute Arturo Lupoli had an immediate chance that was blocked, but the ball then came through to Fagan on the far post. Fagan should have done much better than roll a simple effort into Henderson's arms.

At the other end Porter was shown inside by Mears, but Bywater was equal to the young winger's shot.

Most of the late possession went to Leicester, though Derby had a couple of good opportunities to break quickly in stoppage time that they failed to use.

REACTION

Rams boss Billy Davies felt his side allowed Leicester City back into the game by 'dropping off the tempo' in the second half of Good Friday's 1–1 draw.

Derby were in control at the break through Craig Fagan's first goal for the club, while the home side offered very little by way of attacking threat. But it was a different story in the second half of the Walkers Stadium encounter as the home side came out strongly and equalised through Matty Fryatt.

Stephen Bywater had to be at his sharpest as Leicester had chances to win the game – but the Rams also felt they could have taken all three points.

'I felt that in the first half we were in control, and Craig Fagan scored an excellent goal for us,' Davies said.

'But in the second half we came out and I felt we dropped off the tempo slightly. We allowed them too much possession and, when you come down to this type of match, you've got to take your chances to kill them off – and we had some very good ones.

'We had some good chances at the end, but we've got to be ruthless and kill people off.

'But these things happen, we will dust ourselves down and get ready for what will be another difficult battle against Coventry on Monday.'

REPORT – 9 APRIL 2007
DERBY COUNTY 1
COVENTRY CITY 1

Marc Edworthy was in the wars early on as he went down after an accidental collision with Leon McKenzie, and left the field with blood coming from his nose.

Howard dropped back into defence and won his first header with great authority.

His stay there was only brief, however, as Edworthy was able to return a couple of minutes later, minus his original shirt.

At his more natural end of the field Howard was then close to reaching a couple of dangerous Jay McEveley crosses.

Michael Doyle's 14th-minute shot straight at Stephen Bywater was the visitors' first effort, coming after Derby failed to clear their lines.

Bywater dived to gather Isaac Osbourne's low drive on 22 minutes, but he was never in any danger of being beaten.

David Jones's flag-kick caused great concern as it swirled towards the far post and only a last-ditch finger away from Andy Marshall stopped it finding the back of the net.

The best chance of the game came three minutes before the interval and only a brilliant save from Bywater denied Jay Tabb.

McKenzie had robbed McEveley in the corner of the Derby box and lifted over a fine cross that Tabb met, but Bywater was at his sharpest to keep the effort out.

At the other end Darren Moore rose to meet a Jones corner, but Marshall produced an equally outstanding block.

Elliott Ward opened up the second period with a header downwards from Stephen Hughes's free-kick, though it was a simple task for Bywater to gather.

And while Derby were having plenty of the ball they weren't looking particularly dangerous, and all too often fast breaks came to nothing in the final third.

There were strong Rams penalty appeals with 20 to go as Jones's shot seemed to strike Ward's arm inside the box, but again Eddie Ilderton was un-moved. And the frustration grew on 72 minutes as Coventry went in front. Mears failed to deal with a long ball, allowing McKenzie in to poke the ball past Bywater and hammer it into an empty net.

But within seven minutes Derby were level.

McEveley smashed over a deep cross to the far post where Howard headed it back across goal, but slightly behind Oakley.

No matter. The skipper pulled out what looked like an almost

DERBY: Bywater, Mears, Edworthy, Moore, McEveley, Oakley (C) (S. Johnson 90), Barnes, Jones, Fagan (Bisgaard 70), Howard, Lupoli (Currie 76).
UNUSED SUBS: Camara, Grant.

COVENTRY: Marshall, Hall, Page, Ward (C), Hughes, Doyle, Kyle (Adebola 81), McKenzie (Mifsud 76), Osbourne, Tabb, Virgo.
UNUSED SUBS: Steele, Cameron, Turner.

ATTENDANCE: 29,940.

Matt Oakley celebrates after scoring in the second half of the game.

David Jones fires a ball in towards the goal.

Craig Fagan running at the Coventry defence.

impossible volley to loop the ball over Marshall and lift some of the tension around Pride Park.

Derby piled forward in search of a second goal and were an inch away from finding one when Barnes flashed his shot across goal from a long way to the right.

Bywater produced a good save to deny substitute Mifsud a breakaway effort in stoppage time, while at the other end Bisgaard drove into the side-netting from a narrow angle when a pull-back would surely have won the game.

REACTION

Billy Davies says opposing teams are raising their game when they come to Pride Park Stadium.

Speaking after Monday's 1–1 home draw against Coventry City, the Rams boss said 'That could be a very important point because all our games are difficult.

'Teams come to our place and raise their game because we are a big scalp and people want to beat us. That's what we have to live with when teams come here.

'They want the bragging rights and that means we have to work that little bit harder and be a bit more patient.

'Having watched Coventry these last few weeks I can see the tempo of their game raised today and that has happened to us against other clubs too because of our reputation.'

And yoga is to thank for the stretching prowess that led to skipper Matt Oakley's goal against Coventry. That's the verdict of Davies after Oakley's acrobatic equaliser in Monday's 1–1 draw.

'Yoga has definitely helped his flexibility,' Davies laughed, 'and we thank our specialists in that department who have given Matt that extra half inch!'

Battle-scarred Marc Edworthy came out to face the press after the 1–1 draw with Coventry City – and admitted it was all part and parcel of the game.

Edworthy finished the game with a broken nose and stitches in a lip wound after an early accidental collision with City's Leon McKenzie. He's not normally in the wars in his usual position at full-back, but a move into the centre always brings with it further dangers.

'I think you stay out of trouble a bit more at full-back!' he said. 'Every time you play at centre-half you get bumps and bruises, and I got a few today.

'But you've got to go in there and do a job, and unfortunately that's what happens sometimes.

'I've got a broken nose and a few stitches in my lip, but unfortunately nothing can be done now because if you get it fixed you're out for three or four weeks and we can't afford that.

'All I've got to do is bear with it and stay away from the cameras for the next couple of weeks!'

Giles Barnes was all smiles as he got his hands on the Powerade Player of the Month award for March.

The 18-year-old was revealed on Sunday as the Coca-Cola Championship's top performer after an outstanding month which saw him net two vital goals and have a hand in several others.

And he admitted that the support of his teammates and manager

Billy Davies had been a feature in his development – but he has his sights now firmly set on the final four games of the season.

'I'm delighted to have won the award, but I couldn't have done so without the lads and the gaffer, who are all brilliant to work with,' he said.

'We've got four important games left this season and that's what we're all fully-focused on.'

Dean Leacock and Marc Edworthy are both expected to be fit and ready for the Rams' Coca-Cola Championship trip to Ipswich Town on Saturday.

Leacock missed out on the Easter Monday 1–1 draw at home to Coventry City after suffering from a bout of sickness in the run-up to the game.

Edworthy stepped in to replace the 22-year-old but was in the wars himself and finished the game with a broken nose and cut lip. But both, however, should be in Derby's squad for the Portman Road encounter.

'Edy needs some work done in the summer to try and get his nose sorted out,' boss Billy Davies said.

'But we're hoping we can keep him playing to the end of the season and get the best out of Edy – which is what he gives us every week.'

Of Leacock, the gaffer added 'Dean has trained for the last couple of days, but he has lost a bit of weight, which is disappointing. But he is certainly back in training and will most definitely be a part of the squad at the weekend.'

Darren Moore has been found guilty of a charge of violent conduct in last Friday's match at Leicester City's Walkers Stadium. The 32-year-old defender was today banned for four games by an FA Disciplinary Commission.

There is no right of appeal and, barring Play-offs, his season is now effectively over.

Moore, who is still travelling to Ipswich to support the rest of the Rams squad, denied the charge, which referred to an alleged incident not spotted at the time by the match referee.

Manager Billy Davies said 'We are very disappointed to have lost an extremely valuable player at a crucial time in the season. His experience in particular will be a huge loss.

'The key thing now though is to look ahead and plan for life without Darren between now and 6 May.'

Giles Barnes.

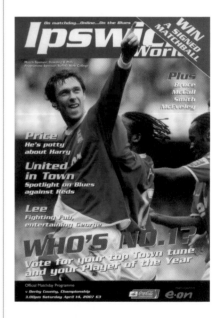

REPORT – 14 APRIL 2007
IPSWICH TOWN 2
DERBY COUNTY 1

The Rams started brightly with a scintillating Giles Barnes run down the right but were soon made aware of Town's pace on the break when the hosts strung together a move that ended with a Fabian Wilnis shot over the bar.

On seven minutes Ipswich came close to opening the scoring when a sequence of passes resulted in Francis Jeffers picking up the ball 25 yards out and flashing a shot narrowly wide of Stephen Bywater's left-hand post.

From the resulting goal-kick, the Rams broke and won a free-kick

IPSWICH: Supple, Wilnis, De Vos, Bruce, Garvan (O'Callaghan 46), Williams, Peters, Walters, Wright, Jeffers (Haynes 79), Roberts (Harding 31).
UNUSED SUBS: Lee, Miller.

IPSWICH: Bywater (Grant 30), Mears, Leacock, Edworthy, McEveley, Jones, S. Johnson (Bisgaard 46), Oakley, Barnes (Teale 83), Howard, Fagan.
UNUSED SUBS: Camara, Pearson.

ATTENDANCE: 24,319.

Stephen Bywater is restrained after his sending-off.

The Rams celebrate their goal at Ipswich.

midway inside the Tractor Boys half when Jason De Vos climbed all over Steve Howard.

The Derby striker headed in David Jones's set-piece, but the flag was up for offside.

Jeffers then shot wide once again before, in a game that was flowing from end to end, the Rams took the lead.

On nine minutes Bywater cleared long downfield, and after the ball took one bounce Howard cushioned a header into the path of captain Matt Oakley, who volleyed a sublime right-footer past Shane Supple from 25 yards.

Ipswich responded immediately, and just a moment after he'd been involved in setting up the goal Bywater was called upon to make a superb fingertip save down to his right-hand side from a Jonathan Walters strike.

There was controversy on 27 minutes as, from an Ipswich corner, Bywater and Alex Bruce went head to head inside the Derby six-yard box and words were exchanged between the pair.

The referee called both players over and instantly sent both off.

As Bywater and Bruce walked off in the direction of the tunnel all hell broke loose, and virtually every player on the pitch was involved in an almighty skirmish.

And just when all that appeared to have calmed down, there was more trouble in front of the technical areas, and Rams boss Billy Davies was sent to the stands.

Lee Grant took over in goal for his first appearance since October.

Oakley's cross to the back post was just beyond the stretch of Howard before Ipswich broke to the other end and Garvan struck a lovely half volley that scorched just wide.

Peters forced a corner in that added-on time as the hosts pressed for an equaliser. De Vos got on the end of Williams's set-piece but could only steer his header over the bar.

The first good chance after the restart came after 50 minutes when Jeffers twisted and turned to evade the attentions of Leacock and then Bisgaard before unleashing a curler from range that flicked the top of the bar.

Grant clutched gratefully onto an O'Callaghan header on 59 minutes as the Rams defended a little too deeply for their fans' liking.

The replacement Derby stopper was then called into action again to expertly palm away a Jeffers drive.

On 68 minutes a curling Jones free-kick from 35 yards was collected well by a diving Supple, but just minutes later, at the other end, Grant could do nothing to prevent Jeffers from equalising after he spun past the Rams defence and picked up a long Fabian Wilnis clearance before placing it low through the Derby 'keeper's legs.

Teale burst through the middle on 87 minutes and tried to curl the ball round Supple, but the real drama came at the other end just seconds later.

Ipswich counter-attacked quickly and sub Haynes charged into the box. He stumbled over under a McEveley challenge and the referee immediately pointed to the spot.

Haynes himself stepped up and slotted a penalty past Grant, who had guessed correctly in going to his left, and into the net.

REACTION

Rams boss Billy Davies knows it's all to play for in the remainder of the Championship campaign despite Saturday afternoon's 2–1 defeat at Ipswich Town.

Although disappointed with his side's defending in the Portman Road loss, particularly in the second half, the gaffer is adamant there's still plenty to play for for Derby, who still sit second in the League table.

Still reeling about the controversial sending-off of his goalkeeper Stephen Bywater in the 28th minute of the game in Suffolk, Davies said 'I'm disappointed, but there is still plenty to fight for.

'I felt that as long as there was no individual errors, that have been costing us dearly of late, then we may have sneaked a goal and the result but again poor defending has cost us.

'But we will regroup, as we are one of three teams still fighting for the top two places.

'When you look at the potential banana skins that are left for everyone we know that anything is possible.

'There will be twists and turns, we just have to remain positive and focused for the remaining matches.'

Stephen Bywater has denied a charge of improper conduct in an alleged incident after he and Ipswich Town player Alex Bruce were shown red cards last weekend.

The FA's Disciplinary Commission will stage a personal hearing for the goalkeeper next Wednesday, and in the meantime he is available to play against Luton Town on Friday night.

On Tuesday the FA ruled that Bywater had been wrongly sent off and dismissed a charge of violent conduct that would have incurred a three-match ban.

There is no special categorisation of punishment in the event of a charge of improper conduct being proved.

Meanwhile, the Rams have recalled teenage defender Lewin Nyatanga from his loan spell at Barnsley. The Welsh international is back at Pride Park to add defensive cover following the suspension of Darren Moore.

James McEveley appeals after bringing down Danny Haynes in the box for a late penalty.

The referee Iain Williamson approaches Billy Davies.

He is then sent to the stands.

Marc Edworthy is shown the yellow card by referee Iain Williamson.

Dean Leacock is shown the yellow card.

And winger Ryan Smith's loan spell with League One side Millwall has been extended to 5 May.

The youngster's original loan period was due to expire after the mid-table Lions played at Huddersfield this Saturday, but he can now play right up to the last game of the campaign away at Bradford City.

Leaders Sunderland, second-placed Birmingham City and the Rams in third are fighting it out for the two spots to guarantee automatic promotion to the Premiership for next season.

Birmingham nipped in to second on Tuesday night with a 2–1 win at Leicester City, but Derby have the chance to go above them on Friday when they host Luton Town.

Whatever happens Davies's side will end up with at least a Play-off spot, but the gaffer says it's still all to play for.

'Yes, that's what we've got to try and do now, pick up the three wins over the three games,' he said when asked if nine points was the target for the remainder of the season.

'When you look at the season so far, we're delighted to be guaranteed a Play-off place – which in itself is a wonderful achievement.

'Obviously now we are in with a good possibility of automatic promotion and, with the teams we're fighting against having just come down from the Premiership, we're thrilled to be in this position, and we'll give it our best shot between now and the end of the season.'

Friday's visit of Luton to Pride Park gives the Rams their first opportunity to chalk up win number one of the desired three.

The Hatters need the points for altogether different reasons, as they know that anything less than a victory will condemn them to League One football for next season.

The match is being screened live on Sky Sports, and Davies knows it's a game his side needs to be up for.

'It's another game and another three points, both clubs need to win the match – that's the way it is,' he added. 'If you're going to go and win a Championship or get automatic promotion you've got to go into these games and be positive and confident.

'We can go in and show the country what we're all about by picking up another three points.'

And it will be a case of mixed emotions for Steve Howard as he lines up in a game vital for his current employers and his old friends.

Howard scored more than 100 goals in a successful five-year spell with Luton, and he admits that their current plight is hard to take in.

But Derby's need for the points is just as great, and there'll be no chance of split loyalties come kick-off.

'They were up there fighting for the Play-offs then all of a sudden sold all of their players and went into free-fall,' Howard said. 'It is hard to see as I've got a lot of friends there.

'The lads look at it the same way, they're really down and a bit annoyed at the way things have happened for them.

'It's a good set of lads down there though, and they'll keep battling to the final whistle. They'll be fighting for their lives as they want to stay in the League, but we need the points more than them, we're focused on promotion.

'It will be hard to take if they go down [at Pride Park] as I've got friends there and I want them to do well, but our need is greater – simple as that.'

REPORT – 20 APRIL 2007
DERBY COUNTY 1
LUTON TOWN 0

An early chance came Gary Teale's way as he met David Jones's free-kick with his head, but he was under enough pressure from the Luton defence to make sure he missed the target.

The Rams came closer on 13 minutes thanks to a clever free-kick routine that saw Matt Oakley's 25-yard shot cannon off the top of the bar with Dean Brill beaten.

Luton had a penalty claim rejected on 22 minutes as Leon Barnett nodded on David Bell's free-kick and the ball bounced up on to the arm of Leacock, but referee Richard Beeby waved the appeals away.

Derby had spot-kick calls of their own thrown out as Howard appeared to be held as he looked to be closing in on Currie's corner.

The big number nine then saw a header cleared off the line by Chris Coyne on 27 minutes, but the rebound was wasted as Jones drove wide from 14 yards with his right foot.

Jones's left foot is more renowned, and on 33 minutes he whipped over a delightful corner that Leacock rose to meet, but his header was deflected wide.

The ex-Manchester United man's flag-kicks were all dropping dangerously inside the six-yard box and giving Luton plenty to think about. And a minute later his next effort led to a deserved opening goal for the Rams.

Leacock powered a header goalwards, and, although Brill palmed it away well, the ball came out for Nyatanga to bundle home from close range.

Luton had a miracle escape six minutes into the second period from another excellent Jones free-kick.

Leacock's header downwards was deflected up on to the bar by Teale, and the ball came out to Howard, but once again he saw his effort scrambled off the line.

The visitors' first shot on target came 57 minutes in as Calvin Andrew twisted and turned on the edge of the box, but his effort was no real danger to Stephen Bywater. But the action was soon back at the other end, and Jones clipped the outside of a post with a lovely curling free-kick.

Drew Talbot should have done better from three yards as he met Lewis Emanuel's fine low cross but somehow sliced the ball behind him.

Oakley broke through midfield on 70 minutes and slipped in Lupoli, who saw his shot well saved by the feet of Brill, but Howard couldn't get his rebound effort on target.

Bywater produced a superb save from Idrijaz's 20-yard curler as the visitors stepped forward at pace, looking for any route back into the game they could find.

It was all Luton in the closing stages with time ticking down on their spell in the Coca-Cola Championship.

Bywater again saved from Langley and only the feet of Brill stopped Lupoli from putting the seal on the win, but Derby were looking for three points – and got their wish, while for Luton defeat meant they were relegated from the Championship just two seasons after winning promotion.

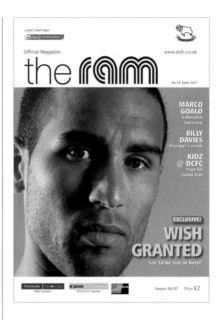

DERBY: Bywater, Edworthy, Leacock, Nyatanga, McEveley, Teale (Pearson 72), Oakley (C), Jones, Currie (Lupoli 65), Barnes (Fagan 79), Howard.
UNUSED SUBS: Grant, Mears.

LUTON: Brill, Foley, Emanuel, Coyne (C), Heikkinen, Spring, Barnett, O'Leary (Langley 72), Bell, Andrew, Talbot (Idrijaz 65).
UNUSED SUBS: Perrett, Boyd, Keane.

ATTENDANCE: 28,499.

Dean Leacock leaps into action during their 1–0 win over Luton.

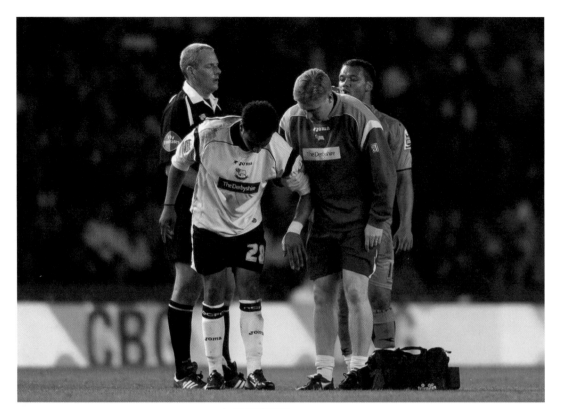

Giles Barnes has to come off with an ankle injury.

Steve Howard comiserates with his former Luton teammates after their relegation is confirmed.

REACTION

A break from Rams action will see Billy Davies in the crowd at Oakwell on Saturday watching Barnsley play next opponents Crystal Palace.

The Rams boss has given his players the weekend off ahead of the trip to Selhurst Park on Sunday next week.

'I will be enjoying some time with the family,' said Davies, 'but I'll be watching Palace because next week we will be back on the training ground and taking stock with two matches to play.

'It was never going to be easy against Luton, but I thought we created a lot of chances, and no one could have complained if we'd scored four or five, especially as we might have had a couple of penalties.

'Matt Oakley hit the bar from an excellently-worked free-kick in the first half, but I thought we were off the pace after the break and dropped too deep.

'That said, it was a fantastic three points and puts pressure back on the others chasing a top-two spot.'

Lewin Nyatanga reflected on a 'dream comeback' after returning to the Derby County line up to score the winning goal in the Friday night success against Luton Town.

Nyatanga's last appearance for the Rams was back in September when he played in the Carling Cup exit at Doncaster Rovers.

Since then he has been out on loan at Sunderland and Barnsley but was recalled to Pride Park at the start of the week with Derby short of centre-back bodies.

And he timed his return perfectly with a close-range strike that lifted the club back up to second in the Coca-Cola Championship ahead of the weekend's fixtures.

'It's a dream comeback really – three points for Derby, and to get the winning goal, it's brilliant,' he said. 'Hopefully I can keep going and build on that.

'It's been a strange week, but that's football though, things do change quickly. But to get the three points is the perfect end to the week.'

Goalkeeper Stephen Bywater has been handed a one-match suspension and a fine of £2,000, having admitted improper conduct following his dismissal in the game at Ipswich Town.

The 25-year-old will miss Sunday's penultimate match of the season at Crystal Palace as he serves his ban.

Bywater had his red card in the defeat at Portman Road overturned but was then charged with improper conduct following an incident with Ipswich's Alex Bruce.

He admitted the charge and attended a personal hearing with an FA Disciplinary Commission on Wednesday, where he was given the punishment.

Rams boss Billy Davies said 'We're disappointed to lose Stephen for the next match, but in the circumstances it's the best we could hope for, considering he won the original appeal and then had to face this charge of improper conduct.'

Bywater has also been warned by the FA as to his future conduct.

Derby County will not be appealing the decision, and as a result the Rams have recalled goalkeeper Lee Camp.

Camp, 22, has been out on loan at Queen's Park Rangers since 12 February and played 11 times for the Loftus Road club. But Bywater's ban has left Derby with Lee Grant as their only senior goalkeeper.

The Coca-Cola Championship promotion race looks like going right down to the wire – and Rams boss Billy Davies is aware that a slip-up for any of the top three could prove costly.

Birmingham City currently head the way with a single-point advantage over second-placed Sunderland, who in turn are a point ahead of Derby in third.

Automatic promotion to the Premiership is between those three teams, with two other clubs waiting to capitalise should one falter at the last.

'Any type of slip at all and the teams will know they're in a difficult position again,' Davies said.

'What we've got to remember is how tough the opposition has been – Sunderland have had a very long unbeaten run, while Birmingham have got £10m of strikers.

'We know that the challenge is difficult as we know where they have been in the last couple of years and also where we have come from this season. But we're very proud to have secured at least third place and to be pushing things right down to the wire.

'The only message to our players is six points from the next two games, to keep the pressure on as much as we can and take it to the last game.

'That has always been our focus, and I have always said that if we can do that there will be a little twist of fate, either this week or next.'

Dean Leacock makes a first playing return to his old childhood stomping ground when the Rams travel to Crystal Palace on Sunday. The 22-year-old grew up close to Selhurst Park and many of his family are fans of the Eagles. He has even been a ball-boy there, but has yet to tread the turf during his playing career.

Lewin Nyatanga at full-time.

Matt Oakley.

The Croydon-born ace has likened Sunday's game to 'going home' – but he says it's all about getting three points towards Derby's promotion ambitions.

'I grew up two minutes away from there; I could see the stadium and the lights, and on a matchday I could hear the noise,' he said. 'It is like going home, and it will be good to go back down there and see the family.

'But three points is the target for us as we need a win to put pressure on Sunderland and Birmingham.'

REPORT – 29 APRIL 2007
CRYSTAL PALACE 2
DERBY COUNTY 0

Wins for Sunderland on Friday and Birmingham City on Saturday meant that Derby needed three points of their own to keep the automatic promotion race alive.

Derby started out playing some bright football, particularly through Giles Barnes and David Jones, though the first chance of the game fell to Palace.

Dean Leacock could only get a touch to Julian Speroni's long clearance, and the ball came through to Clinton Morrison, who could only loft the ball over Lee Camp and narrowly past the post with Lewin Nyatanga putting him under pressure.

The early possession was all Derby's, but threats on goal were scarce at both ends.

Even when space opened up for Jobi McAnuff on 22 minutes, the tricky winger cut in from the left but sliced his shot so badly it ended up going out for a throw-in.

Matt Oakley then fired over on 26 minutes after Jones's right-wing corner was only half-cleared out to the edge of the box.

And two minutes later Palace were in front.

Carl Fletcher scuffed his 25-yard shot, but the ball came through to Morrison, who had been left to wander in behind the Derby defence. The striker was onside and had time to take a touch before stroking his shot past Camp from just inside the box.

Morrison almost made it two shortly afterwards as Camp could only palm out Mark Kennedy's cross into his path, but this time the ex-Birmingham man was off-target.

Howard came close to equalising with 11 minutes left of the half as he rose to meet Darren Currie's corner, though his headed effort went narrowly over.

Currie was the architect of the Rams' best opportunity so far with a clever 37th-minute pass that Matt Oakley ran on to but could only turn straight at Julian Speroni.

Howard then fired a left-footer from 25 yards that was straight down the goalkeeper's throat.

Barnes threatened in stoppage time after collecting Jay McEveley's drilled pass and turning inside Mark Hudson, but again he couldn't find the required accuracy.

Camp grabbed Ben Watson's firm drive shortly after the break, before

PALACE: Speroni, Lawrence, Hudson, Cort, McAnuff, Morrison (Ifill 76), Watson, Kennedy, Borrowdale, Fletcher (C), Kuqi (Scowcroft 72).
UNUSED SUBS: Kiraly, Freedman, Butterfield.

DERBY: Camp, Edworthy (Mears HT), Leacock, Nyatanga, McEveley, Teale, Oakley (C), Jones, Currie (Fagan 64), Barnes (Lupoli 50), Howard.
UNUSED SUBS: Grant, Pearson.

ATTENDANCE: 19,545.

Speroni had to show great athleticism to leap up and claim the ball after Mark Hudson deflected a cross goalwards, with Howard waiting to pounce.

The Rams were forced into a second change just five minutes into the second period as Barnes was helped from the field with a knee injury, with Arturo Lupoli taking his place.

But the game was opening up, and it was soon Watson's turn to threaten for the home side, forcing an excellent low save from Camp on 55 minutes.

McAnuff should have doubled the lead on the hour when he broke the offside trap, only to fire wide in a one-on-one position with Camp.

But it was surely game over on 66 minutes as Kennedy was given far too much space on the left to stride forward into the box and smash an unstoppable effort past Camp.

It should have been three shortly after as Kennedy was again left in space to square low across the box, but his ball was too far in front of the three waiting Palace attackers.

Lupoli almost pulled one back out of nowhere with a smart low shot that Speroni did very well to get across and turn away for a corner.

The flag-kick was only half-cleared and turned back in by Teale, but Lewin Nyatanga could only shoot well over the bar as the ball bobbled around.

The final whistle brought with it an end to Derby's hopes of automatic promotion, but at least they've got another crack in the Play-offs, so their next target will be the semi-finals – and hopefully a date at the new Wembley Stadium.

REACTION

Billy Davies felt nerves got the better of the Rams as their automatic promotion hopes ended with a 2–0 defeat at Crystal Palace.

Lee Camp makes a save.

Lewin Nyatanga wrestles with Clinton Morrison.

Steve Howard with the ball.

Giles Barnes is withdrawn with a knee injury.

Derby were under pressure after Sunderland and Birmingham City won their matches, leaving Davies's side needing a victory of their own to take the race to the final day.

'It was one step too far; unfortunately on the day we just allowed nerves to get to us a little bit and never functioned as we can do,' he said. 'We had an average age of 24 out there, and with key players missing at a very crucial period we're very proud of what's been achieved, but we're disappointed in the end.

'There was a lot of pressure on us and we've seen that today.

'The opposition were out here for a Sunday stroll with nothing to play for, and the game is easier when you're in that kind of situation – it's not so easy in our position.

'But I'd rather look at the positives – it has been a fantastic season, we have had 10 months in charge of a group of players who have worked extremely hard and now we look forward to the Play-offs.'

Skipper Matt Oakley is looking forward to taking on the Play-offs for the first time.

The midfielder's career had been spent exclusively in the top-flight until last season with Southampton, but they never seriously threatened an immediate return after relegation in 2004–05.

But he has the chance of heading back to the Premiership once more with Derby after the Rams' defeat at Crystal Palace confirmed that they will finish third in the table.

Oakley admitted that there was a feeling of disappointment about not taking the automatic promotion race right down to the wire, but he's excited about what still lies ahead.

'I think we've had a fantastic season, and, while we're disappointed that we've not forced the other teams into the last day of the season, the boys will come back and we've got another shot at it,' he said.

'We'll see where we go in the Play-offs – we didn't play well today, but we have been in good form up to now.

'Coming here was always going to be a hard game as Palace is never an easy place to visit; I personally haven't picked up many points here.

'It's a difficult place to come, and they didn't give us anything today, so fair play to them, they took the points.'

Giles Barnes is to miss the Coca-Cola Championship Play-offs with the knee injury he suffered in Sunday's 2–0 defeat at Crystal Palace.

The 18-year-old was helped from the field five minutes into the second half at Selhurst Park, and it was originally feared he had suffered ligament damage.

But scans have found tissue problems instead, and he will be an absentee as the Rams look for a place in the Premiership via the Play-offs having missed out on automatic promotion.

'Giles has damaged the tissue that holds the kneecap in place,' Derby boss Billy Davies confirmed. 'There is no ligament damage and no operation is needed, so it will be a case of treatment and rehabilitation work.

'He should be fit for pre-season training.'

Davies also confirmed that Marc Edworthy only took a knock to his ankle during the South London reverse, and that he should be OK in a few days.

There is positive news about the progress of defender Michael Johnson. The experienced centre-half went off during March's 5–1 win over Colchester United with a hamstring injury that has sidelined him ever since. But he is now back in training, and Davies added 'He should be fit and in contention for the Play-offs.'

The travelling Rams fans have been vocal all season.

TABLE

	P	W	D	L	F	A	Pts
Birmingham	45	26	8	11	67	41	86
Sunderland	45	26	7	12	71	47	85
Derby	**45**	**24**	**9**	**12**	**60**	**46**	**81**
West Brom	45	21	10	14	74	55	73
Wolves	45	21	10	14	55	55	73
Southampton	45	20	12	13	73	52	72
Stoke	45	19	15	11	61	40	72
Preston	45	21	8	16	63	53	71
Colchester	45	20	9	16	70	54	69
Sheffield W	45	19	11	15	67	64	68
Cardiff	45	17	13	15	56	50	64
Plymouth	45	16	16	13	61	61	64
C Palace	45	17	11	17	57	51	62
Ipswich	45	17	8	20	61	58	59
Burnley	45	15	12	18	51	47	57
Norwich	45	16	9	20	54	68	57
Leicester	45	13	14	18	48	60	53
Coventry	45	15	8	22	45	61	53
QPR	45	14	10	21	53	67	52
Barnsley	45	15	5	25	53	78	50
Hull	45	13	10	22	50	65	49
Leeds	45	13	7	25	46	70	46
Southend	45	10	12	23	46	76	42
Luton	45	10	10	25	53	76	40

May

So it's the Play-offs following that defeat at Selhurst Park to close April and hand the automatic promotion spots to Birmingham and Sunderland, who will fight it out for the title on the final day of the season.

There's no pressure on Derby's last-day encounter at home to Leeds United, who are relegated to League One after going into administration and incurring a 10-point penalty.

Results elsewhere will determine who Derby face in the semi-final, with six teams their potential opponents for a place at Wembley.

Stephen Pearson is fit and raring to get his Derby County career going again. The Scotsman joined from Celtic in the January transfer window and was already looking a valuable signing before being struck by a foot injury at the end of February.

He's been on the sidelines since – except for a substitute appearance against Luton last month – but is back in full training and set to return to the side for Sunday's game against Leeds United.

'I'm fully fit now, and after being out for quite a while it will be nice to be back involved,' he said. 'I've missed quite a bit of football so it's crucial that if I play on Sunday I try and get as much match-fitness and sharpness under my belt as possible.

'It's always frustrating when you're injured as you want to play as much as possible.

'But injuries happen in the game so hopefully that's me over it now, and I can look forward to the next few weeks.'

Billy Davies insists that it doesn't matter who the Rams end up with in the Play-off semi-final – only that they will be in for a tough test.

Derby could come up against any of West Bromwich Albion, Wolverhampton Wanderers, Southampton, Stoke City, Preston North End or Colchester United in the last four.

Sunday's results will decide who they take on for the right to head to the new Wembley Stadium in search of a place in the Premiership.

'It doesn't really matter who we get,' Davies said. 'We're there and have got to take on the challenge and get the job done over the two matches.

'Hopefully then this club will be looking forward to what is without doubt a wonderful day at Wembley and a fantastic day out.'

Stephen Pearson, back from injury for the final game of the season.

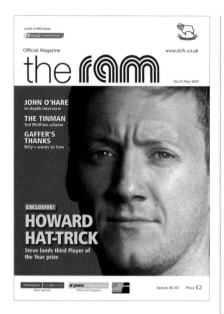

DERBY: Bywater, Mears, Leacock, Nyatanga, McEveley, Bisgaard (Currie 45), S. Johnson (C), Pearson, Fagan, Howard (Macken 66), Peschisolido (Lupoli 80).
UNUSED SUBS: M. Johnson, Malcolm.

LEEDS: Ankergren, Thompson (C), Gray, R. Elliott, J. Johnson, Carole (Howson 52), Foxe (T. Elliott HT), Rui Marques, Cresswell, Blake (Delph 52), Bayly.
UNUSED SUBS: Stack, Moore.

ATTENDANCE: 31,183.

Seth Johnson looks over referee Phil Crossley after a collision between them.

REPORT – 6 MAY 2007
DERBY COUNTY 2
LEEDS UNITED 0

Both sets of fans were making plenty of noise in the early stages, and then the volume level went up further five minutes in with a loud ironic cheer as referee Phil Crossley went crashing to the floor.

He and Seth Johnson collided completely accidentally, though it didn't look too good for the match official as medical assistance was on in a hurry and a stretcher called for.

The game was held up for some 10 minutes to allow treatment for Crossley, who left the field on a stretcher and was replaced by fourth official Carl Boyeson.

To all intents and purposes it meant the game was starting all over again, and it was Derby who had the first opportunity, with Bisgaard shooting wide from just outside the box.

The Rams looked to have pace on the break through Fagan, and with 24 minutes on the clock he ran half the length of the field with the ball at his feet before shooting just wide of Casper Ankergren's right-hand post.

Leeds, to their credit, were playing some neat football and had their first chance of the game on 35 minutes as Sebastien Carole looked to get in on Thompson's chipped pass, but Lewin Nyatanga got back to block well.

But Derby were soon back on the front foot with Pearson and Bisgaard again involved on the edge of the Leeds box before the ball came through to Fagan, whose shot was deflected by a blocking foot and excellently turned away by Ankergren.

The board went up to signal 10 minutes of stoppage time at the end of the first 45, which was no surprise following the earlier break for referee Crossley's injury.

And in the fourth of those added minutes the Rams should have taken the lead.

Peschisolido held the ball up well and fed Pearson on the left, whose low cross was crying out for Howard to smash it home from close range, but somehow Derby's leading scorer put his effort wide of the post.

Peschisolido then dipped a volley wide, but there was still time for one last attack, and though it looked like the chance was gone Derby rescued things to take the lead.

Darren Currie celebrates his first goal.

Skipper-for-the-day Seth Johnson picked up Mears's over-hit cross and pulled back a clever ball from the left that Currie stroked home from 10 yards.

Bywater made his first real save of the game two minutes into the second period as he threw himself away to his left to grab Thompson's 25-yard free-kick.

Bywater pushed over Thompson's 57th-minute free-kick, though Leeds failed to make the most of the corner.

The former Bolton, Aston Villa and Celtic man was looking dangerous with his set-pieces, and on 64 minutes he forced Bywater into another smart save.

Leeds were reduced to 10 men with 18 minutes to go after an act of stupidity by Robert Bayly on his first start for the club. He went through Fagan with a late challenge, then got up and aimed a head at the Derby man, leaving Boyeson with no option but to bring out the red card.

Macken came close to opening his Rams account with seven minutes left on the clock after meeting McEveley's cross from the left, but his header rattled back off the crossbar.

But the lead was doubled on 85, from the most unlikely of sources.

Currie's excellent pass split the Leeds defence and through rushed Mears to squeeze his shot past Ankergren and over the line.

The full-back then advanced down the right a couple of minutes later and smashed a low effort that Ankergren turned past his near post.

Morten Bisgaard lies injured on the pitch.

REACTION

Billy Davies says the omens are good as the Rams prepare for Saturday's first leg of the Play-off semi-final at Southampton's St Mary's Stadium.

'After the disappointment of the past couple weeks, I have felt the pulse coming back into the squad this week,' the boss said after Sunday's 2–0 home win over Leeds United.

'All is very positive with good performances from the players who came in and with Michael Johnson back on the bench and Darren Moore available again.

'We can look to go to Southampton, get a result and bring them back to Pride Park.'

Goalscorer Tyrone Mears said he was trying to blow the ball over the line as a first strike in Derby County colours beckoned.

Tyrone Mears squeezes the ball under the Leeds 'keeper.

The full-back was the most advanced man on the field with five minutes to go as he put the seal on Sunday's 2–0 win over Leeds United.

But he almost didn't break his duck after visiting goalkeeper Casper Ankergren got a foot to his shot, and it looked for a short time as though it would fall agonisingly short.

'I've had a good touch inside the defender, and Micky Gray's tried to take me down, but I've touched it past the 'keeper and I'm blowing it over the line!' Mears said.

'I thought he would get back to it, but hopefully if it hadn't have gone in the referee would have given the penalty.

'I like to get one goal a season and that was a good one to get at the end!'

Billy Davies and the Derby County staff and players parade the pitch at the end of the match.

FINAL TABLE

	P	W	D	L	F	A	Pts
Sunderland	46	27	7	12	76	47	88
Birmingham	46	26	8	12	67	42	86
Derby	**46**	**25**	**8**	**12**	**62**	**46**	**84**
West Brom	46	22	10	14	81	55	76
Wolves	46	22	10	14	59	56	76
Southampton	46	21	12	13	77	53	75
Preston	46	22	8	16	64	53	74
Stoke	46	19	16	11	62	41	73
Sheffield W	46	20	11	15	70	66	71
Colchester	46	20	9	17	70	56	69
Plymouth	46	17	16	13	63	62	67
C Palace	46	18	11	17	59	51	65
Cardiff	46	17	13	16	57	53	64
Ipswich	46	18	8	20	64	59	62
Burnley	46	15	12	19	52	49	57
Norwich	46	16	9	21	56	71	57
Coventry	46	16	8	22	47	62	56
QPR	46	14	11	21	54	68	53
Leicester	46	13	14	19	49	64	53
Barnsley	46	15	5	26	53	85	50
Hull	46	13	10	23	51	67	49
Southend	46	10	12	24	47	80	42
Luton	46	10	10	26	53	81	40
Leeds *	46	13	7	26	46	72	36

* Leeds deducted 10 points for going into administration.

Darren Currie is available for selection for the Play-offs after his loan from Ipswich Town was extended to the end of May.

The experienced winger, who opened his Derby County account with a goal as a substitute in Sunday's 2–0 home win over Leeds United, has made four starts and three appearances from the bench since joining the Rams at the end of March.

Billy Davies leads Derby County into the Play-offs after his first season in charge with the message: 'enjoy it'.

Davies only took over at Pride Park last June but has guided the Rams to third in the table after a thrilling race for the automatic promotion places.

Derby finished just two points adrift of the top two, but they have a second bite at earning a place in the Premiership via the Play-offs.

Their first test is a two-leg tie against Southampton, who finished a further nine points behind in sixth position.

Ahead of Saturday's first-leg game at the St Mary's Stadium, Davies said 'Obviously we were disappointed to miss out on automatic promotion so narrowly, but it's very exciting to be in the Play-offs.

'My message to the players all week has been to enjoy every minute of it – the build-up, the training sessions, the butterflies in the stomach, and of course the matches.

'These are wonderful events, but more importantly they are wonderful memories for those involved.'

For Davies, it's a third successive crack at the Play-offs after he guided Preston North End to top-six finishes in each of the last two campaigns.

They were beaten in the semi-final by Leeds United last season, but 12 months previously they went all the way to the Final, where West Ham United overcame them by a single goal.

The gaffer admits he has taken the events of recent years on board as he looks to take Derby to the top flight at the first attempt.

'You always learn from past experiences, and there were certain things I did that I may have done differently, but that's hindsight and it's a wonderful thing,' he said.

'What I'll do is explain to the players the situation we're now in; what it's like to be involved with.

'We're very proud of the season and what we've achieved so now we will try and take this team into the Play-off Final.'

Darren Moore is happy to be back in contention to play again this season – even though it means the Rams have missed out on automatic promotion.

Moore was suspended for the final four games of the Coca-Cola Championship season and hoped he wouldn't be needed again as Derby would have finished at least second. He has been welcomed back into the frame by the Rams boss ahead of Saturday's first-leg at the St Mary's Stadium.

'I'm absolutely delighted to be back in contention,' the strapping centre-half said.

'Over the last few weeks I've been involved, but it's been like a bit-part really because you're training and doing everything, but when it comes to the game I'm just a supporter. But now it's good because I feel like I can be back involved on all fronts so I'm really pleased.

'I said before that I would have gladly taken the punishment if it meant that we went up automatically.'

REPORT – 12 MAY 2007
SOUTHAMPTON 1
DERBY COUNTY 2
PLAY-OFF SEMI-FINAL FIRST LEG

Marek Saganowski had the first opportunity four minutes in as he got to a bouncing ball ahead of Dean Leacock and attempted a 30-yard lob that Stephen Bywater stepped back to catch on his line.

At the other end the Rams went close when Seth Johnson's free-kick was only cleared out to the edge of the box where Fagan dived in quickly to head just wide.

But seconds later a quick one-two on the edge of the Derby box saw Southampton open the scoring.

Some sharp passing fed the ball out to Andrew Surman, who took a touch before curling a superb left-footed effort past Bywater and into the top corner.

Southampton failed to sufficiently clear a 24th-minute corner, and it produced the Rams' first shot on target, a 20-yard Howard effort that was no trouble to Bartosz Bialkowski.

Gareth Bale's dangerous free-kick was flicked goalwards by Chris Baird, forcing Bywater into a fine sprawling low save, then from the second of two quick corners Bale's cross dipped just wide of the far post.

But out of nowhere Derby were level on 36 minutes.

Johnson's corner was only half-cleared out to Oakley, who lifted the ball back into the box where Howard rose to plant an excellent header back across Bialkowski and send the travelling support wild.

Saints looked to break back quickly and could have restored their advantage had Saganowski not smacked Djamel Belmadi's excellent through pass against the top of the crossbar.

It was then Derby's turn to attack quickly and Oakley was close with a curler from just inside the box that flashed narrowly wide of the far post, with Bialkowski beaten.

Bywater opened the second half with an excellent block from Kenwyne Jones's edge-of-the-box effort with the game already appearing to be opening up more.

Derby then threatened in front of their own fans through Howard, who turned 20 yards out and smashed a powerful effort just wide of the upright.

SOUTHAMPTON: Bialkowski, Ostlund, Baird (C), Pele, Bale (Skacel 56), Surman, Guthrie, Viafara, Belmadi, K. Jones (Best 56), Saganowski (Rasiak 85).
UNUSED SUBS: Davis, Cranie.

DERBY: Bywater, Mears, Leacock, Moore, McEveley, Fagan, Oakley (C), S. Johnson (Nyatanga 90) Pearson, Howard, Macken (Teale 76).
UNUSED SUBS: Camp, Edworthy, D. Jones.

ATTENDANCE: 30,602.

Steve Howard scoring from Oakley's cross.

Steve Howard scoring Derby's second from the penalty spot.

And 10 minutes after the break Derby won a penalty as Oakley's excellent pass picked out Pearson on the left, who cut inside and was hauled down by Pele.

Up stepped Howard to take his tally to two for the afternoon and 19 for the season with a powerful effort that beat Bialkowski low to his left.

The Rams fans behind the goal were making as much noise as they had done all afternoon, and they were almost in dreamland just after the hour as Macken was desperately unlucky to see his 25-yarder cannon back off the post.

Jay McEveley produced an excellent block to deny Saganowski, who should then have levelled on 69 minutes when he hit the crossbar once more – this time from much closer in after Belmadi's pass.

As time ticked on the Rams were guilty of giving away a few too many free-kicks in dangerous areas, though thankfully for them Skacel didn't have his best crossing boots on with most of them.

Derby could have made the game safe on 88 minutes as Howard flicked on Mears's long throw into the path of Teale, but the Scotsman couldn't get enough purchase on his close-range shot.

Southampton won a free-kick right on the edge of the D as three minutes of stoppage time began, but Derby stood firm to block it out and clear.

REACTION

Billy Davies will be making sure his players don't take their foot off the gas ahead of Tuesday's Play-off semi-final second leg with Southampton.

The Rams travelled south to the St Mary's Stadium on Saturday and came away with a 2–1 first-leg victory thanks to Steve Howard's double. But with a single-goal advantage and at least 90 minutes to come, Davies is keen to ensure the players don't think they've already guaranteed themselves a place in the Wembley Final.

'It certainly is half-time, and we won't forget that,' he said. 'We've already said that to the players, and they know that themselves.

'I have said for a week or so that I felt the pulse was coming back into the team, I could feel the whole situation getting better.

'As far as I'm concerned it's a fantastic result in the first game.'

Skipper Matt Oakley felt the Rams fully deserved to be heading back to Pride Park with the advantage in their Play-off semi-final.

Now the Saints – Oakley's former club – know they've got to win Tuesday's second leg to deny Derby a place in the Final at Wembley.

'We made a bad start by conceding in the first few minutes but showed great character, and I thought we were the better side by quite a way in the second half,' Oakley said.

'In the last 15 minutes they came back into it and put some pressure on us, as we knew they were going to.

'But we'd had chances and been unlucky with Jon Macken's strike that hit the post so it could have been a greater victory.

'It's nice to be going back to Pride Park now with a 2–1 win.'

Steve Howard acknowledged his most important Derby County goals to date. The 31-year-old was pleased with his afternoon's work but knows that it's not all over yet, with a fantastic Pride Park atmosphere in the pipeline for Tuesday.

Steve Howard after scoring his second goal.

'It was nice to get the two goals, especially on an occasion like this as I thought we played really well and deserved the win,' Howard said. 'We were back to our best and we've been saying in the dressing room that it's what we needed. Hopefully that will continue on Tuesday and we'll be OK. There's still a long way to go, and Tuesday will be tough again, but today is a good start.'

REPORT – 15 MAY 2007
DERBY 2
SOUTHAMPTON 3 AET
Scores level at 4–4 on aggregate, Derby win 4–3 on penalties
PLAY-OFF SEMI-FINAL SECOND LEG

Pride Park was a sea of noise as the game kicked-off, and with a little over a minute on the clock it felt like the roof was going to come off as the Rams went in front.

Matt Oakley's corner was headed goalwards by Darren Moore and crept over the line despite the last-ditch efforts of Skacel.

But such is the nature of football, no sooner were the Derby fans in raptures than they were quietened down with a bolt from the blue.

Stephen Bywater raced out of his box to head a long ball clear, but it fell to Jhon Viafara, who from 30-yards out volleyed an excellent effort back into an unguarded net.

Derby's two-goal advantage was short-lived, and it was back to how we started the night.

Steve Howard then warmed Davis's fingers with a stinging low drive that the goalkeeper did well to push out.

Southampton seemed more comfortable with matters after the early drama, though Davis was giving a few causes for alarm with his handling of high balls into the box.

Twice he dropped one in front of goal, but on neither occasion did the ball fall kindly for a Derby foot to finish.

Andrew Surman threatened a repeat of Saturday's stunner in the 26th minute, but this time he cut inside on to his right foot and couldn't find the target.

DERBY: Bywater, Mears, Moore, Leacock, McEveley, Fagan (Currie 105), Oakley (C), S. Johnson (Jones 86), Pearson, Macken (Barnes 61), Howard.
UNUSED SUBS: Camp, Edworthy.

SOUTHAMPTON: Davis, Pele, Saganowski (Rasiak 73), Skacel, Cranie, Makin (Belmadi 70), Baird (C), Viafara, Guthrie (Idiakez 82), Best, Surman.
UNUSED SUBS: Bialkowski, Wright-Phillips.

ATTENDANCE: 31,569.

PENALTIES
Best wide 0–0
Jones scored 0–1
Surman scored 1–1
Howard scored 1–2
Skacel scored 2–2
Barnes scored 2–3
Rasiak scored 3–3
McEveley scored 3–4
Idiakez over 3–4

Celebrations after Derby's first goal.

Southampton's Leon Best hooks the ball into the roof of his own net to make it 2–2.

Derby piled on the pressure in the 35th minute and wouldn't let Saints clear their lines, culminating in Seth Johnson's low 25-yard drive skimming just past the post with Davis beaten.

Saints started the second period brightly and had a lot of possession in and around the edge of the Derby box, but they were met with some stiff resistance in the shape of a number of last-ditch blocks.

And it was no real surprise when they took the lead on the night and levelled it up on aggregate.

Leacock failed to cut out a long pass in the 53rd minute and that sent Best clear, but he cleverly fed the advancing Viafara to his right and the Colombian took time to steady himself before smashing his shot past Bywater.

The visitors kept up the pressure and could have added a third through Best after Derby failed to clear a corner.

It was time for a change for the Rams with 61 minutes on the clock, and it was an earlier-than-expected return for Barnes as he took over from Macken.

The teenager's impact was immediate as he sparked off a move that saw Pearson cross low to the far post, where Fagan slid in but his powerful shot rebounded off the upright and to safety. It was quite an arrival as he then helped to spark off the pressure that led to Derby's second goal of the night.

He forced Southampton into giving away a corner, a second flag-kick then followed and Johnson's delivery was turned past his own goalkeeper by Best.

Barnes had a chance to make it three on the night and five overall with eight minutes left on the clock but flashed his shot just wide. But with 90 seconds remaining the Saints were back in front on the night and back level overall.

Belmadi made ground, and although Mears won a good tackle the ball rolled across perfectly for Rasiak to smash it past Bywater from just inside the box.

Skacel could have won it in normal time, but he fired over after being fed by Rasiak.

Derby opened up extra-time on the attack and a neat move involving Jones and Pearson ended with Fagan just not able to stretch quite enough to reach the Scotsman's low cross.

From a free-kick the ball was nodded down to Fagan, who managed to loop it back up and over Davis, but Baird got back to head off the line with Barnes ready to make sure.

And with a minute of the first period of extra-time remaining Jones turned on the edge of the Southampton box but saw his shot beat the post by inches.

In stoppage time the young midfielder curled over a corner that Howard rose and forced Davis into tipping over the bar. From the resulting flag-kick Barnes's header dipped just wide of the post.

Derby began the second half of extra-time as they had ended the first,

Stephen Pearson jumps past a Southampton player.

but once again the ball wouldn't quite run for them in key areas, despite some excellent moves. They had a good chance when Howard rose to meet Jones's free-kick but couldn't direct his header goalwards.

Southampton had their first real break with six minutes remaining as Best strode away, but he shot too early and his effort was no trouble for Bywater.

Both sides had chances to get the ball into the other's box, but it came down to the lottery of a penalty shoot-out.

REACTION

Rams skipper Matt Oakley is looking forward to the prospect of his first visit to Wembley after leading his side to an exciting penalty shoot-out win over Southampton.

The Derby captain was almost lost for words after being part of a dramatic semi-final spot-kick victory over the Saints that saw scenes of celebration at the end that haven't been witnessed at Pride Park since the stadium opened in 1997.

After the game Oakley said 'I don't know what to say, I'm speechless. Like on Saturday it was another end-to-end game with plenty of opportunities.

'It's an honour to lead this team out, especially in this fashion and against my old club, who deserve great credit.

'We have exceeded expectations, and to think we only just missed out on the automatic places.

'No one would have begrudged if we had gone up that way, but going into the Play-offs people may have thought we would be down, but we have come back and shown how strong we are.

'It will be my first time at Wembley so personally it is great, but also for everyone at the club, not least those tremendous fans.'

Billy Davies surveyed some emotional scenes after guiding the Rams to Wembley and admitted 'It's unbelievable.'

Derby will play for a place in the Premiership on 28 May after overcoming Southampton 4–3 on penalties after a 4–4 aggregate draw.

The victory was sealed by ex-Ram Inigo Idiakez blazing his spot-kick over the bar, and it sparked joyous celebrations and a pitch invasion from the fans.

And after going through all the emotions possible in the 120 minutes that preceded penalties, Davies was quick to praise the Pride Park crowd.

'When you look at that it's unbelievable, it makes the hairs on the back of your neck stand up,' he said.

'Just seeing these emotions from all of these people, it really is unbelievable.

'It's about the achievement now – forget about the football, this is fantastic.

'The fans were magnificent tonight, and I'm sure we'll take plenty to Wembley.'

The Rams' opponents at Wembley on Monday 28 May were confirmed on Wednesday evening when West Bromwich Albion saw off local rivals Wolverhampton Wanderers 4–2 on aggregate in their semi-final.

Tony Mowbray's side already held a 3–2 advantage from the first leg at Molineux, and they confirmed their place in the Final thanks to a second-half Kevin Phillips header at The Hawthorns.

The tension mounts for the fans and players.

Steve Howard scores his penalty.

The Rams celebrate, while a despondent Idiakez walks back to the Southampton players.

West Bromwich Albion will face a 'different' Derby County in Monday's Play-off Final, according to Rams boss Billy Davies.

The two sides met twice in the space of a month earlier in the season, with both winning their respective home games.

Davies says that the matches, a 2–1 win for Derby at Pride Park followed by a 1–0 success for the Baggies at the Hawthorns, will have no bearing on Monday's Wembley encounter.

'We're a different team now than we were then, particularly in the first game at Pride Park when we didn't play well but eventually won it,' the gaffer said.

'They outplayed us then, but when we went to their place, we were the better side in the second half but lost out.

'But this is different. We're a different animal now, we've got some crucial players coming back in at a very good time that may help us on the day.'

It's a third successive crack at the Play-offs for Davies and a second Final in three years. But he rates taking Derby to Wembley as a greater achievement than reaching a Cardiff Final in 2005 with Preston, and then taking the Lilywhites to the semi-final last year.

'There are lost of comparisons but this, without doubt, is the best achievement to date for Billy Davies, and hopefully it will be third-time lucky in the Play-offs,' he said.

'No matter what happens though I'm very proud to be leading this team out at Wembley, and I'm very proud to be in the Play-off Final.

'I'm also very proud to have given the supporters and everyone at this club some great memories at a time when we're very much still developing and in transition.'

David Jones says the Rams have to put the Wembley occasion out of their minds by the time Monday's Play-off Final arrives.

'It should be a great day, but we can't let the occasion get the better of us,' the 22-year-old said. 'We've got to concentrate on the 90 minutes and the main thing is that we get the result we want.

'It will be nice to put on a good performance to end the season and show that we deserve to be in the Premiership, but the result is all that counts.

'We're not bothered if we win 1–0 with the worst performance ever!'

Steve Howard wants to win the Play-off Final as a reward to boss Billy Davies for taking the Rams to within 90 minutes of the Premiership.

'It's mostly down to the gaffer – he's a very passionate bloke, who thoroughly deserves it,' Howard revealed.

'Nobody would deserve winning at Wembley more than him.

'He's been there and done it in recent years and has passed all of his experiences on to us.'

Derby finished one place and eight points above the Baggies in the Coca-Cola Championship but now it comes down to a one-off game on Monday afternoon. And Seth Johnson believes that it will be an encounter with plenty of quality on show from both sides.

'You look at the West Brom side and see that they've got a lot of attacking flair and good players going forward,' he said.

'I think it will be a good game, they have got some great players, but we have got to try and impose ourselves on the game and have a real good go at them.

'Even though we know they're a good side going forward, we also know that they've got flaws at the back and we've got the players who can hurt them.

'I think it should make for an entertaining game and a good spectacle.'

Billy Davies's address to the fans gathered at Pride Park to see the team off to Wembley.

Wembley

DERBY: Bywater, Mears, Leacock, Moore, McEveley, Fagan (Edworthy 82), Oakley (C), S. Johnson (Jones 87), Pearson, Peschisolido (Barnes 57), Howard.
UNUSED SUBS: Camp, Macken.

WBA: Kiely, Robinson (C), Perry, Greening, Gera (Ellington 70), Kamara, Koren, Koumas, McShane (Carter 70), Phillips, Sodje (Clement 81).
UNUSED SUBS: Chaplow, Daniels.

ATTENDANCE: 74,993.

REPORT – 28 MAY 2007
DERBY COUNTY 1
WEST BROMWICH ALBION 0
COCA-COLA CHAMPIONSHIP PLAY-OFF FINAL

Albion were on the attack with a shot inside 40 seconds from Kamara, following a long run that should have been halted, though Stephen Bywater was alert with a sprawling low save.

The Baggies seemed more settled in the first few minutes, but with nine minutes on the clock Derby should have been in front.

Howard flicked on a long ball to Peschisolido, picked it up again and slid in the Canadian, who seemed to lose his footing in the act of shooting from just inside the box and could only roll his effort straight at Dean Kiely.

It lifted the Rams, though they were almost caught out three minutes later as Jason Koumas embarked on a long solo run from near halfway that ended up with him inside the Derby box.

Tyrone Mears came in from the side and took the West Brom man down, though replays showed the full-back got to the ball first with an excellent challenge.

Derby – resplendent in a smart new kit especially for the Wembley occasion – were starting to find their feet and forced their first corner with 17 minutes on the clock, but Matt Oakley's delivery came to nothing.

A driving Oakley run then set up Craig Fagan, who came inside but hit his shot safely past the far post.

Derby's next opportunity came shortly after the half-hour mark following a patient move involving Howard, Fagan, Johnson and McEveley, though Oakley ultimately fired wide under pressure from the edge of the box.

Howard and Peschisolido combined to flick a McEveley cross to the far post, where Fagan drove it back across goal, but no Derby foot could get a vital finishing touch.

Koumas was next to threaten at the other end, though his shot from a narrow angle never really looked like dipping far enough to drop below Bywater's crossbar.

The Welshman was looking ever more threatening down the left, and on 41 minutes he made great ground before firing over a dangerous cross that Bywater managed to push just out of Zoltan Gera's reach.

Seconds later Phillips clipped the top of the bar from 20 yards after good build-up play involving Kamara and Gera.

Neither side made a change during the interval, but Albion again began strongly, and it was Koumas who forced Bywater into a low save.

Oakley was a few yards wide of the far post on 52 minutes with a skimming low drive, but it certainly got the Derby fans – behind the goal their players attacked in the second half – up off their seats.

At the other end the Albion fans were also in full voice and were given something to think about as Koumas, this time in the centre, flashed a 25-yard effort narrowly wide.

Giles Barnes was introduced into the action on 57 minutes, taking the place of Peschisolido. And the Rams were a flying save away from going in front shortly afterwards.

Fagan's low cross was superbly met on the half-volley by Oakley, who held his head in his hands as Kiely flew to turn the effort over the bar.

It was probably the game's best moment up to then and a wonderful reaction save from the Irishman – but on the hour he was helpless as Derby took the lead.

Howard took the ball forward on the break and fed Barnes, who made an excellent run down the inside right.

He played the ball across low for Stephen Pearson to finish from close range and score his first goal in a Derby shirt.

The joy was almost short-lived as Koumas broke and Kamara could only poke his low ball wide of the target. Bywater fumbled Gera's powerful 67th-minute effort but grabbed the ball at the second attempt with Kamara lurking.

And it was skipper Robinson who had their next chance, rising at the far post to meet a Koumas free-kick, though Bywater casually plucked the ball out of the air and didn't appear even slightly concerned.

Albion had appeals for a penalty rejected on 84 minutes as Carter went down, but once again it was an excellent challenge by Mears, while referee Graham Poll was once more well-placed to see exactly what happened.

Such was the tense nature of the occasion that Howard dropped back as an extra centre-half with four minutes of stoppage time under way.

The first two minutes were spent dealing with free-kicks into the box, while Jones and Bywater saw yellow for delaying a free-kick and time-wasting respectively.

Clement's free-kick deflected wide right at the death, but Derby cleared the corner and it was all over – sparking scenes of wild celebration among the supporters, staff and players.

Derby County are back in the Premiership.

Manager Billy Davies:

'It's a fairytale story when you think about how far behind everyone else this club was at the start of the season.

'Going up the steps, receiving the trophy, it's indescribable – it's the proudest moment of my life to be honest, and I'm going to enjoy it.

'The lads have proved they're good players, and they'll get better with time.

'I said to the chairman last week that Stephen Pearson would be the match-winner, and he was.

'He is such a wonderful young talent, we were disappointed to lose him for 11 weeks with the injury so we're delighted for him – he thoroughly deserves it.

'We didn't play as we could do in the first half, I think we gave the ball away too much and were a little bit tense. But we were certainly very well prepared and organised through the week.

'We have earned each other's respect from day one, and that has been reflected in the attitude and effort today to put this club into the Premiership.

'It's a memory nobody will ever forget, the achievement is fantastic and now we will go and enjoy it.'

Stephen Bywater:

'I'm feeling tired now! I'm so excited, going upstairs, collecting the medal, the lads are so happy – it's unbelievable.

'This is a massive achievement for the club, the fans, and I'm so happy to be a part of it.

'The match was a case of being calm under pressure, I can't really say too much more as I'm shattered!

'The lads have worked really hard and deserve to go up, so now we're looking forward to a good summer.

'It's been a long three weeks since the end of the League season and hopefully now we can show the fans we deserve to be in the Premiership next year.

'The fans were magnificent today. I couldn't really hear the West Brom fans as ours were singing constantly.

'In the last five minutes they were cheering all the time, getting behind us, and that gave everyone a lift.

'The atmosphere was brilliant and that was mainly down to the supporters, who have been magnificent all year.

'I've played all season when I can, the gaffer has put faith in me by playing me and buying me from West Ham.

'The lads are great, the goalkeeping coach has worked really hard with me.

'It has been a magnificent season – one I'll never forget.'

Chairman Peter Gadsby:

'It's fantastic – a heck of a rollercoaster, but we've got there.

'It was a nervy 90 minutes, never mind the last 20! To be honest we felt fine, Billy always said he felt the legs would show later in the game.

'Ironically it's Stephen Pearson, one of the players we signed in January to boost the squad, who has scored the goal – so that all paid off.

'We had a feeling something special was happening when we got to the top and just kept going and going.

'Billy has been in this kind of position before and one of the things he had was experience, he was very confident, and it's worked.

'I'm just delighted for the rest of the board, the fans, everyone who's been a part of it – this is just sinking in.

'Derby has been in the Premiership before and hopefully we can take to it and give it our brand of entertainment.'

MD Mike Horton:

'We as a board have supported the manager and the players all year, and the players have put it back in.

'Today is the culmination of all of that hard work.

'The board deserve it, the players and staff deserve it, the people of Derby deserve it, and I'm delighted for everyone.

'The scenes out there [on the pitch] are fantastic, I'm absolutely soaked, but at least they didn't get me to jump on the pitch!

'It puts us on the map again. The townspeople of Derby, the shops, hotels, restaurants, everything.

'Derby County's name will be in the national newspapers on a regular basis and hopefully that will bring some prosperity into the town, and put the club back as being one of the top teams in the Midlands again.

'Billy has been a godsend from the day he came – he's enthusiastic, committed, his personality is infectious on the team and you can see the results.'

Marc Edworthy:

'It's fantastic to finish the season in this way – we've been up there for most of the campaign, and it's nice to cross the line.

'They always say that third place struggles in the Play-offs but we were resilient, it was a fantastic team effort and it's a great feeling to win.

'We're hard to beat. We've got that resilience, the players stick together, and the lads who weren't in the squad have played their part.

'It's been a huge team effort, the staff, the squad, everyone together in the background, and if you put all that together you've got a good combination.

'I've heard a lot of reports about the new Wembley, and it's a special place, a fantastic arena that's worth the wait.

'I'm sure our fans enjoyed it – they gave us fantastic support once again – and it's great for them to say they've won at the new Wembley.

'I was out of breath at the top of the stairs! It's always nice to get up there as if you lose you don't get the chance in a Play-off Final.

'I was fortunate to win at the old Wembley [with Crystal Palace in 1997], and now I've won at the new Wembley too.

'You've got to enjoy the good times when they come along, cherish them, and when the bad times come along you've got to ride them out.

'We're going to enjoy this occasion. It's been a fantastic season and to finish it like this is even better.

'All the promotions I've had are individual in their own way.

'I had a fantastic time at Palace, I was lucky enough to win at the Millennium Stadium with Wolves [in 2003] and now winning with Derby is good because it's been a brilliant season.

'They are all individual, but to win the Play-offs three times is fantastic.'

David Jones:

'Obviously I'm delighted, but it's not really sunk in yet that we'll be in the Premiership next season.

'I don't know when it will! I'll go back to the hotel, see the family, and maybe tomorrow it will sink in.

'I can't believe it. We were in line for automatic promotion for a time, but when it actually happens it's a shock.

'The last few minutes were nervous at 1–0, but the lads stayed strong, we defended well and we've deserved it.

'I was put in there to add more energy in closing down and to keep my position.

'You can't really affect the game too much with getting on the ball at that time because all you're doing is defending.

'But you don't want to let anyone down after the lads have put you one-up!

'It was a big team effort, that has been the case all season, and today typified that.

'I'm delighted for everyone – we've got the result, and now we're back in the Premiership.

'I think Manchester United will be the one I look for. It will be really good to be involved in a game like that, and I hope it will come true now.

'Walking up the steps was a special moment and one that will stay with me forever.'